HAPPY PROGRESSING PATIENTS

HOW TO SKYROCKET YOUR CONFIDENCE, THRIVE IN PRIVATE PRACTICE, AND HAVE A FULLY BOOKED CALENDAR AS THE 'GO-TO' PHYSIO IN YOUR TOWN

"It's simple little things you can implement on a daily basis, straight away into your clinic, and get incredible results with. I was already getting some very good results but the guys have an unbelievable step-by-step system that you can just follow and if you have any problems you can ask them for advice and you really know where you're going to go next. The biggest difference for me from the mentorship, I guess, is just how much I'm actually enjoying working in the clinic every single day. Patient numbers have increased, my clarity has increased, and the results have gotten better."

David Grey, David Grey Rehab, Waterford, Ireland

"I used to work every evening and weekends up until ten at night, I thought that was just part of the job. So what I'm doing now is only two evenings and that is huge. I have three small kids – you know, it's massive to be at home at a reasonable time during the day. I'm now at that stage where I can take Saturdays off. It's huge. It's also paying off debts and you're bringing in your weekly (covering outgoings), and you've still got more than you need. To have that consistency is massive, it takes a lot of that stress, worry, and anxiousness away."

Liz Cummings, NMT and Clinic Owner, Ireland

"It's helped me step back from the business two days a week. I only work in the business now for three full days and two half days. That allows me two days a week. The big thing I do is work as the head coach within the clinic. I look after the physio team. Don't hesitate, go buy it and make that investment. It will be the best investment for the business. I think the clinical mentorship is the best investment you can make in your clinical expertise and Mastermind is the best investment you can make for your business."

Marty and Julie Loughran, Physical Therapists and Clinic Owners, Cookstown, Northern Ireland

"I took on my first full-time therapist three months ago which is a lot of me helping mentor them and taking them through assessment and I just wouldn't have had the confidence. I would never have thought I could have been that person that is helping to guide somebody else and that has come from the mentorship where I have confidence in my knowledge. I have confidence in applying that knowledge and feel like I'm making a real difference to people."

Laura Franklin

"[The mentorship] has freed me up. I've got some personal ambitions outside of the practice that will require some of my time, dedication and attention. What the mentorship allowed me to do was to put the first piece of the foundation in place, making sure the clinical systems are established and really fortified. And now I know that whether it is me, my associate Byron, or any other clinical team member who comes in the door at any point, they're going to be at a level where I know our patients are being taken care of to the highest standard that is higher than anyone else's."

Carson, Chiropractor and Clinic Owner, USA

"I wish I had learned this in school. I just feel like I'm on a completely different level. In terms of clients I was seeing maybe 10–15 people a week and now consistently 25 plus, sometimes 30 a week. It's just about that consistency and confidence that each person that comes through I know that I can push and really get them to the goals they want to achieve."

Greg, Physical Therapist and Clinic Owner, Canada

"When I think about the situations I've encountered in the last couple of quarters, I don't think I would have been able to navigate them successfully if I didn't have the mentorship to rely on. So it's given me that focus and helped me to implement the systems and I've had opportunities come out that have shown me that those systems we put in place are quite beneficial to the clinic and are going to help in the long-term success... It's a fantastic investment and very much worthwhile."

Dr. Sandra Vaughn, DPT Clinic Owner, Barbados

"I highly recommend David's mentorship program. Since I started working with him and his team I look different on pain and injuries. I didn't want to just treat symptoms. I wanted to understand why something is happening and this is the main thing David gave me. He also has a biopsychosocial approach which brings you to another level as a physio."

Almedin, Physiotherapist and Physio for NK Maribor Football Club, Slovenia

"This mentorship has filled the gap in all the missing links I needed. I have a better understanding of subjective and objective assessment and how to match the two. Most of all, a complete picture from where the patient is in the rehab continuum to where he needs to go. The step-by-step approach removes a lot of guessing, stress and yet is fully individualised to the patient. No cookie cutter, simply clarity on what needs to be done in order to return to life/sports. Hands down the best investment I have ever made."

Giovanni Frapporti, Doctor of Chiropractic, Lombardy, Italy

"This by far was the best mentorship program I have ever taken. It will give you clarity and confidence. Hands down the best!... If you're a personal trainer, chiropractor, anyone in health, it doesn't matter who you are because the modules and everything transfers over to real-life movement. It is by far the best investment I've ever made. If I didn't do the mentorship I don't know where I would be. It gave me a better understanding on how to structure treatment plans, and how to speak to people. It gave more clarity on how to assess someone better virtually and how to write up and structure a program for them that makes sense to them, not to you, to them."

Edwin Santiago, Personal Trainer, Miami, USA

"How you are treated on the course itself, it's like a family and that was really important. I could see that everybody was on the same page and willing to help each other regardless, going out of their way. The amount of content and Dave makes it look so simple. When you hear him talk and the presentation, it's like 'I can do it!'. I think we can get this effect of healing faster, than going around and around. It gives me confidence, now I know that I can see someone and won't be second-guessing. Now I feel more confident I can deliver the goods"

**Zeph Nicholas, Sports Therapist
and West Indies Cricket Team, Trinidad & Tobago**

"I think, for me and the medical team, we are probably more confident now in saying 'yeah I'm happy that everything is functioning', rather than relying on the players telling us. We've actually got hands-on with them and that gives me confidence to go to the coaching staff, 'Yep, he'll be good to train today'. It has helped build confidence in what you say to the coaches and the players themselves."

**Bobby Sourbuts, Physiotherapist,
England Men's Rugby Team**

Further praise for David's mentorship, methods and system

"I feel like I can treat anyone in front of me and even with the most complex patients I am able to assess the patient and take them through a graded exposure of rehab to get the patients back to things they want to do."

Andy Ellis

"It gives you the confidence and clarity to deal with all sorts of problems and achieve successful outcomes."

Eimear Connolly

"I am a much more confident and happier therapist. Following the system makes my days calmer and less stressful. My energy levels are higher and I have regained my passion for physio."

Laura Franklin

"I no longer feel burned out or exhausted, I now have a clarity and clear plan every time with my patients. It has given me the spark I used to have as a therapist and I truly love what I do again."

Jenny Richmond

"My client retention is incredible and I no longer advertise my client base, it is all word of mouth. In fact I need to take on another therapist to keep up with demand."

Toni Stanton

"Word of mouth for my business is continuously growing and I'm busier than ever (I haven't even advertised yet)."

Leon Cassin

"I feel much more competent in managing some of those much more complex patients and have had some great results with patients that I might otherwise have thought I couldn't help."

Alison McKeown

"I now assess and rehab clients completely different to how I used to and I'm seeing amazing results."

One2one therapy

"To sum it up, I personally felt I'm among the elite therapists, at least my confidence felt that way, and that energy I carried now changes/affects/influences patients' life."

Eu Gene Chong

"I'm now the physio where the complicated cases are referred. People have come to me from all over the county and some from outside the county."

Leon Cassin

"I'm getting great results, for the first time in my career I have real confidence in my own ability, and I'm now getting people travelling to come and see me, which is a testament to the mentorship."

Ed Vos

"Learning this system has helped improve my skills immensely as a therapist and has helped to grow my business and referrals."

Eryn Simon

ISBN: 9798362766887

Imprint: Independently published

Copyright 2022, David O'Sullivan

All views expressed in this book are those of the author and are not intended for use as a definitive guide. This work is owned in full by the primary author, David O'Sullivan. No part of this publication may be reproduced or transmitted in any form whatsoever without the written permission of David O'Sullivan: dave@thegotophysio.com

This book was produced in collaboration with Write Business Results Limited. For more information on their business book and marketing services, please visit www.writebusinessresults.com or contact the team via info@writebusinessresults.com.

WRITE BUSINESS RESULTS

HAPPY PROGRESSING PATIENTS

HOW TO SKYROCKET YOUR CONFIDENCE, THRIVE IN PRIVATE PRACTICE, AND HAVE A FULLY BOOKED CALENDAR AS THE 'GO-TO' PHYSIO IN YOUR TOWN

DAVID O'SULLIVAN

Acknowledgements

I am privileged to have enjoyed some amazing life experiences as a direct result of being a physiotherapist. There are many people who have helped me on this journey and too many to thank by name, but here are a few.

To my parents Tony and Kay, for all the sacrifices they made to help me study in Carlow and then in England on my journey to becoming a physiotherapist. Dad photocopied and printed hundreds and hundreds of pages about different universities in England and drove me to Carlow open days. Mom always made sure I had enough food and clean clothes going back to Carlow each weekend.

To Georgina, my wife, thank you for putting up with me during this journey. I have spent a lot of time away from home working in pro sport and also working unsociable hours. You rarely complained and made, and continue to make, massive personal sacrifices which allow me to do what I do.

To Ava and Ruby who continue to humble me every day and put me back in my place! For allowing me to watch you grow up to be beautiful and intelligent girls while also getting to observe your movement "patterns" along the way!

To Meirion Jones and Martin Higgins, my first two mentors. Everyone needs a good mentor to save you time and mistakes. You took me under your wings and gave me a chance. Without you two, I have no doubt I wouldn't be where I am today.

To all my team at ProSport Physiotherapy and ProSport Academy who make my life easier and allow me to do the things I enjoy such as treating and teaching. To Shane Mooney, our head physio, who has been there every step of the way and played a massive role in the step-by-step system.

To all my past patients who believed in me and stuck with me when I didn't have all the answers. I have made many mistakes and learned a lot from my patients, which I now hope I can pass on to thousands of therapists all over the world so they don't have to make the same errors.

To all my 'Go-To' Physio Mentorship therapists who trusted me to mentor them. The questions you asked, and continue to ask, continue to challenge me to think and improve the step by step system. I have learned a lot from the therapists in the Mentorship and they continue to add to and improve the step-by-step system for me. We have the best "Physio Community" in the world. Thank you.

To all my coaches that I have had over the years who helped me build the clinic and academy. I had no idea it would grow to this level. You all saw the potential before I did and pushed me to go beyond what I thought was possible.

To all the past players and coaches I have worked with at Leeds Rhinos, Munster Rugby, Huddersfield Giants, Warrington Wolves, England Rugby League and England Rugby Union. I had some amazing experiences and this step-by-step system was built and refined in these amazing sporting organisations. I am privileged to have worked with so many great people in such a short period of time.

To all the team at Write Business Results for helping me get this book out of my head and onto paper.

To all the therapists out there who follow my work on social media, subscribe to my emails, listen to my podcasts and purchase this book. There are few other things that excite me more than hearing your success stories of implementing these concepts and getting results for people in pain that have failed with traditional approaches. Thank you for trusting me and implementing this approach with your patients.

Finally, to all my friends and family in my life who have supported me on this journey. You know who you are.

Dave

Dedication

To Georgina, Ava and Ruby – DRAGOS! xoxo

Contents

Acknowledgements — 12

Dedication — 14

Foreword — 19

Introduction — 21

Part One: 8 Pillars

Chapter 1: Humbling Lessons Learned From Professional Sport — 31

Chapter 2: There Is No "Magic Bullet" — 41

Chapter 3: My Road to Success — 51

Chapter 4: An Overview of the 'Go-To' Therapist Method (and How to Always Give More in Value than You Take in Payment) — 59

Part Two: Subjective and Objective Assessment

Chapter 5: Making Sense of Your Patient's Story and Having Confidence and Clarity in Your Treatment Plan — 85

Chapter 6: Making Sense of the Objective Assessment   99

Chapter 7: Designing a Long-Term Strategy for Success   124

Part Three: Patient Adherence and Buy-In

Chapter 8: Designing a World-Class Customer Experience   145

Chapter 9: How to Design a Treatment Plan that Gives   155
Massive Value to You and Your Patient

Chapter 10: How to Get Complete Patient Adherence   163
and Buy-In

Part Four: Delivering World-Class Results

Chapter 11: Curing Symptoms with Hands-On Treatment   179

Chapter 12: Lower Level Rehab that Gets You Instant Results   191

Chapter 13: Bridging the Gap from Low to High-Level Rehab   208

Chapter 14: How to Know Exactly When the Patient   219
is Ready to Return to Running or Other
High-Load Activities

Chapter 15: Return to Running Acceleration and   227
Deceleration Progression

Chapter 16: Build Resilience Under External Loads and   237
Increased Stress

Chapter 17: Putting It All Together with a Complex Patient Who Has Failed with Traditional Approaches — 251

Part Five: Growing and Scaling a Private Practice Sustainably

Chapter 18: Choosing the "Right Way" to Grow Your Reputatiox Clinic and Impact — 277

Chapter 19: Systemising Your Business for Ultimate Freedom — 288

Chapter 20: What Is Possible for You and Your Practice with a Step-By-Step System? — 303

Epilogue — 313

Foreword
by Kevin Sinfield, OBE

Throughout my time in rugby, as a player, administrator and coach I have worked with some outstanding people. Dave would be right at the top of that list. He is the best physio that I have ever worked with. His holistic approach of looking at the body as a whole to find the true cause of the problem rather than just treating the symptoms made him different. He always made each patient feel special with a high level of care, and he has an incredible level of enthusiasm and energy to fix people.

Dave successfully "fixed me" on many occasions. His methods were transformational and I knew he would get me right, so that I could play each weekend. He filled me with confidence and belief and I trusted him, which is so important.

The reason I'm telling you this is because I want you to trust him too. What Dave shares in this book can help you unlock similarly transformational results for each and every patient in your physio practice.

Dave and I go back a long way. We first met at Leeds Rhinos when he joined the club as an assistant physio and I was captain. His strong Irish accent was warming and he was good to be around. The physio room was often a place of great banter, and Dave certainly encouraged and nurtured an enjoyable environment.

He was direct, had fingers and elbows made from granite and was often brutal with his hands-on work, but I always knew he would fix me and so did the rest of the team. I was very fortunate throughout my career, injury wise, but much of that was down to Dave's management and constantly pushing me on, finding progressions and improvements. On finishing playing, at every opportunity I have tried to recruit Dave to ensure his skill set is available in any environment I have worked in. Whether this has been club or country, his involvements and experiences are highly sought after. He is a good man with strong values and it was great to be able to work with him again during The Extra Mile Challenge last November raising funds and awareness for motor neurone disease. Having Dave involved gave everyone great confidence that we would complete it in one piece.

I am delighted to write this foreword for his book because I know it will help, support and encourage therapists to have more confidence to treat patients in practices across the world. If you apply what he shares in the coming chapters, you will quickly be able to make sense of each patient's symptoms, explain the problem so that they can understand it, and then devise a plan that will enable each of your patients to get results fast. The book also provides progressions to keep your patients improving to deliver long-lasting great results.

Introduction:
Building a 'Go-To' Clinic the "Right" Way

Building a fully booked clinic with happy, progressing patients while still having time for yourself and your family can be stressful. In 2015 when I was transitioning from pro sport to grow my private practice, I struggled initially. I actually found it harder in private practice to get results than in pro sport.

Once I figured out why that was (which I'll share with you in the coming chapters) everything changed for the better. I was finally able to keep patients progressing without dropping off when the pain eased. I was able to create raving fans quickly and predictably which allowed me to rapidly build a thriving word-of-mouth private practice. I then hired more therapists to help me gain the freedom to spend more time with my family.

And that is when the opposite happened!

I'd give the new therapist a full schedule of patients only for their diaries to be empty again a few weeks later. This really frustrated me and led me to become even more stressed, burnt out and anxious about the future.

I'd go home at night after a full day of patients and instead of switching off and being present with my family, the clinic consumed me. I'd spend the evening half listening to my wife while I was constantly worrying about finding new patients to fill my therapists' diaries.

I turned to Google Ads and spent thousands of pounds trying to find more new patients only for the same thing to happen again – patients dropping off after a few sessions.

I quickly realised that a scalable and sustainable 'Go-To' Private Practice is not built on the number of new patients you get, it's built on the number of patients you ethically keep progressing. In other words, a 'Go-To' Clinic is built on the number of patients you don't lose.

The question to ask is: what are patients who don't get results and drop off really costing you? Confidence? Growth? Revenue? Referrals? Reputation? Freedom? Let's take the emotion out of it and do the maths...

If you increase your therapists' patient visit average by just two sessions that the patient actually needs...

The numbers don't lie...

100 of your patients having an average of 3 sessions each
£50/Session = £15,000

100 of your patients ethically having an average of 5 sessions each
£50/Session = £25,000

40% increase in revenue **WITHOUT** having to worry about **finding the equivalent of 66 new pateints to earn the same revenue!**

Or by the three extra sessions that your patients ethically need...

> ## Double your revenue and save hundreds of hours by not having to always find new patients!
>
> **100** of your patients having an average of 3 sessions each
> **£50/Session = £15,000**
>
> **100** of your patients ethically having an average of 6 sessions each
> **£50/Session = £30,000**
>
> Double you revenue **WITHOUT** having to waste time & worry about **finding 100 new patients to earn the same revenue!**

I quickly realised there are three ways to grow a private practice, as outlined by Jay Abrahams[1] when talking about the three ways to grow a business:

1. Find more patients.

2. Keep patients progressing and ethically increase the patient visit average.

3. Get past patients to come back to see you for more or to buy another service you offer.

It makes no sense to me to spend time, energy and money getting more new patients when you are not optimising those you've already got. If you do not do a good job with option two on that list, option three will not happen. And that was what was

---

[1] Abraham Group, *Three Ways To Grow Your Business*, available at: https://www.abraham.com/topic/three-ways-to-grow-your-business/

happening to me. I was finding new patients for my therapists. They were losing them after a couple of sessions.

When I realised my therapists were making more money than I was at the end of the month – even though they were sitting in empty treatment rooms while I saw all the patients – I said enough was enough!

I stepped back and shadowed my therapists for a full week during EVERY SINGLE session! I quickly realised they were making three big mistakes that were causing patients to stagnate, cancel or drop off completely. Here are those three big mistakes so you, or your therapists, never have to make them again.

Mistake #1
Value Was Not Exceeding Price

The first thing you must do is to ensure your therapists are ALWAYS giving more in value than you take in payment.

> *A successful private practice is not built on how many new patients you can get in the door, it is built on how many you can ethically keep progressing!*

In order for a patient to book another session, the value must exceed price. Said another way, a sale will never be made if price exceeds value.

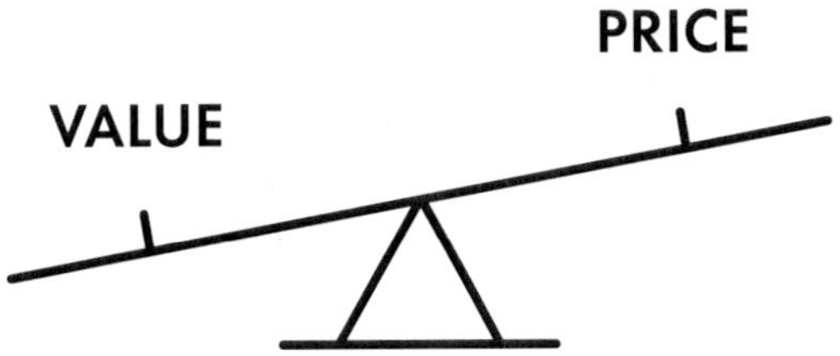

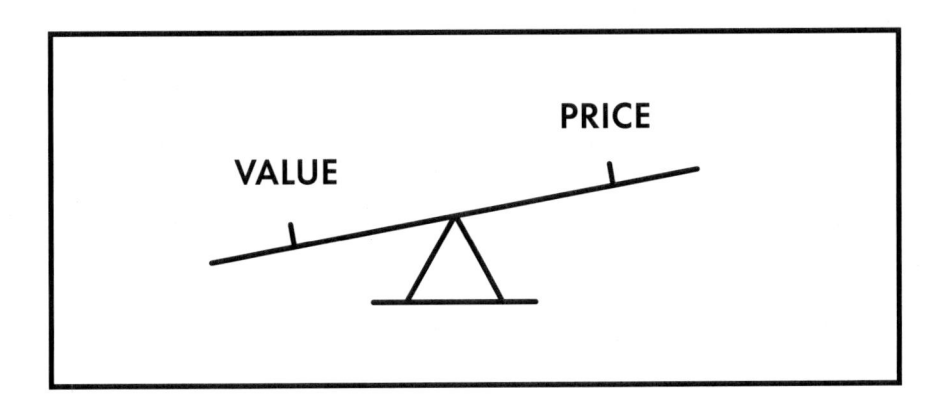

It is the therapist's job to design a treatment plan that increases the ACTUAL and PERCEIVED value. You can do this by not making the next mistake my therapists were making.

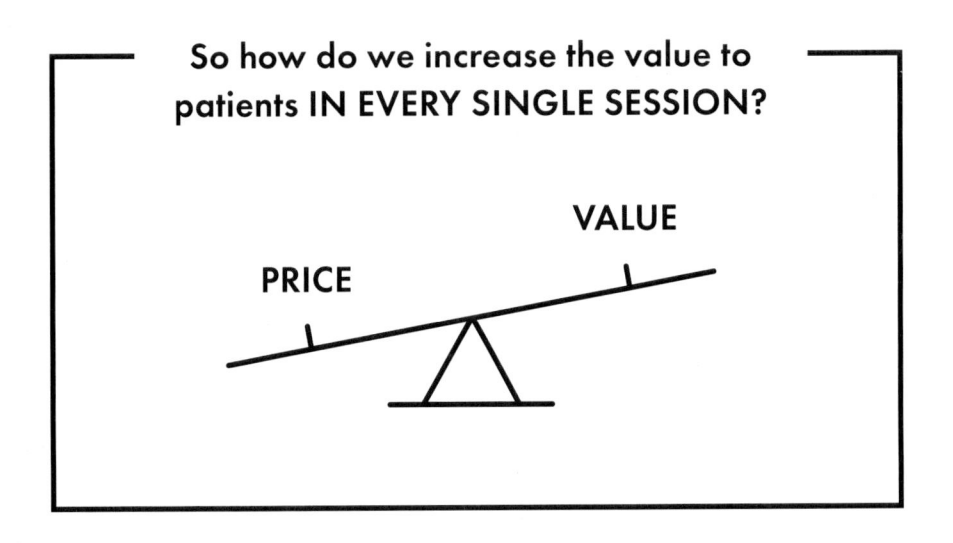

So how do we increase the value to patients IN EVERY SINGLE SESSION?

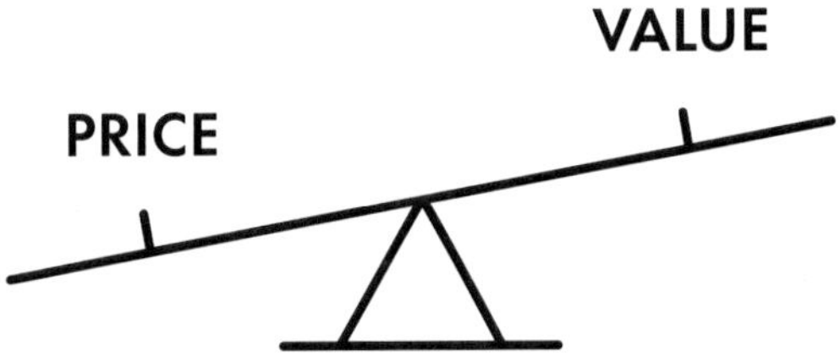

Mistake #2
Not Solving The Most Valuable Problems For The Patient

My therapists were focused on the patient's external problems, such as: back pain, knee pain, ankle pain etc.

They didn't realise that patients buy "solutions" to their internal problems.

The treatment plan was all about the "back pain" while the main problem the patient wanted to solve was being able to pick their kids up or do the gardening. They didn't see the value in lying on their backs doing exercises that weren't solving their internal problems.

If you want to charge more money, solve the most valuable problems for your patients!

Mistake #3
Not Understanding That A Patient's Motivation And Behaviour Will Change From Session One To Session Two

As time goes on, the motivation a patient has to achieve their dream outcome will naturally drop. That's life!

Fogg's Behaviour Model States: Behaviour = Motivation x Ability x Trigger.

My therapists were not taking this into account when prescribing exercises in later sessions. As motivation dips, the patient must be able to incorporate the exercises into their life with simple triggers.

There must also be an instant reward in the form of pain relief etc. immediately after doing the exercise. The patient must feel the difference and see the improvement from the exercise or they will not continue them once motivation drops.

> *The thing that brings the patient into your clinic is an internal problem. The thing that keeps them long enough to achieve the solution is the milestones that the patient hits along the way so they can see (and feel) they are on the right path.*

The exercises must hit these milestones and not simply be "strengthening muscles".

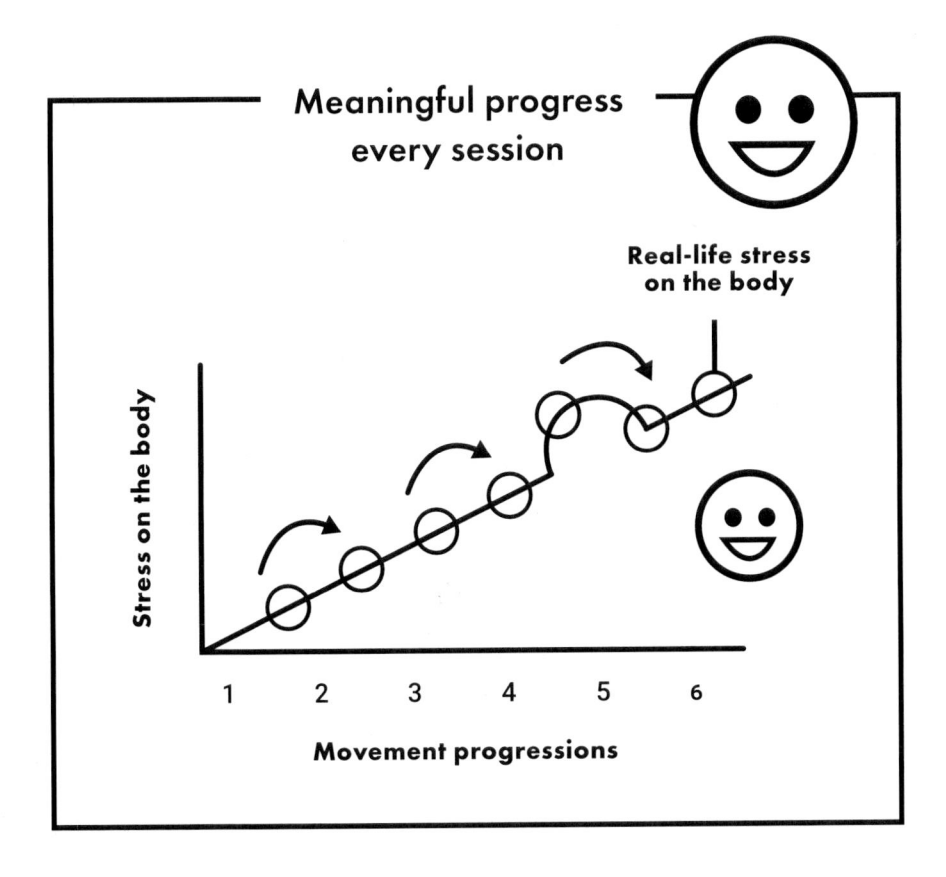

Meaningful progress every session

Real-life stress on the body

Stress on the body

1 2 3 4 5 6

Movement progressions

After finally understanding what was NOT happening, it became clear that implementing another business system or doing another in-service training, CPD/CEU course with my therapists would not help solve this problem once and for all.

It was clear that there are different skills required to not only survive but to also thrive in private practice that we were not taught in university courses.

I believe every ethical therapist should be able to build a fully booked 'Go-To' Clinic the right way by letting their patient results do the talking while still having time for their family!

This book will teach you these skills so you can not only enjoy a fully booked practice of happy progressing patients but also have a framework to ensure that all your therapists are delivering the same high standard of care so you can have the freedom you deserve.

Part One:
8 Pillars

I can show you hands-on techniques, rehab exercises and all the "tactics" in the world, but at the end of the day, if you can't get your patients' pain to settle and keep them progressing, the rest will be useless. Very often in private practice strategy is 80 per cent of the battle and the "tactics" is the final 20 per cent. Get the strategy right in the first session with your patient and the rest becomes easy. When you really think about the customer's journey in private practice, the physiotherapist really needs eight fundamental skills to thrive.

The patient will come into the initial assessment, very often not knowing what to expect. You, as the physiotherapist, need to be able to build rapport quickly with the patient and ask personal questions about their history in order to make sense of the symptom in the subjective assessment. You then must be able to demonstrate confidence in the objective assessment and control this part of the session with the "expert authority" using verbal commands where the patient has to listen to your instructions and perform the movements you need them to do in order to make sense of their symptoms.

You must then be able to communicate this effectively to the patient in order to get "buy-in" and "adherence" to the treatment plan. If there is time left over in the first session you must make a great first impression with some hands-on treatment, if appropriate, and usually give the patient some exercises to do at home until the next session.

Sessions two onwards follow a similar structure yet there are different skills needed in these sessions as a physiotherapist, especially when the pain begins to ease. The levels of motivation required by a patient to come back may naturally tend to drop as the sessions progress and therefore the therapist must do certain things at certain times in the customer journey to ensure the patient stays engaged, motivated and, above all else, progressing in each session.

If you want to confidently treat every patient who walks through your door to reach their desired outcome while increasing the ceiling of what they can achieve then the first this first section of the book will give you an overview of the FOUNDATIONAL 8 pillars that you really need to master to be successful in private practice. I've made all the mistakes in the process, which you'll find out shortly, so you don't have to. You get to work smarter, not harder, in your journey to becoming the 'Go-To' Physio in your town.

Chapter 1:
Humbling Lessons Learned From Professional Sport

What the f*%k is a syndesmosis injury?

My heart started to race and I could feel my internal physiology start to change. I was nodding and acting as confidently as I could, hoping and praying the Head Physio could not detect that I had no clue what a syndesmosis injury was. I quickly tried to think back to what we were taught back in university and was pretty sure we hadn't covered that!

It was my first day as a newly graduated physiotherapist and my first day with Leeds Carnegie Rugby Union, as they were known back then. I remember it like it was yesterday...

I was nervous yet excited. I always had a clear vision in my mind of working in sport and becoming the 'Go-To' Physio yet now I had to walk the talk. The self doubt naturally started to kick into my mind as I walked through the training ground door. Am I good enough? Would it be easier if I had just gone straight into the NHS as a band five physiotherapist instead of jumping straight into pro sport? Expectations and pressure would be so much higher here.

My first player was Lee Blackett, now head coach of Wasps Rugby Union. I took Lee out to the communal physiotherapy area and started to press and prod on his ankle (around the peroneals) and went back to my old reliable deep tissue massage to the muscles around the area. That would surely buy me some time, I thought!

Lee winced in pain as I got deep into the tissues. I then did some very low-level rehab with him... praying that the Head Physio wouldn't look out of his window and see what I was doing. Would I get found out just an hour into my first job? Was I being too aggressive with him at this stage of the injury? Was I not being aggressive enough with my rehab? All of these thoughts flooded my brain.

Externally I was acting confidently although I did notice the pitch of my voice was raised noticeably... yet internally I was in agony! I quickly sent him on his way before the Head Physio found out I had no clue what I was doing! Welcome to the real world of pro sport, I thought to myself. You wanted this!

Long story short, I got through my first day at Leeds Rugby and went straight home and looked up what the f*%k a syndesmosis was... hoping and praying I hadn't caused more damage to the player and he'd come in OK the following morning.

My first three months at Leeds Rugby was very much a reality check for me. I felt like I'd been lied to at university. I'd use all the new special tests, mobilisations, eccentric loading protocols I learned in university and on placements, but I quickly learned most patients don't present like the textbooks or how my university lecturers led me to believe. In fact, very few do.

To make it even worse, when you are working in professional sport, there really is nowhere to hide...

Unlike private practice or the national healthcare setting where the patient goes away for a week, Lee and all the other players are there all day, every day with you. Fortunately for me things started to settle down after three months with Leeds Rugby.

I moved over full time to work exclusively with Leeds Rhinos Rugby League after initially splitting my time between them and Leeds Carnegie.

I was fortunate to have a great mentor in Meirion Jones, the Head Physiotherapist at Leeds Rhinos at the time, who got me into Leeds Rugby in the first place after doing a student placement with him the year before.

Meirion was a great mentor and taught me a lot in those first 12 months that, looking back, must have saved me years and years of trying to figure things out myself. I was strong with my hands-on treatment at this point and also had a big interest in strength training so I was able to hold my own. In fact I was beginning to develop a reputation for having "thumbs of steel"!

In my second year at the club, Meirion got promoted to Head of Medical for Leeds Rugby, overseeing both medical departments, while I got promoted to Lead Physio for Leeds Rhinos within 12 months of qualifying.

This brought new challenges for me as I now had the added responsibility of speaking to the Head Coach every morning and having to give timelines and progress reports on players' injuries.

To be honest, I really struggled with speaking to the Head Coach at the start, making up timelines and a prognosis as I went along. I felt an internal pressure to say what they wanted to hear rather than what they needed to hear.

Often, once I said the words, I felt instant doom and even more pressure on myself, cursing myself as I walked back downstairs to the physio room, knowing I was setting unrealistic expectations and would need to face the consequences later on when the player was not ready in time. Yet I didn't let that beat me. If anything, I saw it as a challenge I now needed to overcome and looking back it probably helped me.

You see, I was desperate to be that 'Go-To' Physio who could get players back quicker than everyone else and help people that had failed with traditional approaches! In this new role I was also desperate for the players and coach to respect me.

So, every evening after work, I spent every waking hour reading *T Nation*, strength coach websites, physio forums, you name it. I was in search of that "magic bullet", looking for any shortcut or cutting-edge technique I could find.

I was also spending hours reading research papers but was becoming more and more disillusioned with these, finding that the research results demonstrated in the papers did not translate to the real-life results they were promising.

There was a common theme emerging for me in that second year. I was getting short-term changes with hands-on techniques extremely easily, but not getting long-lasting changes.

I found myself repeating the same treatments day after day, praying for a different result! The players were appeased short term, but I knew deep down the pain would return again and they'd be back the following day. This was beginning to frustrate me more and more.

Around this time, I had also set up a private practice clinic above a running shop in Huddersfield under the company name, "ProSport Physiotherapy" with Meirion and another one of my great mentors, Martin Higgins.

They looked after the clinic in Leeds while I built up the Huddersfield clinic. What surprised me most was that I found it EVEN HARDER in private practice than pro sport! The same problems of short-term changes were showing up in private practice.

The initial assessment and the second or third session were great! I was getting short-term changes really easily. However, by the fourth session, the hands-on treatment wasn't working as well and that's where I was really beginning to feel the pressure, especially when the patient was handing over their hard-earned money at the end of every session.

There was an expectation on me that, because I was a pro sport physio, I had all the answers, yet deep down I felt like an imposter taking these people's hard-earned money. I was going through the motions in the subjective and objective assessment, spending 90 per cent of the session "appeasing the patient", performing my favourite hands-on treatment techniques and "buying myself some time". Then I was rushing through two to three rehab exercises in the last five minutes of sessions, hoping and praying the patient would return the following week.

Yet every patient was generally following the same pattern... things would go "OK" for the first two to three sessions and the patients would leave with a smile on their face. Then my stress levels would INCREASE and my patient's happiness levels DECREASE after the fourth session progress slump. Inevitably patients would drop off or cancel and make some polite excuse.

I'd tell myself some sob story about how the patient must not be doing their exercises properly or were just not committed enough when in fact, looking back, it was 100 per cent my fault! The truth is I was going through the motions. I was using hands-on treatment as a comfort blanket to "buy myself time". I felt comfortable with hands-on treatment and relied on it excessively. Back then there was no genuine clinical reasoning happening.

Time was probably the biggest healer for most of my successes, yet I believed the hype that I had "thumbs of steel" and that must be making the biggest difference. I wasn't asking myself the higher-level critical thinking questions that I will share with you in the coming chapters, that I now know are so important to getting long-lasting results.

A hands-on treatment approach only will get you so far in "changing the pain experience" but as I like to say now: **"Getting rid of pain is easy; keeping pain away is the true art."**

The true secret to keep patients progressing – who have failed with traditional approaches or have had their pain experience for some time – is to give them the right stimulus at the right time in a graded exposure manner.

To put it another way, prescribe the hands-on treatment and right rehab exercises at the right time. As Goldilocks said, not too much, not too little, just the right amount. It's simple really yet not that easy to figure out how to do in the real world... as I then found out with Munster Rugby.

Munster Rugby

In the late summer of 2011, I flew over to Limerick for a job interview with Munster Rugby. When I saw the advertisement go up, my heart skipped a beat. This was it. This was what I was imagining myself doing while I was a student and watching Munster win Heineken Cups in 2006 and 2008. This was my dream job.

After two gruelling interviews, I got offered the job. It was a difficult decision personally to move back to Ireland and professionally to leave Leeds Rhinos, but this was the big one I had been dreaming of for all those years.

So, after another grand final win at Old Trafford in October 2011, I packed up my things and got the ferry from Holyhead to Dublin to begin my new career with Munster Rugby. I landed at the University of Limerick in high spirits and keen to impress and earn the respect of the players and staff.

Looking back, I was a fraction of the therapist I am now and to be honest am embarrassed at some of the things I did back then. Externally things were going great...

I had made a good first impression with the players and staff. Paul O'Connell, who was captaining Ireland at the time, damaged his MCL playing against France in the Six Nations and requested to leave the Ireland camp to do his rehab with me, rather than stay in camp, so he'd be ready for the Heineken Cup quarter-finals against Ulster.

Ronan O'Gara, who was based in Cork, and would typically be looked after by the Cork-based physios, would ask me to hang back for treatment at Thomond Park when the rest of the team had left. I'd then drive him back to the team hotel in Limerick, him sitting in the passenger seat of my old Ford Focus. I'd have to pinch myself twice to think, is this really happening?

Word started to spread and Donncha O'Callaghan and Tomás O'Leary would do the same and request treatment from me when they travelled to our Limerick-based training centre. That was a big boost for my ego and I was still hungry to learn and improve, spending every waking hour when I went home at night looking to improve.

I wish I could say it was a fairy-tale ending for me at Munster Rugby but unfortunately (or fortunately, as I like to look at it now) I had inherited some tricky cases from the get-go with some high-profile players.

It still pains me at times to think back at my time with Munster and knowing what I know now. Believe me, I wish to god I had my time back there with those players with my current skill sets, because I would have done things so differently. You see, I was still a very hands-on dominant therapist first and foremost.

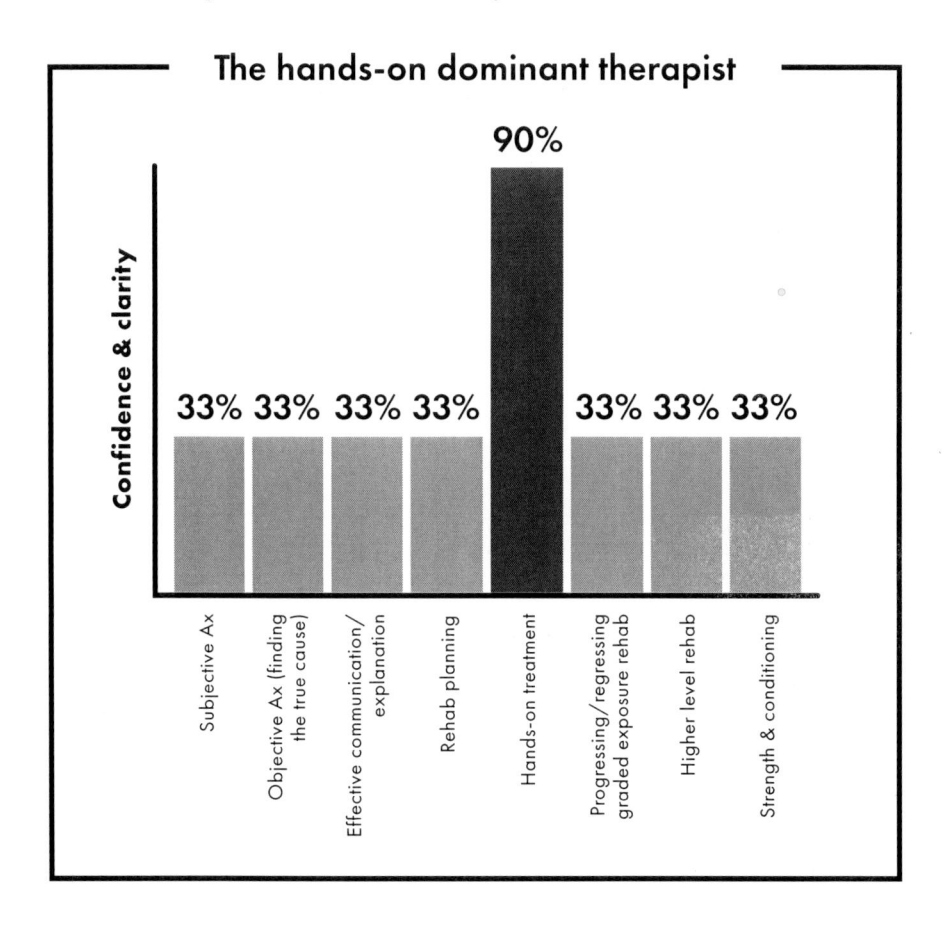

The hands-on dominant therapist

Confidence & clarity

Category	%
Subjective Ax	33%
Objective Ax (finding the true cause)	33%
Effective communication/explanation	33%
Rehab planning	33%
Hands-on treatment	90%
Progressing/regressing graded exposure rehab	33%
Higher level rehab	33%
Strength & conditioning	33%

The majority of my sessions would be spent with the players on the bed wincing in pain as I dug my thumbs and elbows in as hard as I could. I got addicted to the short-term relief that hands-on treatment gives and, in all honesty, so did the players.

They'd jump off the bed and feel good for a few minutes or hours before having to come back the next day and request the same thing again. I'd go home at night with my hands aching and have serious doubts of how I could continue to do this, day in, day out for the next 40 years of my career.

Looking back, I was also very strong with my strength and conditioning background, and most of my rehab exercises were simply strength-focused exercises.

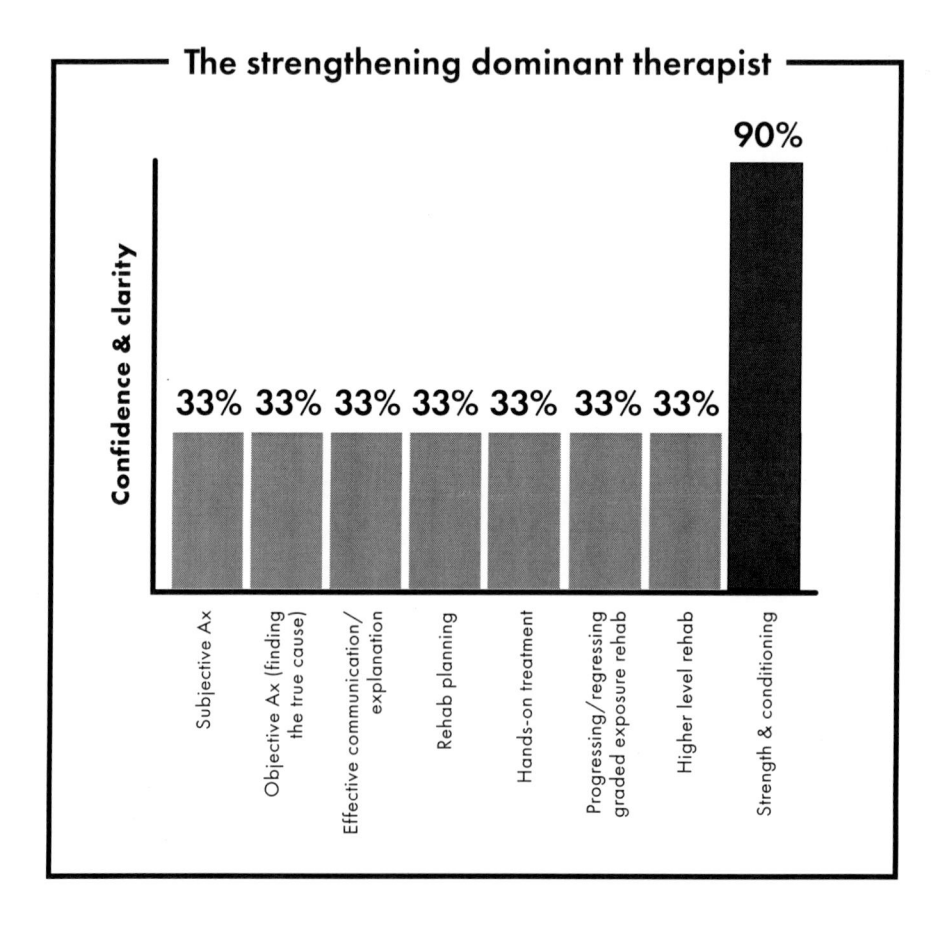

The strengthening dominant therapist

Category	Confidence & clarity
Subjective Ax	33%
Objective Ax (finding the true cause)	33%
Effective communication/explanation	33%
Rehab planning	33%
Hands-on treatment	33%
Progressing/regressing graded exposure rehab	33%
Higher level rehab	33%
Strength & conditioning	90%

I didn't understand that the nervous system could "cheat" with these exercises, which we will cover in the next chapter – and looking back, these guys were animals.

They were ridiculously strong athletes, yet I was on a wild goose chase trying to get that extra 1.5kg on the bar which didn't translate to moving well without pain in the real world. It all came to a head when two of the players had to retire on my watch.

Back to reality and lessons learned

There was a defining moment, however, at Santry Sports Surgery Clinic for me with one of those players when I said enough was enough…

We left the surgeon's office at about 4pm and headed for the car in an awkward silence. To be fair, the player was upbeat and I could sense almost a feeling of relief and a weight lifted from his body. The drive back to Limerick was also a strange one knowing this would be hitting the national headlines shortly and, essentially, that he wouldn't be my player anymore.

Probably, deep down, I was relieved too as I had explored every single avenue I knew how (at the time) to try and help him. But this was one of the few cases I saw on a day-to-day basis where pain truly did mean damage.

The player's "headspace" was right but it could not overpower the signals that were coming from below telling him that the load was exceeding the tissue's/joint's capacity to tolerate load for running and change of direction. To cut a long story short, one of my childhood heroes had just retired and I wasn't able to help him.

Even though I had joined the team halfway through this player's rehab plan, that hurt my pride and ego a lot, in all honesty. It proved a reality check for me. I was starting to believe the hype that I was the 'Go-To' Physio. Yet in that year, I had two players retire on my watch. I took that very personally.

As I said, for one player, pain did mean damage and the load placed on the joint was just too much to allow him to do the one thing he loved doing, while the other player had a "healthy" body but the constant setbacks proved too much for him.

Here were two players who, in reality, needed to be managed very differently from the start. I managed both players with a strong hands-on treatment and strengthening approach. No amount of hands-on treatment would have solved the joint capacity and load tolerance issues with player A, and no amount of hands-on treatment and strengthening exercises would solve the "confidence" issues for player B.

I knew I needed to change my approach if I wanted to be that 'Go-To' Physio. So, off I went again, on my crusade, with my hunger and desire to help people who had failed with traditional approaches stronger than ever. Yet my biggest lesson and the final "penny" dropping was just around the corner with the Huddersfield Giants.

Chapter 2:
There Is No "Magic Bullet"

We rushed towards platform 11 in London Kings Cross Station... We were about to miss our train back to Huddersfield. We picked the pace up and got into a gentle jog. We just made it.

As we both settled into our chairs for the two-hour trip back up north, Luke said the two words that made me want the ground to swallow me up: "It's back."

I looked at him deflated. That gentle jog was enough for the pain to return. Rewind to three hours earlier and Luke had arrived in London hoping for some relief for his hip. I was doing *another* CPD course, still searching for the "magic bullet". I was with Huddersfield Giants at this point, having returned to the UK from Munster Rugby, and was struggling with Luke.

His hip was getting worse and I was losing confidence in my own ability to help him. I was £10,000 deep and five levels into this latest course at this stage. Yet, in every level, if something came up that didn't resolve, or things got a bit complicated, we'd be told, "This is an advanced level issue." I didn't have time to wait.

In pro sport, I needed results yesterday, never mind waiting another three months to finish the final levels of this course. So I persuaded the club and Luke to make the trip down to London to see the creator of this special technique.

It started well and he got some quick wins. The hip range of motion improved. The pain started to disappear. A smile came across his face. We were all riding that "high" you get when you see a patient have "hope" for the first time in a long time.

I asked the "guru" what we needed to do next with Luke to keep the gains. The answer? "Nothing! He will be fine now!" the guru reported confidently. Luke shook his hand, thanked him and had a glint in his eye.

I was a little bit more sceptical after my two players had to retire with Munster, yet I dared to dream it could be this easy!

Fast forward three hours and the pain was back after a gentle jog, never mind 80 minutes of a rugby league match or a week's training. That was the defining point for me when I finally stopped searching for that "shiny object" or "magic bullet".

I had tried them all... Functional neurology courses, breathing technique courses, 3D movement courses, hands-on courses... I was EXHAUSTED! Constantly on the look-out for the next best thing.

After I had composed myself and tried to stay positive with Luke, I made the decision there and then to stop chasing this "magic bullet". I finally committed to getting rid of all these gimmicks and "quick fixes" and instead truly committed to building MY OWN graded exposure system. You see, at the time I was also reading Louis Gifford's *Aches and Pains* books and these were really beginning to resonate with me. I loved how simple he kept things and his teaching style; he has definitely had a massive influence on how I teach – and even how I'm writing this book, although I never had the pleasure of meeting him.

Back to that transitional train journey! On the train on the way home, I grabbed a piece of scrap paper and I mapped it all out from start to finish, with the skills I'd need to truly be a 'Go-To' Physio that could get long-lasting and life-changing results. This was when the first draft of the 8 Pillars of the 'Go-To' Therapist was born.

The Huddersfield Giants' training centre was my laboratory. I went in with fresh eyes and one core question at the heart of my research that I wanted to answer: **What needs to happen to get long-lasting results?**

There were five big things that clicked into place for me at this time:

1. Second order consequences.

2. The motor adaptations literature.

3. Understanding there are physical and emotional stressors.

4. Defining the root problem.

5. The 80/20 Rule.

1. Second order consequences

On my quest to work smarter, not harder, I began to obsess over systems and mental models. I knew I wasn't treating the true source of the problem but it wasn't until I came across the mental model for "second order thinking" that things began to fall into place.

First order thinking is fast and easy. It happens when we look for something that only solves the immediate problem without considering the consequences of that action. For example, massaging the hamstrings of a patient complaining of tight hamstrings. The hamstrings might feel OK for five minutes but usually the tightness will return again shortly thereafter.

Second order thinking is more deliberate and considers the possibility of being wrong. Second order thinking considers the **consequences** of being wrong. For example, what if their hamstrings "feel" tight but their receptors are becoming sensitised due to increased tension as a second order consequence of an elevated rib cage?

To see what I mean, relax your neck, exhale for as long as you can and then slowly go to touch your toes. Pay attention to when you first notice the "tension" in your hamstrings. Now repeat the movement, but this time keep a proud chest, inhale and go to touch your toes without allowing your ribcage to depress. Your hamstrings will "feel" tight much quicker as a second order consequence of what the ribcage and pelvis is doing.

Therefore, taking this principle, if I wanted to help my patient to get rid of their "tight hamstrings" once and for all, would it make more sense for me to start at the ribcage in order to bring about a second order consequence at the hamstrings without needing to constantly massage the hamstrings and only get short-term relief? This is an example of second order thinking, rather than jumping in and just treating the symptoms.

This set me on the right path, but it wasn't until I came across the motor adaptations literature that I began to see how I could use this principle to be successful more consistently.

2. The motor adaptations literature

I was in the airport waiting to fly back from Portugal on a pre-season training camp with Huddersfield Giants when I first came across the motor adaptations literature from the likes of Paul Hodges, Kylie Tucker and François Hug. It was like a eureka moment for me!

In a nutshell, the motor adaptations literature shows when a noxious stimulus and/or a pain experience is present there are some important strategies the human body implements to deal with this. The key findings are:

There are NO known predictable responses to noxious stimulus/pain experience. This is why it is critical to understand that there can be no "cookie cutter" approaches to dealing with someone in pain.

- Different people react in different ways. You must treat the person in front of you first and foremost.

- Activity of muscles above and below the area of injury/pain increases when degrees of freedom are reduced, or the nervous system wants to decrease stress on a certain part of a muscle or joint.

- When there's an option to offload stress on injured/painful tissues we take it. This has implications for rehab which is done using two limbs.

- Research shows that when a noxious stimulus is present, the nervous system is capable of producing the same force through the knee joint as that prior to the noxious stimulus being present but the direction of force through the knee joint changes. This may be a useful short-term solution but long term what are the consequences?

- Once the noxious stimulus is removed, the previous movement strategy prior to stimulus doesn't necessarily return (protective movement behaviour remains).

The final point is the most important of all to understand. The nervous system may NOT go back to the previous strategy after the pain experience has gone and may continue to use the adapted strategies.

Short term, it was a useful strategy to "survive" but long term, what are the second order consequences?

This got me thinking about my athletes. Could the current pain experience/symptoms simply be a second order consequence of a previous injury and the motor adaptations their nervous system is now using? Could I have just been treating the symptoms the whole time and not the true cause? If this was true then the answer to all my problems was in the subjective assessment and the patient's previous injuries. And all my problems would be solved!

Not so fast!

This worked well for some patients but not others. This forced me to take a step back again and apply the second order thinking model. What is pain? Is it a first order consequence or a second order consequnece? Of course, it was a second order consequence. But to what? Stress! It all starts with a stressor.

3. Stress and reactions to stress

On my crusade to find the "magic bullet" I had already taken a lot of breathing courses and learned about various other "techniques" that looked at the diaphragm. I had mistakenly thought the diaphragm was the problem. The diaphragm, just like a tight hamstring, is also a REACTION or a second order consequence.

The stressor was SPECIFIC to the person in front of me. It finally clicked that stress can come in many forms, both emotional and physical. The respiratory system can become sensitised just like the musculoskeletal system. Stress can increase the heart rate which can also affect the breathing rate and breathing depth.

An increased breathing rate usually means a decreased exhalation time, which means a reduction in the diaphragm's ability to lengthen during the exhalation. This also means a reduced ability to access "rest and digest" for the patient.

Think of someone having a panic attack or hyperventilating for an extreme example of a lot of inhaling (shortening the diaphragm, elevating/protracting the ribcage) and not a lot of exhaling (lengthening the diaphragm and depressing/retracting the ribcage). This simplified things further for me and I could now see that there could be an emotional and/or physical stressor in the person's story.

If I could piece the clues of the subjective assessment together, this would allow me to apply the second order thinking principles together to design a treatment plan that would give long-lasting changes.

4. Defining the root problem

In addition to second order thinking, I also became interested in the power of asking yourself better questions to help focus your mind, which I'll show you how to apply to the subjective assessment and treatment plan design in the coming chapters. It wasn't until later that I got real clarity on the power of questions from Keith Cunningham, a U.S-based business coach, when he spoke about separating the problem from the symptom in his book *The Road Less Stupid*[2].

Previously, I was accepting the patient's symptoms as the problem to be solved and jumping in and treating the first thing I saw with a patient without first defining the true problem. The first person to define a problem (the patient) often dictates the problem to be solved (the symptoms), according to author Shane Parrish. Our instinct is to jump in and start designing treatment plans to solve the problem right away, but this can backfire with patients in the form of symptoms returning if we haven't defined the problem properly. Before we, as therapists, accept this problem, we need to know if it's the right problem to be designing a treatment plan for in the first place.

Often therapists (and patients) can waste a lot of time trying to solve the wrong problems (symptoms). They jump straight in without spending the time defining "root problem". Keith Cunningham says, "The key to defining the root problem is discovering the obstacle that is impeding your progress" (from where the patient is to where they want to be). In order to do this, we must first define where we are currently (point A) and then where we want to get to (point B). We will cover how to communicate this to the patient later, in the effective explanation chapter.

Both Shane and Keith agree that how we state the problem can quickly change how our minds see the problem and put us on the path to success! Most of the time, the symptoms the patient presents with is NOT the problem we need to solve. How we define a problem shapes the solutions (treatment plan) we come up with.

---

[2] Cunningham K., (2017), *The Road Less Stupid: Advice from the Chairman of the Board*, Keys to the Vault, first edition

Shane Parrish[3] has helped me focus on the root problem with some really great questions to ask yourself before designing a treatment plan for a patient:

- Am I just accepting the patient's (or doctor's) definition of the problem?

- Is the problem back pain or that the patient cannot do certain tasks because of the back pain?

When we design the solution to the true problem, it creates fewer problems in the future. The first step is, therefore, to ask yourself when a patient comes through your door: "Is this the symptom or the root problem?"

The next step is to ask yourself what would have to be true for this problem to not exist in the first place? For example, with the case of an inflamed knee joint, what would have to happen to make the knee joint not get inflamed in the first place? Said another way, what muscles or other joints would be doing their jobs so the knee joint wouldn't become inflamed in the first place? All of a sudden you are designing a very different treatment plan to the one addressing just the knee joint.

The third step is to ask yourself, would this solution pass the test of time? Will this problem just pop up again for the patient in three months, three weeks or three years? For example, with the inflamed knee joint, if I just treat the knee joint and help it to settle down, what happens when the patient goes back to the real-world activities?

This is one of the biggest mistakes I see therapists make all the time, especially when I consult with professional sports teams. The therapists and patients spend so much time and energy doing all the "evidence-based" rehab. On paper they are doing everything "right" according to the literature, but it does not address the root problem and so the patient stagnates again when increasing the load on the injured area.

Settling the inflamed knee joint will solve the problem for a few weeks until the patient increases their load again. Solving the hip or hamstring issue that wasn't doing enough work in the first place will solve the root problem and so, when the patient

---

[3] Parrish S., (2021) 'How to Write a Problem Statement', *Farnham Street Blog*

goes back to the real world, everything is doing its job. Do we completely ignore the symptoms then? Not at all. So, what do we do in the real world with real people?

5. The 'Go-To' Physio 80/20 rule

It was around this time that I also came across the Pareto principle in a business book (*80/20 Sales and Marketing*[4]) I was reading. You may have heard of the 80/20 rule by the Italian economist Vilfredo Pareto?

Basically, he found that 80 per cent of your results come from 20 per cent of your actions, and it applies to everything. Business, relationships, wealth... so, I started thinking about how it relates to my world with complex patients. I spent a few weeks pondering this principle and how it related to the second order thinking mental model. I aimed to identify the 20 per cent of actions that were really driving 80 per cent of the patient's symptoms. Finally it all clicked into place.

What I was doing previously was spending 80 per cent of my time treating the symptoms with maybe 20 per cent of my time doing some exercises to help address the "true cause". I flipped this on its head and came up with my own version of the 80/20 rule.

The 80 20 rule

80%
Desensitising true stressors & graded exposure to load tolerance

20%
Desensitising symptoms

---

[4] Marshall P., (2013), *80/20 Sales and Marketing: The Definitive Guide to Working Less and Making More*, Entrepreneur Press, Illustrated edition

I started spending 20 per cent of my time on the symptoms aka the second order consequence (because it's still important to address them)... but I flipped it and spent 80 per cent of my time addressing what is *not* doing its job from the person's story (previous injuries) in the first place – in other words, the true driver of the pain experience/problem.

I won't lie, it was scary at the start to change to this approach, especially in pro sport where the pressure was on to get results fast. As I saw results, my confidence grew more and more with each patient. I slowly implemented this approach in private practice and the results were great in the first few sessions. Yet I still hadn't grasped the true concept of second order consequences in private practice and there was a big problem still left to solve.

Chapter 3:
My Road to Success

It was March 2015. My second daughter, Ruby, was seven months old and the unsocial hours of working in pro sport were beginning to take their toll on me and my wife, Georgina. After seven years, the excitement I once got from working in pro sport was beginning to fade. I was getting less patient with the players and even the Head Coach at times, and I knew I was ready to walk away from working in it on a full time basis.

There was only one problem... I was earning decent money (around £50,000 – £60,000ish a year, at the time) and had to come up with a way to replace this "reliable pro sport" income. I was seeing a few patients (10–12 a week) on the side and this was my "pocket money". I was treating my private practice (a "scruffy" room above a running shop) more like a hobby than a business that actually had to provide for my family.

Worse still, I found it harder in private practice than in pro sport to get results back then. I really struggled to ask for money at the end of sessions and to ask patients to come back for more sessions when the pain was beginning to ease. My patient numbers were up and down: some weeks I'd have 12 patients in and others it'd be back down to six or seven. There was no consistency in my patient numbers and that concerned me, as this was soon to be my main source of income for my family without my pro sport wage.

I had reassured my wife we could survive and I could make up the £50,000 a year shortfall in private practice, although between you and me, I secretly doubted myself – the way things were going some weeks. After many back and forth conversations and lots of mental wrestling inside my own head, I took the "jump" and handed my notice in one wet, spring Monday morning.

I now had six months (my notice period) until the end of the season to get to 30 patients a week (then charging £35 per session) so I could replace the pro sport income. With the deadline in place, I went "all in" on my private practice.

I wish I could tell you it went from strength to strength straight away. I really struggled with the now added pressure of having to make this work long term. I was OK for the first couple of sessions with a patient and things would be going well. I relied a lot, and prided myself upon, my hands-on treatment and approach. Some patients did OK, but for the majority the pain returned again quickly once the patient returned to the real world.

Worse still were the patients whose pain was beginning to ease but who needed more sessions to maintain the results, because I actually struggled the most with the "voices in my head". I was implementing the second order thinking principles at this stage and even though I knew deep down they needed more sessions to get long-lasting results, I was afraid the patient would think I was "salesy", so I'd make some excuse like, "give that a few weeks and give me a call if the pain returns". Then, inevitably, the pain returned.

Being brutally honest with you, some patients lost confidence in me eventually and made some "polite" excuses and were never to be seen again. Others didn't even bother to come back. I had to hear it from the running shop manager downstairs. They had gone to the chiropractor down the street. This massively hurt my ego and, quite frankly, seriously knocked my confidence.

I was supposed to be this top pro sport physio who works with world-class athletes day in, day out. Yet I couldn't get the average person's pain to stay away. I felt like a fraud asking for my patients' hard-earned money at the end of the sessions. I knew I had to change my approach as my lack of confidence and lack of long-lasting results was harming my reputation, and hence my ability to grow my practice.

Why was I able to get such great results in pro sport yet struggled to translate this to my private practice? Over the coming weeks I pondered this question. I reflected on what I did in pro sport when a player got injured and the process I went through. I discussed it at length with my mentor, Meirion, who suggested I write down on paper the difference in how I treated patients in pro sport and in private practice. I reluctantly agreed. Yet when I wrote it down step-by-step, the answer was obvious, almost jumping out of the page at me.

The hip-hop music was blasting away in the background in the gym, yet nothing could distract me from this scrap piece of paper screaming the solution to all my problems.

The big question was... how could I have the same success in private practice as I enjoyed in pro sport? You see, after I mapped out what happens in pro sport, it was obvious that all my problems were happening in the initial assessment. I showed it to Meirion and he agreed at once.

You see, when an athlete gets injured, the coach and athlete usually want to know four things:

1. What's the problem?
2. How long will it take to get back?
3. Why did it happen?
4. What's the plan?

It was only then that I realised how much Meirion had mentored me in answering these four difficult questions over the first few years of my pro sport career. When I was working with Leeds Rhinos in my very first Head Physio role, before I went upstairs to speak to the Head Coach, Meirion (then Head of Physio at Leeds Rugby) used to have me go through what I was going to say to the Head Coach with him. He'd then redirect me if I was being too ambitious and allowed me to avoid making the same mistakes as him – That's probably why I'm passionate now to pay this forward so other therapists can learn from my mistakes!

Back to these four questions...

Let's take a grade two hamstring tear as a quick example and look at a timeline of the injury to return to play. The coach and player want and need to know a realistic timeframe of when they can expect to be back training and playing. In this case, usually around four to six weeks is a realistic timeframe.

However, usually around day seven to ten, the athlete may be pain-free on the bed. Now, if I hadn't set the expectations of the player and coach, they may attempt to train or play because the pain has eased. Why would they think any differently? No pain? Let's give it a go and see how we get on!

Can you see the importance of setting patient expectations now? This was EXACTLY what was happening to my patients in private practice! A lot of my patients were expecting hands-on treatment coming in, because that was what I was known for. The guy downstairs in the running shop was telling people about my strong "thumbs", so in all honesty I felt obligated to give the patient what they wanted, not what they actually needed.

I had a false belief that if I didn't give them the hands-on treatment, they'd be unhappy and possibly go elsewhere (I didn't realise back then that patients didn't want hands-on treatment, they wanted the "feeling" that hands-on treatment gave them). After studying that scrap of paper for what seemed like hours, I also realised there was a massive mismatch in patient's expectations.

A useful (adapted) formula I had stumbled across a few months earlier in a business book (Keith Cunningham's *The Road Less Stupid*) finally made complete sense: **Patient Expectations – Current Reality = Patient's Level of Happiness**

I finally realised that if there was a big mismatch in what the patient was expecting and the reality of the injury, prognosis and treatment plan then I would not have a happy patient. I knew I had to step outside of my comfort zone and address the objections in the first session. Sh%t!

That meant I had to reveal the problem, solution and realistic timeframe to the patient, to give myself the best chance of a happy patient who adheres to the plan, gets results and ultimately gives me reviews and referrals to help my practice grow sustainably. Basically I needed to use a pro sport approach in private practice.

Luckily for me I had a mentor who coached me on answering these four questions so that wasn't my biggest mental obstacle! I had to overcome my fear of not just giving patients what I thought they wanted (hands-on treatment) and actually give them what they needed. F*%k it! I took the plunge and went all in with that deadline looming of having to replace my pro sport wage shortly.

From that moment onwards, in the first session I outlined the problem, the solution, the treatment plan and how many sessions I thought it would take, just like I would with my Head Coach on a daily basis in pro sport. It was scary at first yet something amazing happened. I was spending more time on the "explanation" in the initial assessment... and less time doing hands-on treatment YET patients were leaving just as happy.

There were also some other big benefits that I didn't even realise existed by following this process and what happened next surprised me MASSIVELY!

The patient almost had a sense of relief after the "pro sport explanation". They could see a clear plan in place and had a sense of relief that they were going to be OK. This really surprised me. I could see them visibly relax and unwanted tension in their bodies melt away in front of my eyes. They were getting less hands-on treatment in the first session but leaving even happier. What happened next surprised me even more.

They came back in the next session feeling just as good – if not better than before – and even more optimistic (even with less hands-on treatment). I guess that's the power of "pain science education" when you can get it to actually work in the real world without patients thinking you've just said, "It's all in their head".

Patients were then coming in excited for the next step or milestones to tick off on their journey to the dream outcome that I had set out on the whiteboard in the initial assessment. This also weirdly helped focus me on the session ahead. Almost like magic, I had a new sense of clarity in these sessions, focusing on getting the patient to the next level of the graded exposure plan.

I was finding that patients were not only actively engaged in the process and almost addicted to hitting the next milestone on the graph, but I was able to save so much time in sessions. In fact, I was able to reduce my follow up sessions from 45 minutes to 30 minutes, which is plenty of time when you have clarity on the plan and are just working towards the next milestone on the graded exposure ladder.

I was no longer trying to do and treat everything in the same session. I was clear, focused and back to my "pro sport self", except this time in private practice. Not only that but what happened next shocked me most of all...

Usually, sessions three to four, when the pain is beginning to ease, is when I found my patients were dropping off, making polite excuses about "checking their diary and getting back to me", only to never be heard from again. Yet now at this point in their treatment, even when the pain was easing, patients were asking me the magic question: "What's the next milestone we need to hit this week?" They knew there was more work to do to get to their dream outcome *and* they were "selling me" on why they needed to come back next week, rather than me feeling "salesy" asking them to come back the following week even though the pain was easing.

I was able to FINALLY use my pro sport skills and bridge the gap from low to high-level rehab and actually build resilience for these patients. Not only that but I was able to get them to the "thoughtless, fearless, movement" level of graded exposure, in the words of the great Louis Gifford. This was a massive "aha" moment for me.

When I was able to expose these private practice patients to the level of rehab that was bottom-up based (reflexive based), rather than top-down (conscious cueing), that was where it all clicked into place for me about how to scale a private practice sustainably.

You see, the patient's confidence and self belief went through the roof. Their confidence in their own bodies skyrocketed. And that's when it happened... word started spreading like wildfire. I finally understood what a "raving fan" was, but, more importantly, how to predictably create one time and time again. Bridging the gap from low – to high-level rehab and getting the patient to the "thoughtless, fearless movement" stage of the graded exposure ladder was the "secret sauce" to grow a private practice predictably!

I quickly increased my patient numbers per week to 25 and had to open more times in my diary. I worked my ass off for the next three months between pro sport and every waking hour seeing patients in my practice and soon got to 40 patients a week, all the while working full-time in pro sport.

My wife and I didn't mind as we knew it was short term and for the greater good. Long story short, by October 2015 I had already had to hire Shane Mooney, the now 'Go-To' Therapist Head Mentorship Coach, and fast forward to 2022 we have built the clinic to 150+ patients a week with the three-year target set to 220 patients a week.

We have:

- One full-time practice manager
- One full-time admin staff member
- One part-time admin staff member
- One part-time head physio (Shane)
- Three physiotherapists
- Two sports therapists

All the while replicating these results with over 800 therapists in over 30 countries all over the world. Everything I teach can be applied in the real world. I have a severe distaste for "overnight internet gurus" who have not walked the walk. Since 2015, my clinic has grown from 15 patients a week to 150+, without relying on me being in the day-to-day "grind".

In fact, I've now removed myself from the day-to-day running of the clinic and have since been able to go back into pro sport on my terms on a consultancy basis. I've worked in a Rugby League World Cup final in Australia in 2017 with England Rugby League. I've worked with Masters winning golfer Danny Willett around the world, along with Tommy Fleetwood, amongst other world-class golfers like Jason

Day. I treat former superbike World Champion Tom Sykes. I got headhunted by England Rugby Union (as a proud Irishman) in 2019 and worked in a Rugby Union World Cup Final week in Tokyo. All this in addition to working with many other celebrities and world-class athletes on a weekly basis.

I say all of these things not to impress you, but to impress upon you that I've walked the walk at the biggest stages. My step-by-step system is constantly being tested at the highest levels in pro sport and used in my own private practice in Huddersfield, UK.

I still make mistakes. I still flare patients up from time to time. However, I make fewer and fewer mistakes these days because of my step-by-step system. The system is the saviour! With that said, in the next chapter let's look at the eight core skills in the system that every 'Go-To' Therapist needs to have in order to get life-changing results for their patients.

Chapter 4:
An Overview of the 'Go-To' Therapist Method (and How to Always Give More in Value than You Take in Payment)

When I left the Huddersfield Giants in 2015, I had a new problem.

I needed to now grow the clinic to ensure I always had enough patients for my new therapists. Therefore, I set off on my next crusade to learn marketing skills so I could promote my clinic better. What happened next really surprised me!

It actually made me a far better private practice therapist! I began to understand that a "sale" will never be made if the value does not exceed the price. That first got me thinking about ways to increase the value to the patient.

Then I came across the terms "external and internal motivator" for the patient. This enabled me to see what patients really want and need, and allowed me to create solutions for them that made sure I was giving them more in value than I was taking in payment.

I completely revamped my subjective assessment questions to ask much higher level questions that gave me powerful information to design valuable treatment programs. This took me to the next level and patients responded favourably.

Yet it wasn't until I came across Alex Hormozi's Value Equation that I was finally able to see how all of the pieces fitted together in the subjective assessment. My framework for always giving your patient more in value than you take in payment is as follows:

- **Step 1**: Understand the patient's dream outcome.
- **Step 2**: Understand the patient's perceived likelihood of achievement.
- **Step 3**: Find ways to decrease the time delay.
- **Step 4**: Find ways to decrease the perceived effort and sacrifice.
- **Step 5**: Use this information to focus your objective assessment and treatment plan design.

Step 1:
Understand the patient's dream outcome

What is the ultimate result that the patient wants? This is important to understand as your treatment plan needs to be optimised to always be working towards this.

What is the patient's definition of success? This is another powerful question as it allows you to then not only give it to them in your treatment plan, but also exceed it.

Step 2:
Understand the patient's perceived likelihood of achievement

This step allows you to ask the patient questions that give you an insight into their perceived likelihood of achieving their dream outcome. For persistent pain patients, they may have a low perceived likelihood of achievement, while a first-time acute back pain patient may have a high confidence that they will get back to their dream outcome.

This is important to understand so you can be realistic with your own expectations of the patient's progress, as well as gain a key insight into their belief systems that you may need to influence or update.

The best way to increase a patient's low level of perceived likelihood of achievement is to get them some quick wins that show them they are on the road to their dream outcome. This will be an important consideration when it comes to how you design your treatment plan and what you optimise for.

Step 3:
Find ways to decrease the time delay

It is important to ask questions in your subjective assessment to enable you to find ways to decrease the time delay of progress that the patient feels.

There is a reason why liposuction costs 100 times more than a gym membership. There is a decreased time delay to the dream outcome and this is valuable to the patient. The ability to clinically reason the true cause of the patient's problem/pain experience will allow you to get results fast and decrease the time delay towards the ultimate goal/dream outcome.

Step 4:
Find ways to decrease the perceived effort and sacrifice

It is also important to ask questions in your subjective assessment to enable you to find ways to decrease the perceived effort and sacrifice for the patient.

Back to our liposuction example – that costs 100 times more than a gym membership. The other reason a practitioner can charge this much is that, besides the initial post-surgery recovery, the effort and sacrifice for the patient is minimal.

Unfortunately, we live in a world where people want something for nothing and most patients' motivation levels will drop drastically after the first session. This is why it is critical to ask questions in your subjective assessment that allow you to find ways to decrease your patient's effort and sacrifice in your treatment plan. This will be discussed in a lot more detail in Chapter 8, using Fogg's behaviour model.

Step 5:
Use this information to focus your objective assessment and treatment plan design

The final thing to note is that the thing people buy is the long-term value, aka their "dream outcome". But the thing that makes them stay long enough to get it is the short-term experience. These are little milestones a patient sees along the way that show them they are on the right path. You will now use the information gained from the subjective assessment, in your objective assessment and treatment plan design, to ensure you are working towards these little milestones in every session.

Ultimately, we want patients to have a big emotional win early. This gives them emotional buy-in and momentum to "see it through" to their ultimate goal which gives you the best shot of getting results and referrals.

Going through this process will focus you on the person first and foremost and more than likely take you down a completely different treatment approach than the "traditional" route focusing on strengthening muscles.

Using this framework with your tricky cases or your own therapists

I now use this framework to reflect on my own tricky cases but also my therapists' tricky cases to see which of these four variables we have not done a good job with for the patient or can improve on to ensure we continue to give the patient more value than we take in payment.

For example, when I'm looking at my therapists' notes as part of my head physio framework, I am looking at a clear dream outcome, a consideration of the patient's current level of perceived likelihood of achievement and whether the treatment plan has ensured we decrease the time delay, effort and sacrifice in the hands-on treatment approach and exercise prescription for the patient.

The "best therapists" in the world will naturally focus on the bottom two variables

The best companies in the world focus all their attention on the bottom side of the equation (decrease time delay, and decrease effort and sacrifice). Think of Amazon and how you can take your phone out and in two minutes, with a few clicks, order something that will be at your doorstep the following morning. Sure, you could get the same item slightly cheaper if you shopped around and had to wait two to three days to receive it. This increases your time delay, effort and sacrifice.

The best therapists in the world will use clinical reasoning to know where to start to decrease the time the patient has to wait before they experience improvements and design a sustainable treatment plan that is focused on decreasing the effort and sacrifice for the patient.

The top two variables are the "guiding star" that your treatment plan is optimising for. As you hit each milestone you should notice your patient's perceived likelihood of achievement start to increase significantly.

Practical application:
3 simple ways to increase the value to your patient instantly

If you want to instantly increase the value to your patient focus on these three simple steps:

1. Solve an actual problem worth solving for your patient

What is the REAL PROBLEM the back pain is causing your patient? Don't solve a "weak glute", solve a way for your patient to pick their grandkids up pain free without having to think twice. That is a problem worth solving in your patient's eyes. The "weak glute" is just a little piece of the puzzle. It should not be your, nor your patient's, primary focus.

2. Deliver results quicker

Instead of jumping in and treating the first thing that you can see, step back and come up with a strategy rather than a tactic to get your patient the ultimate result. What is the first milestone that you can hit with your patient so that they can "feel" the difference in everyday life? This will allow them to "see" and "feel" the difference and results of working with you, far more than having them lying on their back doing three sets of ten glute bridges that they can only "feel" momentarily.

3. Reduce your patient's effort in the process

At a first glance, you might think I'm talking about doing more hands-on treatment. I am NOT! What I am really talking about here is fitting your rehab exercises into your patient's daily life and routine, and finding triggers that remind them to do the exercises rather than just relying on motivation alone. We will cover this in more detail in the "Treatment Plan Design Framework".

The 3 critical sides to creating raving fans who refer

On a higher level, the 'Go-To' Therapist must do three things exceptionally well in order to achieve the dream outcome for the patient. I call this the S.O.S. B.A.R. D.O.M.S. Triangle.

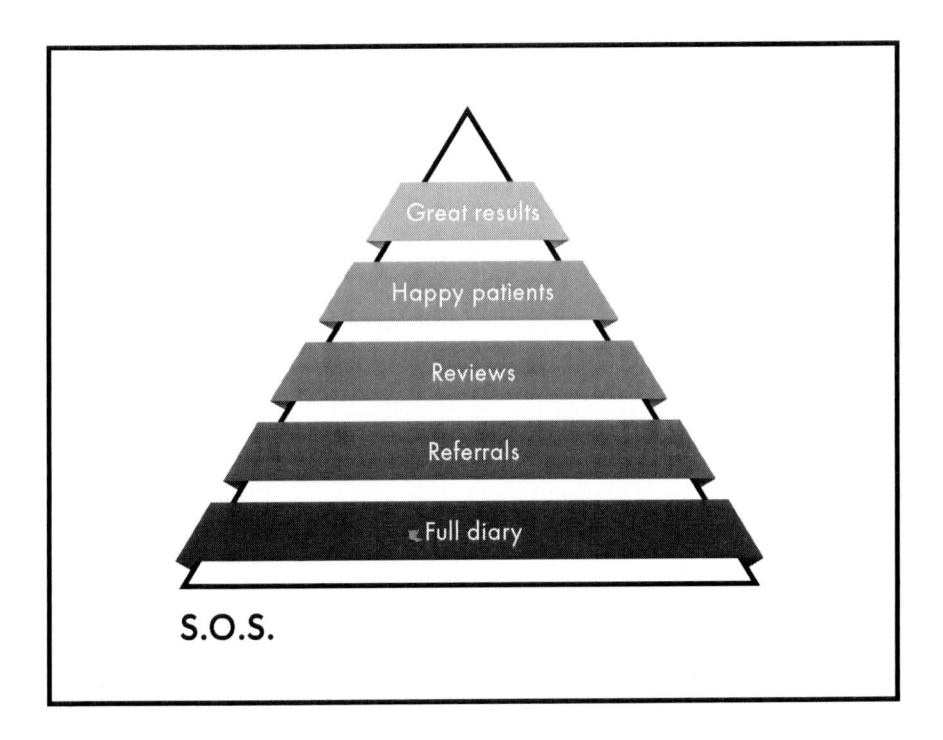

Pyramid (from top to bottom): Great results / Happy patients / Reviews / Referrals / Full diary. Labeled **S.O.S.**

S.O.S. stands for "sense of symptoms". It is critical that therapists can make sense of the patient's symptoms.

Confidence to explain the:
1. Problem
2. Solution
3. Plan (Setting expectations)

Great results
Happy patients
Reviews
Referrals
Full diary

Sense of symptoms

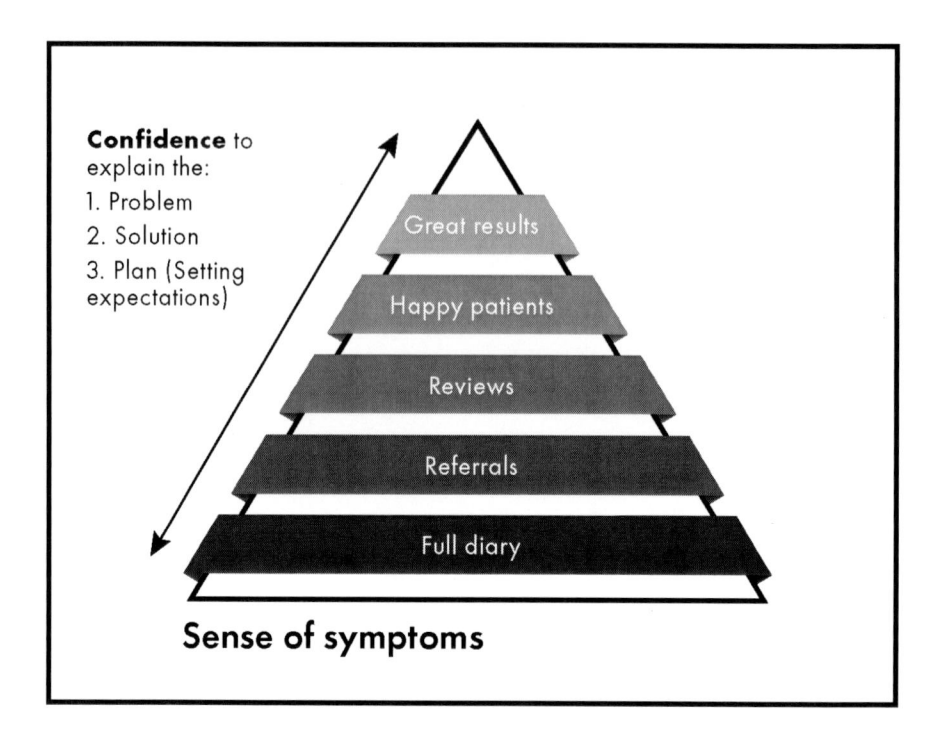

This will allow you to:

1. Always know where to start with your treatment plan.

2. Have confidence and clarity when explaining the problem and solution to your patient.

3. Design a treatment plan that actually SOLVES the patient's problem.

4. Takes away all the guesswork in sessions and overtreating.

The next critical point of the triangle that the therapist must achieve is B.A.R. which stands for "buy-in", "adherence" and "retention".

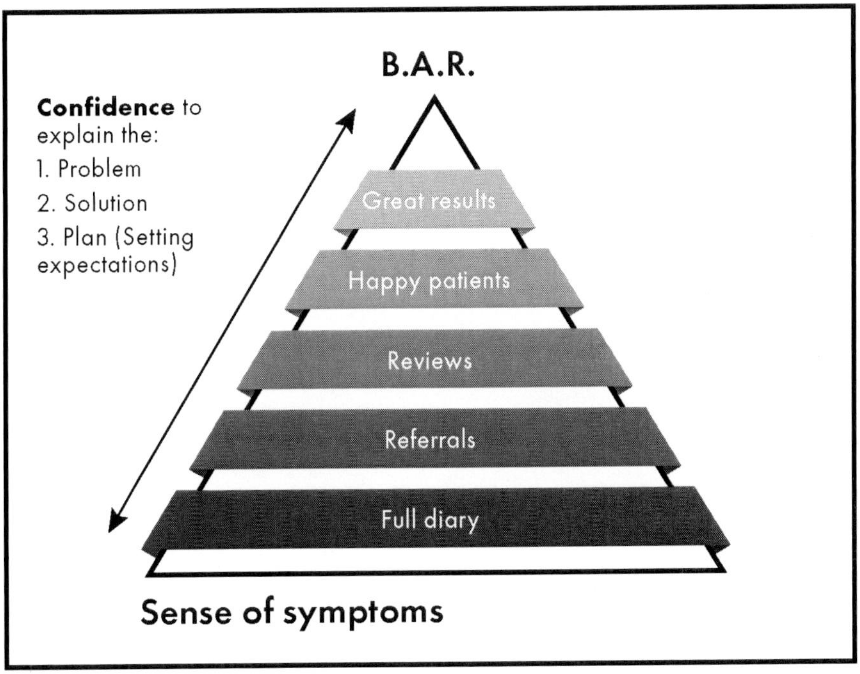
B.A.R.
Confidence to explain the:
1. Problem
2. Solution
3. Plan (Setting expectations)
Great results
Happy patients
Reviews
Referrals
Full diary
Sense of symptoms

This allows you time to:

1. Bridge the gap from low – to high-level rehab.
2. Keep the patient progressing to the "thoughtless, fearless, movement stage" where the patient can feel the difference during dream outcome activities.
3. Create a raving fan.
4. Get referrals.

Buy in - Adherence - Retention

Confidence to explain the:
1. Problem
2. Solution
3. Plan (Setting expectations)

Allows you time:
1. Bridge the gap from low to high level rehab
2. Get to 'thoughtless, fearless, movement stage'
3. Create a raving fan
4. Get referrals

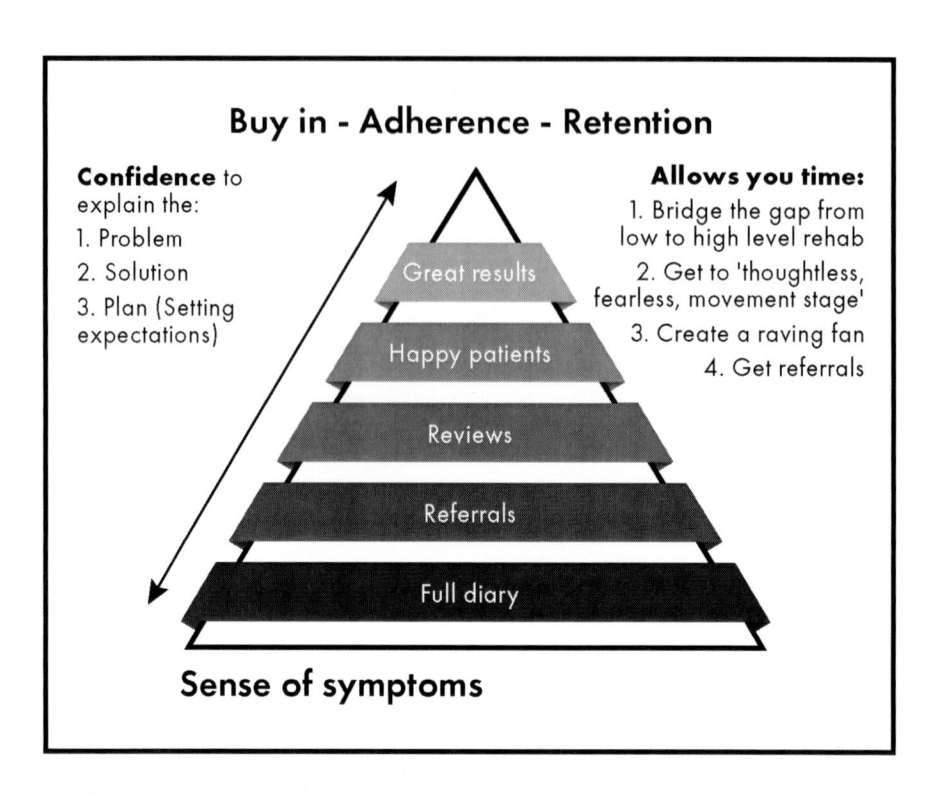

- Great results
- Happy patients
- Reviews
- Referrals
- Full diary

Sense of symptoms

The final critical point of the triangle is D.O.M.S. which stands for "dream outcome", "milestones", "start fast".

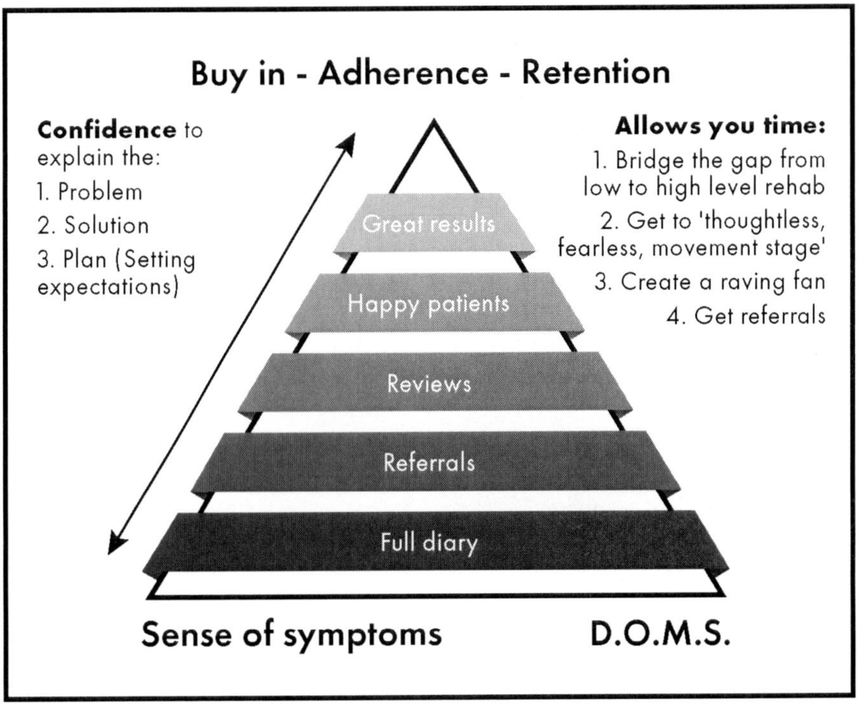

Buy in - Adherence - Retention
Confidence to explain the:
1. Problem
2. Solution
3. Plan (Setting expectations)
Allows you time:
1. Bridge the gap from low to high level rehab
2. Get to 'thoughtless, fearless, movement stage'
3. Create a raving fan
4. Get referrals
Great results
Happy patients
Reviews
Referrals
Full diary
Sense of symptoms
D.O.M.S.

Remember, a physical therapy clinic's ability to grow is not built on the first session but the sessions thereafter.

This allows you to prescribe the right exercises at the right time that:

1. Work towards the dream outcome of the patient.

2. Start hitting key milestones along the way which ensure the patient can see the progress and increases the perceived likelihood of achieving their dream outcome.

3. Deliver the dream outcome.

4. Get referrals.

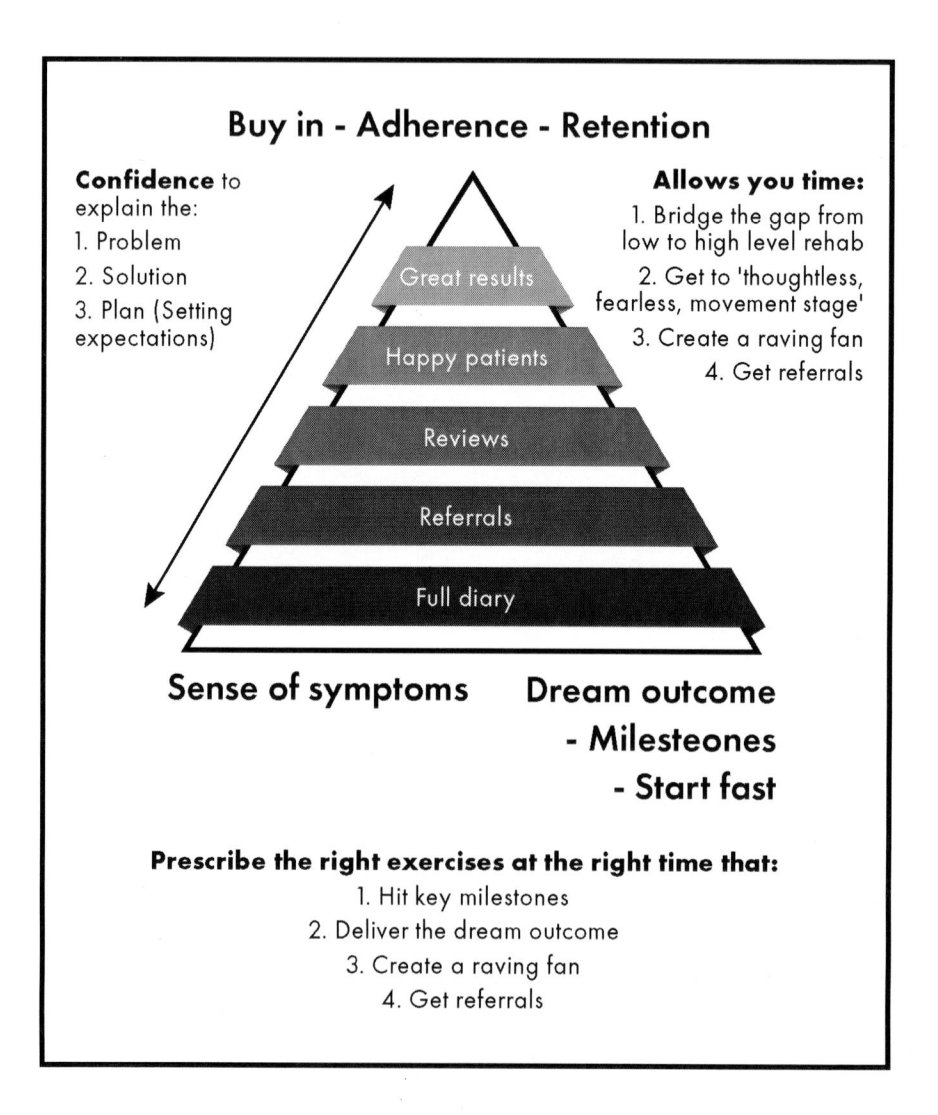

Buy in - Adherence - Retention

Confidence to explain the:

1. Problem
2. Solution
3. Plan (Setting expectations)

Allows you time:

1. Bridge the gap from low to high level rehab
2. Get to 'thoughtless, fearless, movement stage'
3. Create a raving fan
4. Get referrals

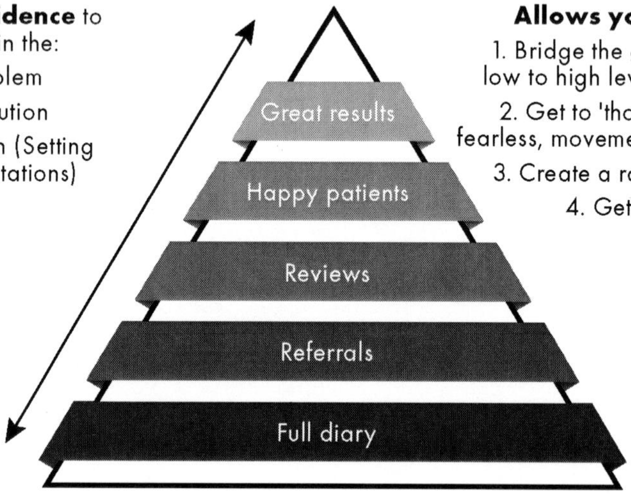

Great results
Happy patients
Reviews
Referrals
Full diary

Sense of symptoms

Dream outcome
- Milesteones
- Start fast

Prescribe the right exercises at the right time that:

1. Hit key milestones
2. Deliver the dream outcome
3. Create a raving fan
4. Get referrals

Practical application:
The 8 core skills you need to always deliver more in value than you take in payment

Now that you understand there is much more to giving value to your patient than just some hands on treatment and a few rehab exercises, let's look at the eight core skills/pillars required of a 'Go-To' Therapist throughout the patient journey.

We will go through each pillar in much more detail in the coming chapters, but for now here is a brief overview so you can see the full picture.

The 8 Pillars to getting predictable results for your patients while always giving more in value than you take in payment:

- **Pillar 1:** Subjective assessment

- **Pillar 2:** Objective assessment

- **Pillar 3:** Effective explanation

- **Pillar 4:** Treatment plan design

- **Pillar 5:** Hands-on treatment

- **Pillar 6:** Low-level rehab

- **Pillar 7:** Bridging the gap from low to high-level rehab

- **Pillar 8:** Strength and conditioning

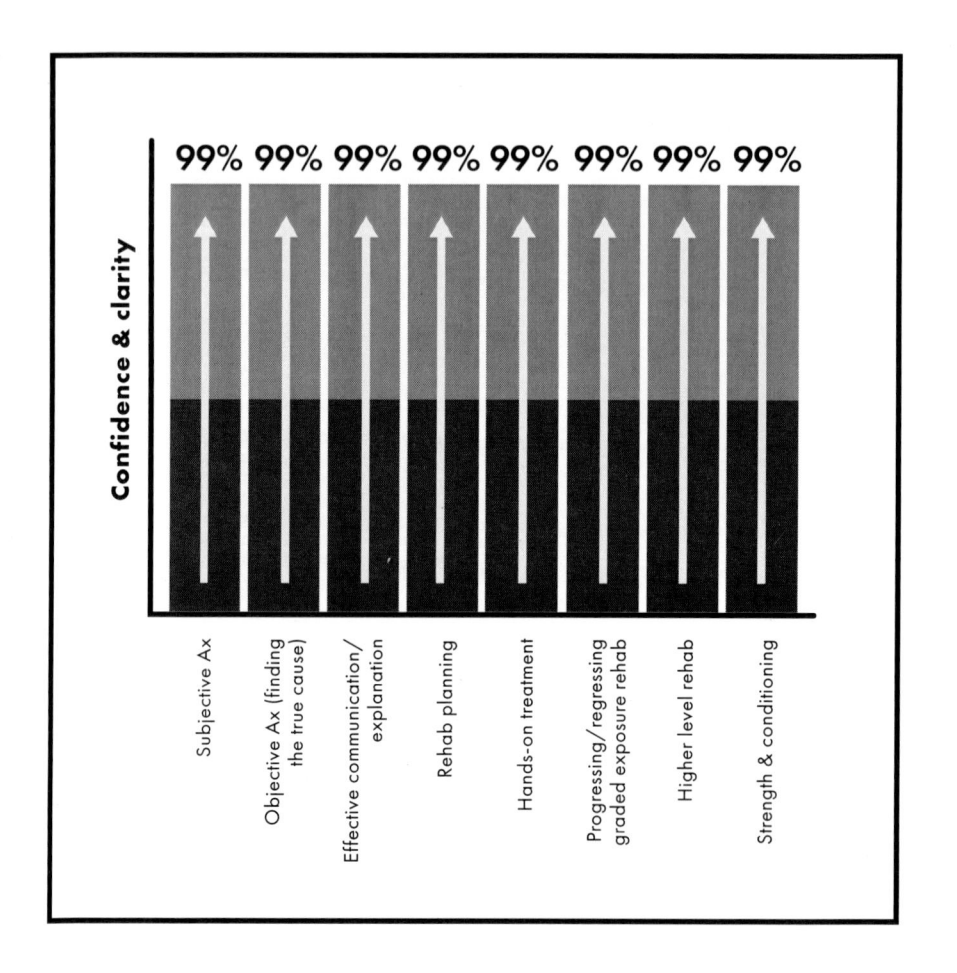

Pillar 1:
Subjective assessment

This pillar contains different mini frameworks that ultimately allow you to make sense of your patient's symptoms in the subjective assessment by asking high-quality questions that give you higher quality information that you can use to piece your patient's story together to form a working hypothesis in your objective assessment.

It should also identify the "northern star" or "dream outcome" that you are optimising for with your patient, as well as provide opportunities to gain an insight into how to design a treatment plan that will decrease effort and sacrifice for the patient.

Pillar 2:
Objective assessment

This is where you will look at your patient's current movement strategies to cross link with their story to see what is doing a good job (or even too good a job) and what is not doing enough work that is causing the sensitised area to produce a pain experience. You will ask yourself three critical questions throughout this phase that we will cover shortly.

Pillar 3:
Effective explanation

This is where you come down to the patient's level and explain the problem and solution to the patient in simple terms in the context of their injury or situation/story.

Pillar 4:
Treatment plan design

Once the patient understands the problem and solution, you will now design the plan with the patient, including key milestones along the way to the dream outcome. You will then also give a realistic time frame and explain how many sessions it will take to set expectations for the patient.

Pillar 5:
Hands-on treatment

If hands-on treatment is appropriate, you will use smaller mini frameworks to clinically reason where to start with your hands-on treatment for a fast start and to decrease the time delay for the patient to start seeing results. You will use the frameworks in this pillar to consider the second order consequences of your hands-on treatment to ensure you're always working towards long-lasting results.

Pillar 6:
Low-level rehab

In this pillar you will use the rehab principles frameworks to design rehab exercises that get results quickly and ensure your patient is not reliant on hands-on treatment. You will work smarter not harder when designing rehab exercises that fit into your patient's daily life.

Pillar 7:
Bridging the gap from low to high-level rehab

In this pillar you will learn how to transition from low-level (top-down cues) to high-level (bottom-up cues) so your patient can move with "thoughtless, fearless, movement" and feel the difference in everyday life.

Pillar 8:
Strength and conditioning

In this pillar you will learn how to use strength and conditioning principles to build resilience for your patient to ensure they can truly withstand the demands of the real world specific to their situation.

Standing the test of time with two World Cup Final weeks

I have used this exact framework in two World Cup Final weeks when making big decisions on whether players would be fit or not. It has given me the confidence to take the emotions out of the decision-making process and ensure it is safe for a patient to return to their daily activities.

A surprising benefit of having a structured step-by-step system in place is the ability to remove the emotion out of the decision-making process and give a realistic prognosis for your patients in high pressure situations.

In November 2017, in Brisbane, Australia I had to make two big calls on two big players in the week of the Rugby League World Cup final. One was a quadriceps strain and the other a "tight hamstring". The step-by-step system allowed me to see exactly where the players were in the process and how much work was left to do. As you'll see in Chapter 15, I was able to use the step-by-step system to my advantage and "show" not "tell" the player they were not ready to return to action. This is also very powerful in private practice where patients may want to return to activities, such as running, too quickly.

As the philosopher Aristotle put it, "The whole is greater than the sum of its parts". When you have a complete structured step-by-step system in place, there are many more surprising benefits that will become apparent as we progress through this book.

Final thoughts

The first two pillars are focused on making sense of the patient's symptoms.

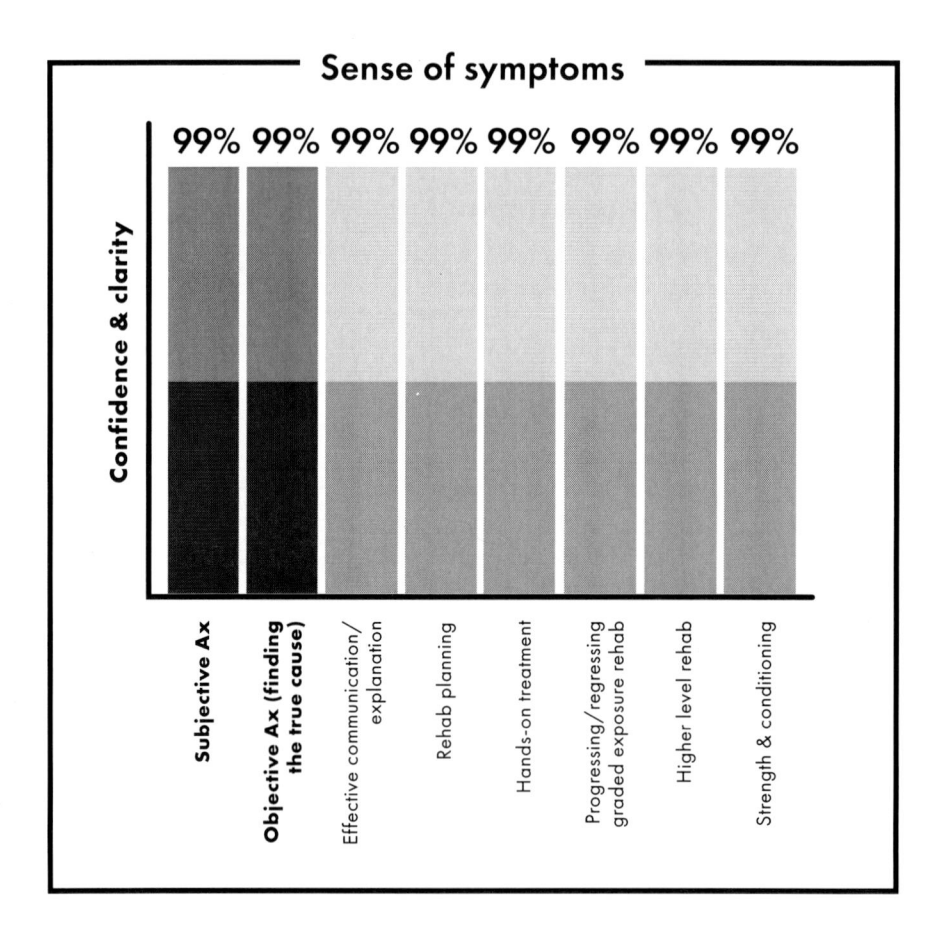

Sense of symptoms

Confidence & clarity	99%	99%	99%	99%	99%	99%	99%	99%
	Subjective Ax	Objective Ax (finding the true cause)	Effective communication/ explanation	Rehab planning	Hands-on treatment	Progressing/regressing graded exposure rehab	Higher level rehab	Strength & conditioning

This allows you to:

1. Always know WHERE TO START with your treatment plan.

2. Have confidence and clarity when explaining THE PROBLEM AND SOLUTION to your patient.

3. Design a treatment plan that actually SOLVES THE PATIENT'S PROBLEM.

4. Take away all the guesswork in sessions and overtreating.

The next two are focused on patient buy-in, adherence and retention.

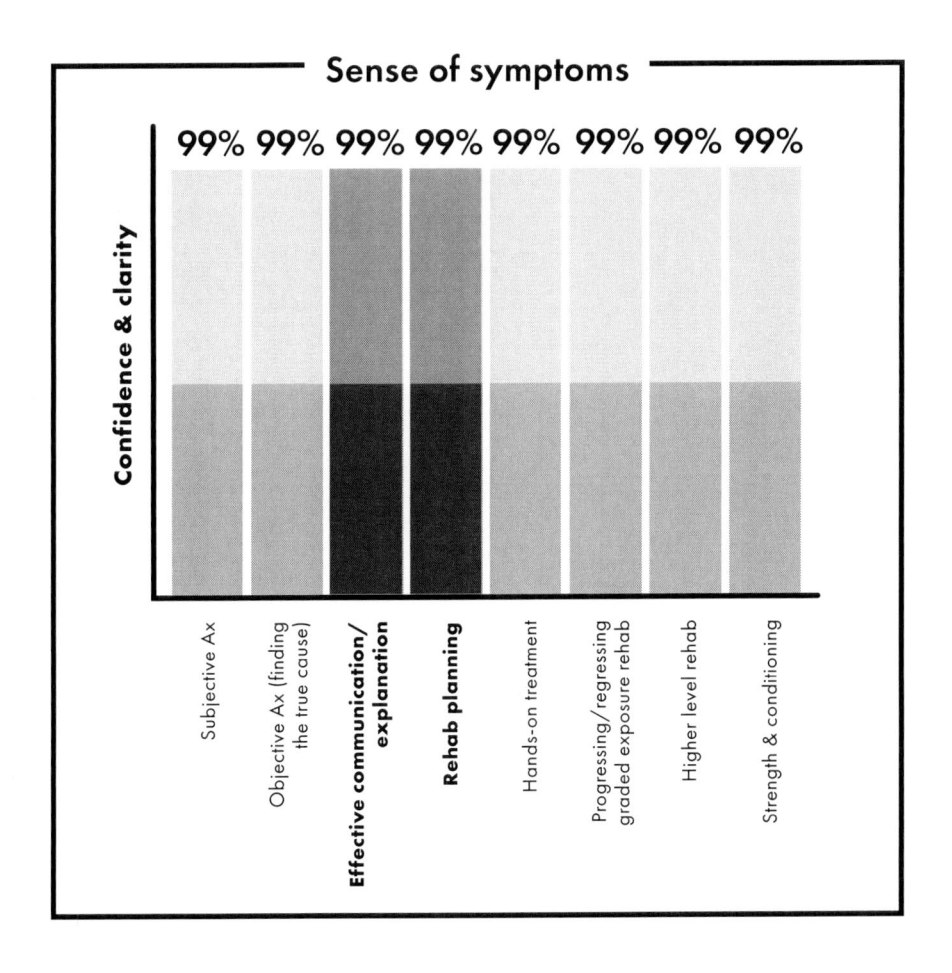

Sense of symptoms

Confidence & clarity

99% 99% 99% 99% 99% 99% 99% 99%

- Subjective Ax
- Objective Ax (finding the true cause)
- **Effective communication/ explanation**
- **Rehab planning**
- Hands-on treatment
- Progressing/regressing graded exposure rehab
- Higher level rehab
- Strength & conditioning

These two pillars allow you to:

1. Design a simple step-by-step treatment plan that is realistic for the patient to achieve their dream outcome.

2. Fit the rehab into their daily life to decrease the perceived effort and sacrifice.

3. Deliver best bang-for-buck approaches with your hands-on treatment and rehab exercises specific to the patient.

4. Design rehab exercises that allow the patient to feel the difference throughout the day and that are therefore exercises they will actually do.

5. Have clear next steps for your patient in the next session so you never lose a patient.

The final four pillars are "walking the talk" and prescribing the right exercises at the right time to achieve the patient's dream outcome.

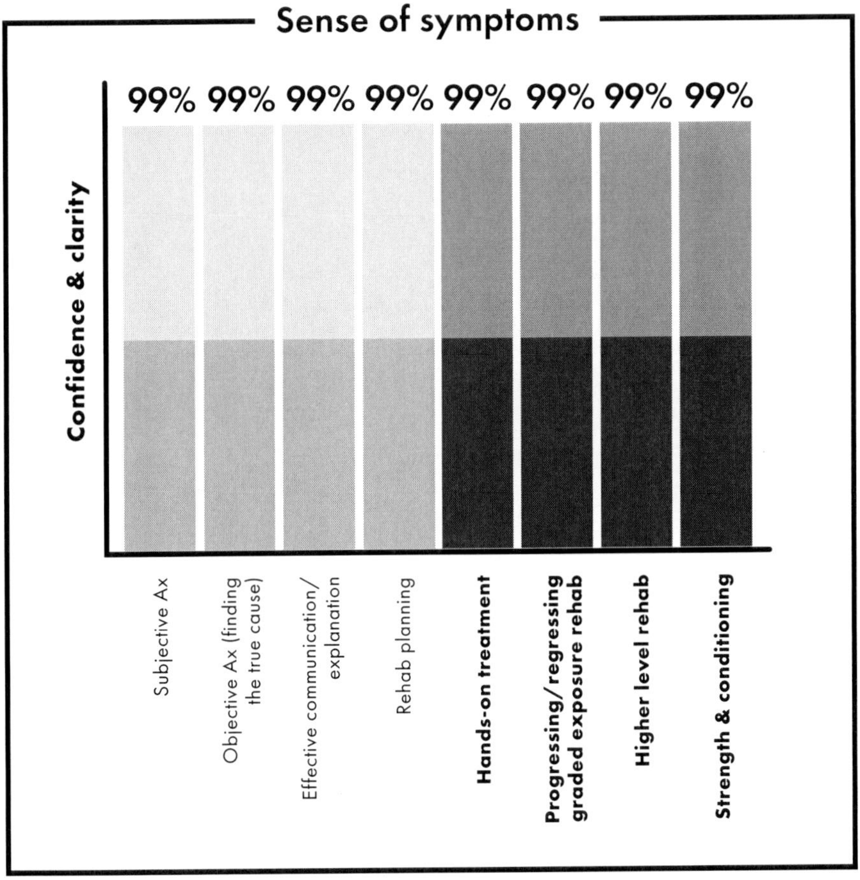
Sense of symptoms
Confidence & clarity
99% 99% 99% 99% 99% 99% 99% 99%
Subjective Ax
Objective Ax (finding the true cause)
Effective communication/ explanation
Rehab planning
Hands-on treatment
Progressing/regressing graded exposure rehab
Higher level rehab
Strength & conditioning

Having these four pillars in place will allow you to:

1. Stop over-treating and create an impact that the patient can "feel" in their day-to-day life.

2. Gain a fast start ensuring that the patient can feel the impact of working with you to reinforce buy-in, adherence and retention.

3. Deliver rehab exercises that are outcome specific and not muscle specific for maximum impact.

4. Hit milestones with your treatment plan that reinforce to the patient they are on the right track to achieving their dream outcome.

5. Remain accountable to always giving more in value than you take in payment so you can sleep well at night.

Each pillar builds on the next to give you and your therapists unshakeable confidence. If you are strong in some pillars but not in others then it will be extremely difficult to make sense of your patients' symptoms and design plans that always give more in value than you take in payment.

In the next section we will look at arguably the most important of all the pillars, but the ones that are frequently skimmed over by therapists.

THE GO-TO PHYSIO MENTORSHIP

Discover Dave O'Sullivan's step-by-step method to rapidly improve patient adherence and progress — while skyrocketing confidence in your clinical care!

" The Go-To Physio Mentorship is one of the most comprehensive, forward-thinking personal development programs available to physical therapists.

Dave and his team are phenomenal. I went from struggling to feeling confident in my abilities virtually overnight . This also took my client numbers from 10-15 a week to 15-20 to 20-30 in the first 3 months — I now struggle to fit them all in the diary!

I would recommend The Go-To Physio Mentorship to any therapist who is willing to go that extra mile to succeed. "

TONI STANTON

Scan the QR code now to find out more about how The Go-To Physio Mentorship can help you and your business grow!

Part Two:
Subjective and Objective Assessment

With clarity comes confidence. With confidence comes power: the power to act and help your patients.

Becoming a calm, confident physiotherapist in private practice all starts with being able to make sense of your patients' symptoms. This is a non-negotiable first step for any 'Go-To' Physiotherapist. It isn't the most sexy part of the profession, such as the hands-on or rehab exercises, yet when you get this part right, the results are sexy!

This section of the book will help you to add more structure and consistency to your subjective and objective assessments. This in turn will allow you to have complete clarity on where the root of the issue is, the confidence to diagnose your patients and then design the best approach for your patient to achieve their dream outcome.

It will also highlight the important difference between "pain free" and moving with "thoughtless, fearless movement" and how you can incorporate this into your assessments. This is a key differentiator if you want your patients to be able to navigate their day-to-day lives without any consideration of their ailment and help them build confidence in their bodies.

It will also show your patients that pain relief is just the beginning of their treatment and allow you enough time to deliver incredible results for your patients so they spread positive word of mouth and generate referrals.

Being recognised as a 'Go-To' Physio that goes the extra length to get remarkable results all starts here in the subjective and objective assessment.

Chapter 5:
Making Sense of Your Patient's Story and Having Confidence and Clarity in Your Treatment Plan

In 2014, the Huddersfield Giants started working with Karl Morris, a sports psychologist based in Manchester. I immediately struck up a close friendship with Karl and a lot of what he was teaching was resonating with me and the approach I was developing at the time.

Karl taught me many things during our time working together, but one of the things he said that truly stuck with me was the phrase from Tony Robbins: "The quality of your life will be dictated by the quality of the questions you are asking yourself." This instantly resonated with me and I began to think about the quality of questions I was asking not only myself but also my patients, particularly in the subjective assessment.

In university, I was taught to ask aggravating and easing questions, 24-hour pattern questions and severity, irritability and nature (SIN) questions. These are all important questions to ask the patient, but they are addressing the symptoms and not the true cause. Most importantly, they are all questions that can easily allow you to be sidetracked and focus only on the pain, forgetting the person in front of you.

The subjective assessment is arguably the most important pillar of the eight as this is where ALL the answers lie to your patient's problems. However, there is so much more to the subjective assessment than just asking questions. The subjective assessment is the big interaction with the patient – first impressions matter.

The aim of the subjective assessment should be thirteenfold:

1. To establish rapport and authority.

2. To make the patient feel understood, accepted, safe and in control.

3. To identify the most important thing that the patient wants from the session.

4. To establish the internal problems that the external problem is causing the patient.

5. To establish the mechanism of injury.

6. To establish the aggravating and easing factors and identify the most valuable problems to solve.

7. To get a clear timeline of the patient's previous physical and emotional stressors.

8. To identify any potential objections or tripwires that could sabotage a successful outcome for the patient.

9. To identify the patient's current perceived likelihood of achievement.

10. To identify the opportunities in the patient's life to start fast with your treatment plan, allowing you to add value immediately with the least amount of effort and sacrifice possible.

11. To rule out red flags.

12. To be aware of yellow flags and understand the patient's medical history and current medications.

13. To recap the patient's story so they can feel understood and heard.

1. Establishing rapport and authority

Whether right or wrong, one of the key essentials for a "sale" is for the person buying to be sold on "you"! They must believe in you and that you can help them. Have you ever worked or met with a world-renowned surgeon? I have had the pleasure of meeting and working with quite a few over my time. Why do I bring surgeons up here? Because the best of the best surgeons all have similar characteristics. They are friendly, calm, confident, make good eye contact and give you confidence and belief.

You too must do the same for your patients. One of the first things I teach in my 'Go-To' Physio mentorship program is the importance of building rapport and authority. You and your therapists need to be friendly, calm and confident yet maintain authority.

The key components of rapport and authority include:

- Eye Contact
- Smile
- Tonality
- Putting the other person at ease (ask them simple questions about the past)
- Observing for "fight or flight'"
- Empathy
- Listening for/observing FEELINGS and EMOTIONS

Would you ever see or hear a world-renowned surgeon with a high-pitched voice, talking fast and nervously? What impression would this give you? Be the world-renowned surgeon in the eyes of your patient and not the giggly nervous schoolboy/girl. Your ability to get results with your patients will not only be about how good your hands-on skills are, but also how much of a people person you are.

2. Make the patient feel safe, understood, accepted and in control

People have four basic human needs:

1. To feel understood

2. To feel accepted

3. To feel safe

4. To feel in control

Be confident, assertive, authoritative, professional and *the* expert in your field who is in charge. Let them know that they are in the competent hands of an expert. Then, set the stage and expectation of the session ahead so they understand what to expect moving forward and feel safe.

Once you've done this, get their acknowledgement and commitment, and let them know they don't need to do any movements or answer any questions if they don't feel comfortable. Remember, for a lot of people it will be their first time at physiotherapy and they won't know what to expect. Setting expectations and explaining what will happen in the sessions will immediately help put them at ease, build rapport and help you get better quality answers to your questions.

3. Identify the most important thing the patient wants from the session

A useful formula to memorise is:

Patients Level Of Happiness = Current Reality – Expectations

Our job is to bridge the gap between current reality and patient expectations.

Remember that cancellations, no shows, and drop offs happen when price exceeds value. However, results, raving fans, referrals, and reviews happen when value exceeds price.

A critical question to start your session with after you've built rapport and set the agenda is:

"What's the most important thing to you that you want out of today's session?"

This is a powerful question to ask, as it gives you an opportunity to meet and exceed the patient's expectations or to adjust their expectations if they are unrealistic.

The patient's answer usually falls into two buckets:

1. "I want some pain relief..."

2. "I want to know what's wrong and how to fix it..."

If the patient answers, **"I want some pain relief..."** you may consider focusing on the 20 per cent of symptoms/undoing motor adaptations first using breathing techniques and/or hands-on treatment if appropriate. You may also consider delaying effective explanation (the third pillar) until the end of the session and then setting expectations about their symptoms, possibly returning due to the acute nature of the presentation, if applicable.

It is important the patient understands we haven't addressed the root cause yet. I have learned the hard way that there is limited value in spending time with a "pain science explanation" to someone who is sitting in a lot of pain. Desensitising the pain experience and then providing the explanation is likely to be of far more benefit to both the therapist and the patient.

The other bucket patients fall into is: **"I want to know what's wrong and how to fix it once and for all..."**

This is a more "mature" buyer who has probably been around the houses and failed with traditional approaches. This is the patient who will get the most value from the effective explanation performed after the initial assessment.

4. Establish the internal problems that the external problem is causing the patient

The external motivator for a patient is usually the back pain, neck pain, knee pain etc. The internal motivator, however, is the thing that motivated the patient to take action, pick up the phone, book an appointment, give up their time and attend the appointment – such as being pain free when picking up their grandchildren/ playing a full round of golf without flaring up an old injury/returning to running after time out.

This is critical to understand as most people put up with pain for long periods of time before seeking help. It is only when the pain starts affecting other parts of their life that they usually decide enough is enough and find the motivation to solve the problem.

Remember: Patients buy "solutions" to their internal problems.

You will add massive value to the patient by optimising their treatment plan to solve their internal problems. However, you first need to understand clearly what these internal problems are.

Probing questions to uncover internal motivators include:

- What is the pain stopping you from doing?

- How is the pain affecting your daily life?

- What was the defining moment for you when you decided to take action and get this sorted?

- Is your pain affecting anything else in your life?

5. Establish the mechanism of injury

Understanding the mechanism of injury is critical for decreasing the time delay in improvements and delivering quick wins for the patient.

With the mechanism of injury or progressive overloading doing specific tasks in the lead up to the pain experience, think about which peripheral tissues are involved. Joints move in three planes of motion. At any particular part of a range of motion, there is a point upon which the joint pivots or rotates, which is called the instantaneous axis of rotation. There are tissues on one side of the axis that lengthen/decompress, and tissues on the other side that need to shorten/compress. This will be a combination of a passive subsystem (osseous and connective tissue), active subsystem (dynamic contractile tissues) and the neural subsystem (nervous system interpretation of proprioceptive input).

The question to ask is: which peripheral tissues may have undergone a protective response and which motor adaptations may be present as a result?

For example, with lifting mechanisms causing back pain, consider iliocostalis and the intercostals as some tissues which may have undergone a protective response. With regards to implementing the 80/20 rule, you may consider spending 80 per cent of your time working on the true cause of the problem, with just 20 per cent of your time dedicated to the symptoms (the iliocostalis, in this example) to ensure you get some quick wins.

If there was no specific mechanism of injury, think about the lead up time to the injury happening. Was there any change in the patient's normal routine? Any sudden increases in load? Then ask yourself which peripheral tissues would be involved? Which tissues should be tolerating a lot of the load, but maybe are not, and which are potentially doing too much (usually the pain experience area of the body)?

6. Establish the aggravating and easing factors

You can also use the principle of tissues shortening and lengthening with the aggravating and easing factors to piece the clues together to uncover which peripheral tissues may be involved.

7. Clear timeline of the patient's previous physical and emotional stressors

It's important for you to draw out the patient's previous injury timeline in chronological order. This not only helps focus your mind but can also help the patient to have an "aha moment" and connect the dots of their story.

The 'Go-to' Physio resilient person

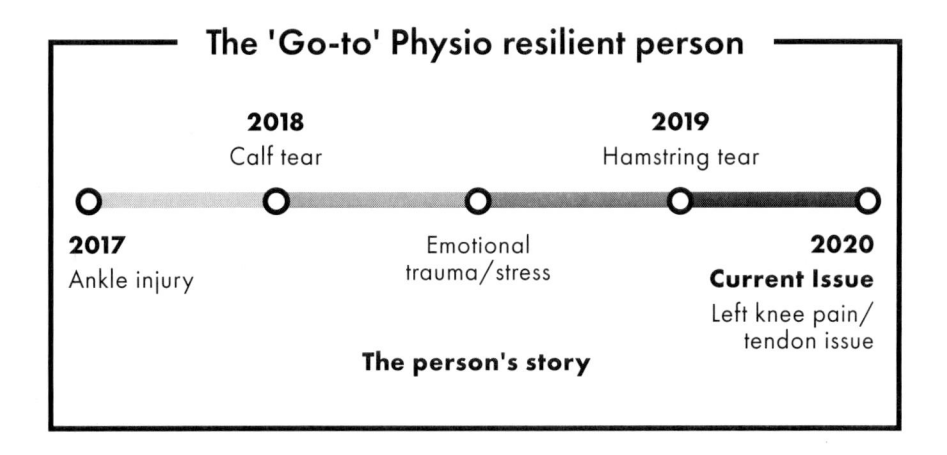

```
2017            2018           Emotional         2019           2020
Ankle injury    Calf tear      trauma/stress     Hamstring tear  Current Issue
                                                                 Left knee pain/
                                                                 tendon issue
```

The person's story

It's important to also note any times of increased stress or trauma on the timeline, as this is where the respiratory system may have become sensitised, leading to second order consequences on the diaphragm and ribcage, followed by third order consequences on the peripheral tissues.

Some good questions to ask around sensitive issues such as emotional traumas and/or stressors are:

- Have you had any major times of trauma in your life?

- Have you had any prolonged stress in your life?

- What's the most stressful part of your day?

- How would you rate your stress management?

- How do you usually sleep?

- Do you wake feeling refreshed?

- How many hours do you typically sleep?

- How is your nutrition on a day-to-day basis?

- Have you noticed any foods that help or hinder your pain?

The patient may not feel comfortable opening up to you in the first session but they may choose to do so in later sessions, so if something isn't making sense early in the treatment sessions, it may be this. Medications may also give you clues about emotional stressors such as anxiety.

8. Identify any potential objections or tripwires that could sabotage a successful outcome for the patient

Asking questions such as as the following can give you lots of valuable information:

- What have you tried previously?

- What helped? What didn't help?

- Is there anything that makes it worse?

It is important to understand what the patient values and may not value. They may have tried massage before but it resulted in a flare up for their injury, for example. In this case, if you talk a lot about massage in the effective explanation and treatment plan, the patient may have a hidden objection.

The most dangerous and difficult objection of all is the **HIDDEN OBJECTION!!**

The questions I've just outlined will allow you to find hidden objections.

9. Identify the patient's current perceived likelihood of achievement

It is important to understand your patient's starting point and current levels of motivation. A highly-motivated patient with a lot of self-belief that they will recover from this injury will be managed very differently from a patient with very little self-belief.

Some good questions to gain insight into your patient's motivation levels are:

- On a scale of 1 to 10, how confident are you that this problem will get sorted once and for all?

- On a scale of 1 to 10 – 1 being not important and 10 being extremely important – how important is this for you to get sorted right now?

NOTE: If it's not important to them... BEWARE! If they don't have a burning desire to solve this problem, it doesn't matter what you are charging, they won't "buy-into" the treatment plan or, worse, they'll buy and then not do the work they need to, potentially damaging your reputation in the process.

10. Identify the opportunities in the patient's life to start fast with your treatment plan, allowing you to add value immediately with the least amount of effort and sacrifice possible

Identifying the most valuable problems to be solved for the patient and where to start solving them is non-negotiable if your aim is to create raving fans.

You must start fast with the patient and find ways to build a treatment plan around their life rather than expecting them to live their life around your treatment plan.

You must use the subjective assessment to gain an insight into how you will do this for the patient.

Understanding your patient's daily routine is critical if you are to include exercises that are easy to implement throughout their day. Some questions to help you develop a treatment plan that will fit into your patient's life include:

- What does a typical day look like for you?

- What are the activities you do repetitively throughout the day? Sit, stand, stairs?

- What are the most stressful parts of your day?

- What are the least stressful parts of the day?

The answers will give you an insight into the best times of day for the patient to incorporate their exercises, which will be important during the effective explanation.

11. To rule out red flags

It should go without saying that it is critical to rule out red flags or any sinister pathologies being present.

Remember that a lack of red flags doesn't rule out serious disease, and red flags in isolation don't confirm serious disease either. It is usually not clear cut; however, my rule of thumb is if it doesn't make sense from a musculoskeletal point of view then it's best to be safe than sorry.

Common red flags include:

1. Bladder/bowel dysfunction which may present as very localised tenderness.

2. Saddle anaesthesia which will be accompanied usually with a history of trauma.

3. Recent unexplained weight loss.

4. Constant night pain.

5. Thoracic pain (metastasis), especially with anyone over the age of 55 years old.

12. Be aware of yellow flags and understand the patient's medical history and current medications

"What do you think is the actual problem?" This is a powerful question which may give you insights into other potential obstacles that may stop you from helping your patient achieve their ideal outcome.

Asking about any medications may also give clues about emotional stressors or a sensitised nervous system. Anxiety and asthma may be relevant for a back pain patient, while a diagnosis of depression may help you decide how much and when to give exercises to a patient.

13. Recap the patient's story so they feel understood and heard

Recapping the patient's story to them not only helps them feel understood and heard, but it is also a great way for you to "connect the dots" and focus your mind. Very often as you repeat the story back to the patient and say the words out loud, you will start to make connections in the patient's story, which will give you enhanced focus as you move into the objective assessment.

The answer always lies in the patient's story

As you can see, there is a lot more to the subjective assessment than you or I were probably taught at university. Asking these questions forces you to stay focused on the person in front of you rather than just the site of pain. Your patient will feel heard and understood and you will gain invaluable information for the objective assessment. If something is not making sense in the objective assessment or with the patient, the answer will always lie in the subjective assessment.

Before progressing to the objective assessment, you must have ruled out red flags and be clear on the following three things in order to design a meaningful objective assessment that gives the information required to design and deliver a value-based treatment plan that solves the patient's more valuable problems:

1. Clear timeline of previous injuries and stressors.

2. What the pain is stopping them from doing.

3. Where they want to get back to.

Once you have this information, let's move onto making sense of your patient's symptoms in the objective assessment.

Chapter 6:
Making Sense of the Objective Assessment

On 2 September 2016, I left Huddersfield on a dark cold morning at 5.45am, travelled to Amsterdam via Manchester Airport and back again late that Friday evening, in order to present my step-by-step system to one of the world's leading experts in the field of human movement, running and motor control, Frans Bosch.

My goal was for Frans to scrutinise and essentially rip apart the 'Go-To' Physio system and find any holes or weaknesses in order to further improve it. After 18 hours, two planes, two trains and two car journeys on the M62, one of my big "aha" moments was getting clarity on human movement and how I could apply this to the objective assessment.

Here is a modified version of a slide that I've seen Frans use previously:

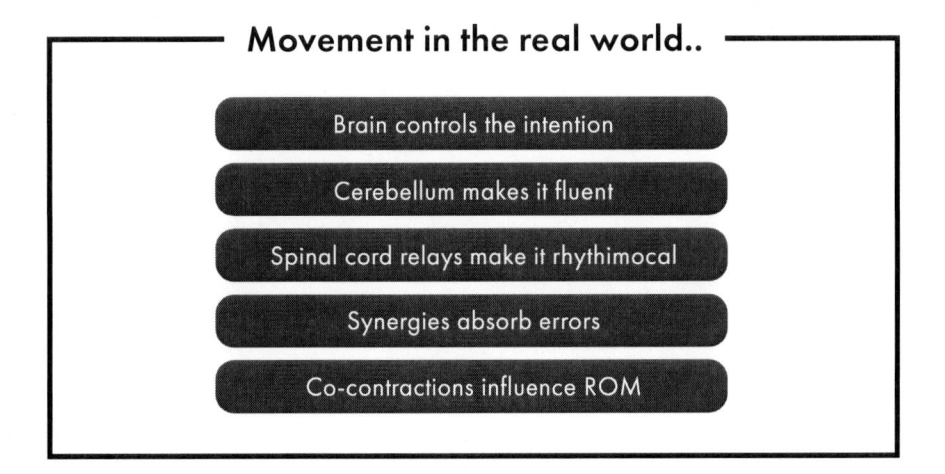

Movement in the real world..

- Brain controls the intention
- Cerebellum makes it fluent
- Spinal cord relays make it rhythimocal
- Synergies absorb errors
- Co-contractions influence ROM

The key takeaway on leaving Holland was that when I am performing an assessment, such as a toe-touch movement for example, the patient's conscious intention is to "touch their toes". The patient makes a conscious decision to move. That is it.

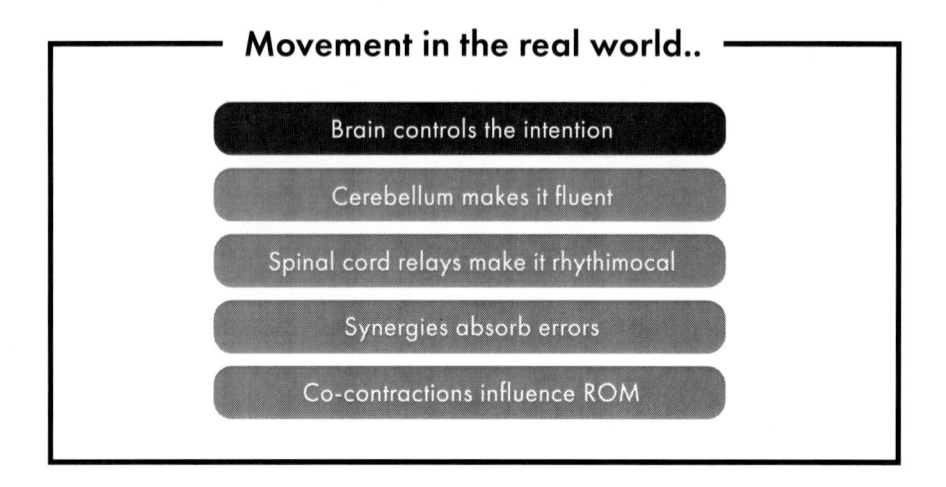

Movement in the real world..

- Brain controls the intention
- Cerebellum makes it fluent
- Spinal cord relays make it rhythimocal
- Synergies absorb errors
- Co-contractions influence ROM

HOW the patient carries out the rest of the movement is essentially influenced by the situation at hand AND previous experiences with the movement. I was now starting to connect the dots between the patient's story, motor adaptations and past experiences doing this movement.

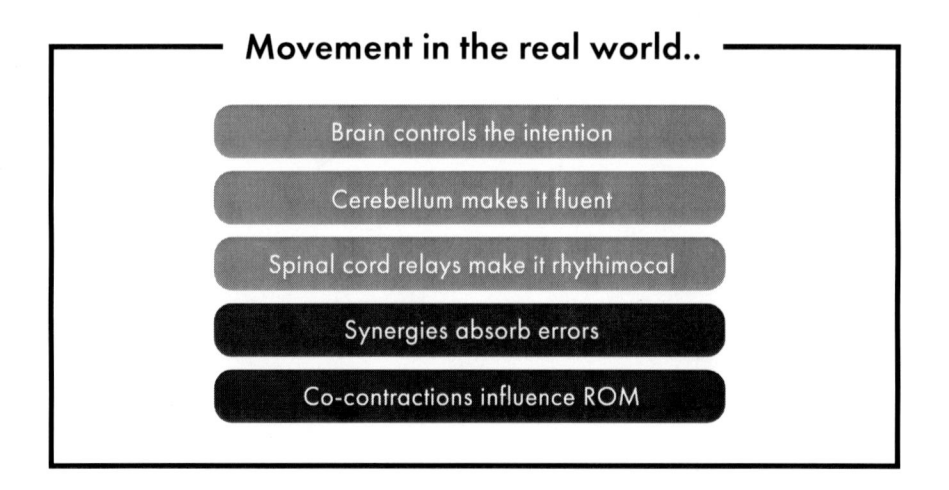

Movement in the real world..

- Brain controls the intention
- Cerebellum makes it fluent
- Spinal cord relays make it rhythimocal
- Synergies absorb errors
- Co-contractions influence ROM

If there are motor adaptations or "perceived threats" to the nervous system present then it is reasonable to assume that other synergies will kick in to help out. Antagonists may also help out, which may influence the patient's range of movement.

Now, instead of just seeing a person touching their toes, I was going deeper and visualising the synergists and antagonists all going to work to achieve this movement together, under the order of the nervous system.

The person is like an iceberg. What you are seeing in front of you is the "ice above the water". What is happening under the water is how the nervous system is organising all of the various bits to achieve the movement.

The power of motor adaptations

A couple of years ago I developed really bad blisters under the ball of my right big toe after a Gaelic football match. The following day I went for a walk with my wife, Georgina, and my kids, Ava and Ruby. I spent the majority of the time walking on the outside of my foot with my shin muscles screaming at me by the end of the walk!

When I got home, I went out to my gym and performed some single-leg dumbbell Romanian deadlifts. As I descended on my right leg, my right foot suddenly jerked and I nearly rolled my ankle. I tried the movement again, doing my best to override this action by the nervous system with 100 per cent pure intent, yet the same thing happened again. My nervous system would not let me "load" that big toe after the walk, even with my complete intention to do so. I ended up having to use a wedge on the outside of my right foot, under my fifth metatarsal, to stop the foot rolling in order to complete the set.

> That was a big "aha" moment for me in relation to the power of motor adaptations. It showed me that the brain is always keeping score and will find a way to keep a "perceived threat" from taking load.

Frans allowed me to finally break free from just going through the motions with patients in the objective assessment and instead start to match movement strategies with the clues from each patient's story. I then started using the power of questions to help focus my mind on making sense of the movement strategy in front of me. I developed the habit of asking myself questions while the patient was performing the movement to "activate" my brain and help me come up with the solutions.

There are three very useful questions to ask yourself during objective assessments to find the root problem. I have adapted these from Keith Cunningham's book *The Road Less Stupid* to apply to the physio profession:

1. What are the possible reasons I am noticing the patient moving this way to achieve that task?

2. What isn't happening that, if it did, would cause the symptoms to either reduce or disappear all together?

3. What is happening that, if it stopped happening, would cause the symptoms to reduce or disappear all together?

When you ask yourself these questions as you go through the objective assessment it allows you to connect the dots with the subjective assessment, as well as helping you come up with solutions to treat the root problem rather than just the symptoms.

It is important to note at this stage of the objective assessment that you are building a working hypothesis that you will accept or reject as you go deeper into the objective assessment. You have to resist the urge to make a definite diagnosis based on just a few tests.

Let's go back to our toe-touch example. You might find the patient immediately gets pain around the lower back and sacroiliac joint area. When you look at the patient while asking yourself the three questions I've shared, you notice the patient does not depress their ribcage as they go to touch their toes. They are unable to "relax" their low back muscles and this coincides with the back pain at the start of the movement. The patient also has a history of prolonged stress and trauma in their story, and an old ankle injury.

Here is how you might answer these questions in your mind as the patient is performing this movement:

1. What are the possible reasons I am noticing the patient moving this way to achieve that task?

The diaphragm may not be lengthening through a full range of motion due to increased stress in the patient's story. This may restrict the ability of the ribcage to depress and "cause" an inability of the low back muscles to relax, which could contribute to a conscious experience of "pain" in this area.

The old ankle injury may be reducing "co-contractions" peripherally in this limb, which, in turn, may cause the nervous system to feel "unsafe". This may cause increased "co-contractions" centrally in the form of stiffening the ribcage and low back area. This may restrict the ability of the ribcage to depress and "cause" an inability of the low back muscles to relax, which could contribute towards a conscious experience of "pain" in this area.

The patient may be used to having a pain experience when going to touch their toes now and therefore actively "holds their breath" when they move. This would shorten the diaphragm and make it more difficult to depress the rib cage and relax the low back muscles.

2. What isn't happening that, if it did, would cause the symptoms to either reduce or disappear all together?

If the ribcage depresses more, this may allow the low back muscles to "relax" and do less work which may decrease the pain experience.

If the diaphragm is able to lengthen, this may help the ribcage to depress more easily, which may then allow the low back muscles to "relax" and do less work. This, in turn, may decrease the pain experience.

If the "co-contractions" improve peripherally, this may help decrease the "co-contractions" centrally, potentially allowing the low back muscles to "relax" and do less work. All of this may decrease the pain experience.

If the patient "relaxed" and exhaled rather than holding their breath, this would help the diaphragm to lengthen, which would facilitate the ribcage to depress and may allow the low back muscles to "relax" and do less work. Again, this may decrease the pain experience.

3. What is happening that, if it stopped happening, would cause the symptoms to reduce or disappear all together?

If the low back muscles could "relax" more and do "less work" during the movement, this may decrease the pain experience.

Can you see how, by asking yourself these questions, you gain far more valuable information by watching a patient perform a simple movement? With this information, you can potentially take action that addresses the root cause of an injury, rather than going into the objective assessment with the intention of "labelling" the symptoms with a diagnosis.

Instead of just focusing on the low back pain and coming up with a traditional "SIJ-type diagnosis", you can now use the three questions to optimise your treatment plan towards the root problem and feel empowered to act on this valuable information to treat the hypothesised root problem at source once and for all. However, you can only do this if you accept the hypothesis you have formed by the end of the assessment.

So, now that you have a simple way of focusing your mind on building a working hypothesis, what movements are useful to have the patient perform in the objective assessment so you can design a value-based treatment plan and start fast, allowing you to get results the patient can "see" and "feel"?

The three-layer objective assessment approach

My own objective assessment follows a three-layer approach that links together as you progress.

1. The first layer is the **Generic Objective Assessment**. This is the 10,000 foot overview.

2. The next layer is the **Passive Assessment** where you start to zoom in on the biggest motor adaptations laid down by the nervous system.

3. The final layer is the **Coordinative Testing** where you stress the nervous system directly to check for any "perceived threats" to certain tissues in certain directions.

The value in using the three-layer approach I have outlined, in addition to the stressor and story method in the subjective assessment, is that as you progress through the assessment you are building a stronger and stronger hypothesis of where to start your treatment plan.

The REAL VALUE, however, is that if you have missed something in either the subjective assessment or one of the layers, then the other layers don't usually make sense as you progress through the objective assessment. This means you won't end up on a wild goose chase, taking your patient's rehab plan in the wrong direction, with the mechanism of injury or progressive overloading doing specific tasks in the lead up to the pain experience – think, "tissues shortening and tissues lengthening".

The Generic Objective Assessment

The Generic Objective Assessment is an opportunity for your patient to do some simple "big" movements like touching their toes, bending backwards etc., and to gain an appreciation of how they are achieving these tasks WITHOUT trying to diagnose based on just these few movements. This is the starting point of the objective assessment; we need to go through the other two layers to further strengthen our working hypothesis of the root problem.

In my 'Go-To' Physio Mentorship, I do not actively cue or look for "ideal" movements. Instead, I am mainly looking at whether the movement is performed with "thoughtless, fearless movement" (a term coined by the late Louis Gifford), and that the patient is happy to challenge their base of support subconsciously.

The part of the movement where the pain experience occurs can give you clues as to what peripheral tissues may be contributing to the pain experience at this moment or, more importantly, what tissues ARE NOT contributing towards the movement efficiently which may result in other tissues having to absorb the movement errors synergistically. Other clues may appear in the form of what the person IS NOT loading in these basic movements.

In order to do this effectively and without bias, I like to use the principle of "challenging the base of support to gain an insight into the patient's nervous system's movement strategies".

Challenging the base of support

Ideally for us to stay balanced as human beings, our centre of gravity wants to be between our base of support.

For example, when we do a side flexion assessment to the right, we ask the patient to have a conscious intent to "reach your right hand down the outside of your right leg", but we're actually assessing whether the patient's left hip wants to challenge the base of support in order to keep them balanced. We are also assessing the ability of the left ribcage to elevate with the diaphragm shortening on this side, while the right side of the ribcage depresses and the diaphragm lengthens underneath it.

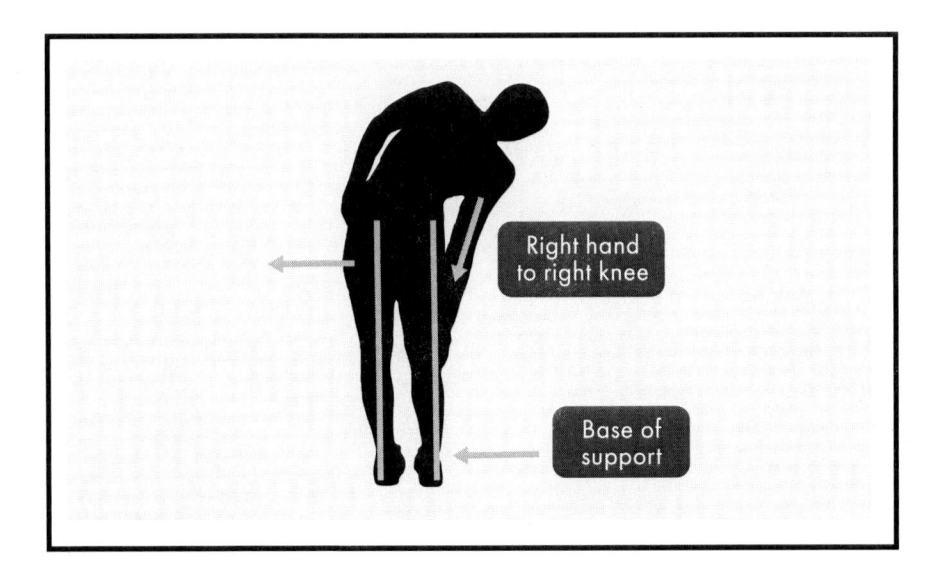

If the left hip and rib cage don't react as above, we may see all the patient's weight become "lopsided" to the right side, with very little weight on their left leg. This is not a good "survival" strategy to have as a human, because we have few movement options in this position and it puts a lot of pressure on the right-sided facet joints, amongst other tissues.

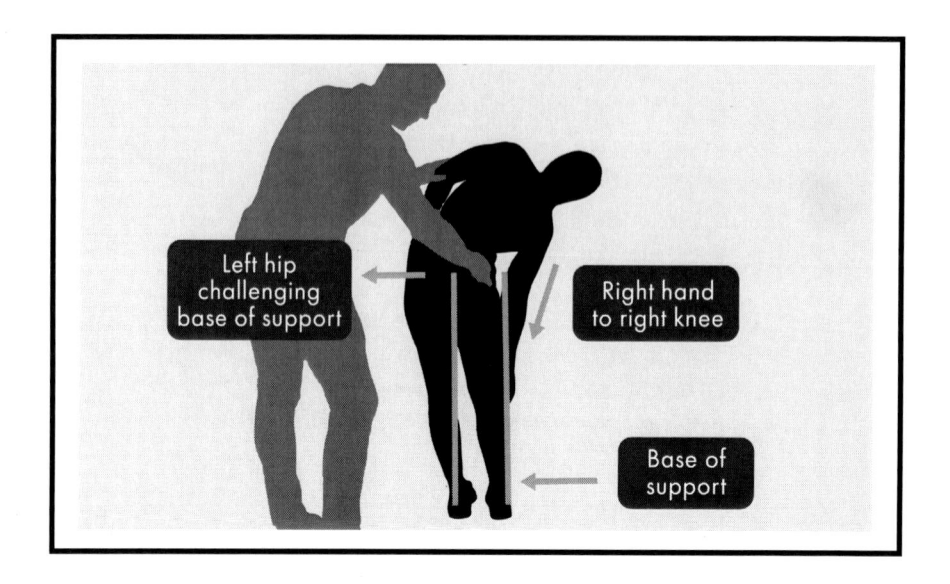

Figure: Silhouette illustration with labels "Left hip challenging base of support", "Right hand to right knee", and "Base of support".

So, if the patient's left hip goes, and challenges the base of support by travelling outside the left foot as they reach right, then we might assume the nervous system is happy to tolerate load at this level of exposure, through the tissues on the left side of the body.

This is just one example and, of course, there are many other strategies a patient with right-sided facet joint pain may use.

Despite this, the principle of "challenging the base of support to gain an insight into the patient's nervous system's movement strategies" is a useful tool in the objective assessment. It provides you with an ideal opportunity to see how their nervous system "reacts" and what "strategies" they use. In a nutshell, when you perform your objective assessment you are looking for the body to want to challenge the base of support, but to keep the centre of gravity between the base of support.

Seeing this response can give you confidence that the nervous system is happy to tolerate load (at this graded exposure level).

For a toe-touch assessment, the hips/pelvis need to travel back while the trunk goes forward. The weight goes towards the heels initially before the trunk brings the weight forward onto the midfoot towards the end of the movement. In doing so, our body sets us up to push into the floor to return back to the start position.

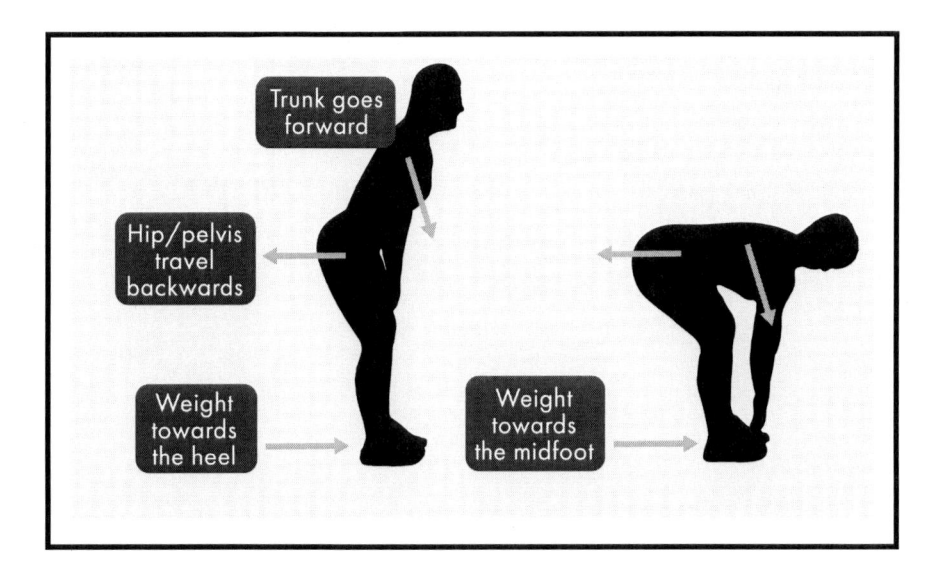

This interaction between the trunk and pelvis is key, and very often the patient has developed movement habits to avoid loading certain tissues and disrupting this key relationship. The answer as to "why" they do this will be in the patient's story.

After using the three objective questions with the patient in positions where they have to challenge their base of support, you can go deeper into the assessment by using your traditional passive assessment.

Applied example using our low back pain patient

The passive assessment is useful to perform after the generic objective assessment. It is also usually the first time you touch the patient and so it is an opportunity to appreciate their ability to relax in general, as well as their ability to relax particular joints.

When performing the passive assessment, pain at certain parts of the movement can give you clues as to what tissues may be contributing towards the pain experience. You use the principle of "tissues shortening and tissues lengthening" to clinically reason which tissues are more likely to be contributing towards the pain experience.

One of the biggest pieces of advice that I want to give you, which was a game changer for me, is to avoid treating the first adaptation you see. Think about the principle of second order thinking. For example, if there is decreased hip flexion and internal rotation, yet no "reason" for this in the patient's history, then this may simply be an adaptation to the true stressor. When you desensitise the true stressor, very often this hip range of motion will be restored very quickly without you needing to actually treat it.

Remember, looking at the body and being "holistic" isn't about treating EVERYTHING; it is simply about working SMARTER and not HARDER. In saying that, if there is a reason for the protective response of a joint, such as pain or trauma, you can use selective tension and various positions to clinically reason which tissues would be a priority to desensitise rather than just throwing everything at it and hoping for the best.

In the scenario with our low back pain patient with a prolonged history of stress, you may find that when you bring her hip passively past 90 degrees of hip flexion she reports a "pinch" in the groin with an abrupt end feel.

Rather than worrying about pathological changes just yet or just triggering the glute muscles with first order thinking, you want to work smarter not harder.

You therefore apply second order thinking principles and want to challenge your working hypothesis that the patient's inability to lengthen the diaphragm through a full range is contributing towards the pain experience.

You may choose to test this by getting the patient to perform a prolonged exhalation and hold their breath at the END of the EXHALATION phase and retest the hip flexion. If the hip flexion range of motion dramatically improves and it reduces the "pinch" then this would further strengthen your hypothesis that the diaphragm (and possibly pelvic floor) may be a main contributor to this back pain patient.

This hip flexion "pinch" can then become a useful key performance indicator for you to recheck later after you influence the "diaphragm's ability to lengthen" rather than just treating the first thing you find.

> Other tissues that come to mind if the exhalation did not improve the hip flexion may be the gluteus maximus tissues or adductor magnus, but, again, this would be cross-referenced with the patient's story and the first part of the objective assessment.

Another great way to clinically reason is to see the difference in hip range of motion supine versus prone. Certain tissues, such as the adductor magnus for example, will be lengthening in supine while shortening in prone. The difference in gross range of motion between supine and prone would allow us to clinically reason which tissues may be contributing to the reduced range of motion.

If there is a reduced range of motion in supine, for example, then the adductor magnus tissues would be one such tissue we'd be interested in examining further; whereas if the prone range of motion was reduced, then the hip flexor tissues are of more interest, as these are lengthening in prone while the adductor magnus tissues are in a shortened position.

It is also worth noting that at this point of the assessment I may be performing additional tests on the bed, for example special tests of the knee joint for a knee pain patient to rule out any serious pathologies.

After you perform the passive assessment you are starting to get a clearer picture on the patient's motor adaptations that have been laid down as a result of their story. All of this means your working hypothesis is strengthened further.

There is one more layer to the objective assessment however to "stress test" your hypothesis and that is the Coordinative Testing component.

Coordinative Testing

In my search for the "magic bullet", I attended various muscle-testing courses and even studied applied kinesiology. I always felt there was "something in it", but couldn't quite get on board with some of the claims made on some of the courses. As always, I try not to throw the baby out with the bath water and, instead, ask myself, why are some of these things helping patients and how can I use this within my own movement model and bring it back to principles?

It took a few years before it finally clicked into place when I came across the "force steadiness" or "torque steadiness" literature. Rice et al (2015)[5] demonstrated that measuring the regulation of submaximal muscle force was more relevant than earlier measures (eg, joint position sense, static force sense) for daily activities like:

- Walking
- Driving a car
- Stepping over obstacles
- Ascending and descending stairs

As well as sport-related activities like:

- Squatting
- Sprinting
- Jumping
- Landing
- Cutting

---

[5] Rice D.A., McNair P.J., Lewis G.N. and Mannion J., (2015), "Experimental knee pain impairs submaximal force steadiness in isometric, eccentric and concentric muscle actions", *Arthritis Research & Therapy*, 17, 259 (2015). https://doi.org/10.1186/s13075.015.0768-1

It has also been my personal experience that most injuries and "pain experiences" happen at submaximal levels of load tolerance.

Kern, et al[6], 2001 found that during daily activities, maximal voluntary activation was used for only 56 seconds (Kern et al. 2001). In addition, moderately active college students used 17 per cent of their maximal quadriceps and hamstrings force in daily activities.

In the 'Go-To' Physio mentorship program, I teach a modification of traditional muscle testing in what I call Coordinative Testing. I am in no way trying to "invent" or come up with yet another method, but rather call it this to focus the therapists' minds on what is happening when we perform the movements or "tests". In essence, we are assessing force steadiness.

Submaximal force steadiness has been studied in various populations, including those with anterior cruciate ligament reconstruction, knee and hip osteoarthritis, a history of falling, and subacute stroke. Previous researchers observed that people with these conditions had less force steadiness and accuracy than their uninjured counterparts.

You can essentially use coordinative testing to test the ability of certain tissues to tolerate load as submaximal directions. This IS NOT a maximal strength test and you are not attempting to isolate muscles, but rather see how the nervous system is self-organising to achieve the task. You deliberately use submaximal loads as this will require more proprioceptive control and "skill" than just maximal "high threshold" strategies. If the patient has to use a "high threshold strategy" for a task that only requires 40–50 per cent of maximal voluntary contraction then this is not very energy efficient.

Movement efficiency is using the right amount of energy, no more, no less to do the job at hand.

---

[6] Kern DS, Semmler JG, Enoka RM. "Long-term activity in upper – and lower-limb muscles of humans", J Appl Physiol (1985). 2001 Nov;91(5):2224-32. doi: 10.1152/jappl.2001.91.5.2224. PMID: 11641365.

From my observation, a patient that builds tension and brings a MAXIMAL contraction (100 per cent force production) to a task that only requires 40–50 percent of Maximal Voluntary Contraction (MVC), for example, is not energy efficient in dealing with the perturbation placed upon the body at this point.

A useful analogy to help explain this to patients is being able to drive a car by only slamming the foot on the accelerator or taking the foot off the accelerator. This strategy is OK short term, and you will get from A to B quickly, but there will be potential problems if you have to slow down (decelerate) and turn corners (change direction).

An inability to bring an efficient motor output to the task is a protective sympathetic response from the nervous system, in my opinion, potentially due to a perceived threat of tolerating load in this direction. The interesting thing is that this direction will usually be due to a previous injury or an inability of the tissues in this direction to tolerate loading due to stress adaptations, for example.

The ability of an individual to produce a steady force during a submaximal voluntary contraction is defined as force steadiness (or torque steadiness) and is an important aspect of force control. Smooth force generation is highly dependent on the sense of force, which is part of proprioception.

Multiple neuromuscular receptors – including golgi tendon organs, muscle spindles (proprioceptors), and pressure-sensitive skin receptors – contribute to the perception of force, by detecting mechanical tissue changes and transmitting action potentials to the central nervous system (CNS).

While the literature at present is measuring force steadiness using a single joint, you are assessing force steadiness over numerous joints, according to world-renowned researcher Roger Enoka when I showed him my approach and discussed it at length. When performing coordinative testing, you use the model Frans Bosch taught me by thinking about the brain's "intention" first and foremost. Movement intent usually happens via the foot or hand and so, rather than do a muscle test where we isolate a muscle, you always start at the hand or foot.

Rather than ask the patient to build tension or "push" into my hand, I prefer to use my fingertips instead of the midhand to assess. This delivers better feedback to feel the "isometric contraction" at submaximal levels. This also ensures it doesn't turn into a maximal strength test. You can ask the patient to build tension for a couple of seconds and then increase your pressure to no more than 50–60 per cent of the maximal voluntary contraction.

What you are looking for is a nice, solid isometric contraction where the patient can hold and essentially have a conversation. If they can't meet the pressure, then you may consider a "perceived threat" to be present and/or a proprioceptive issue between the peripheral tissues and spinal cord.

Coordination testing of the lower limb

For coordination testing of the lower limb, you want to build "intent" from the foot and see how the system reacts to the "perturbation". You don't want to focus on isolating a muscle, but rather put a load in a certain direction and see how the body reacts. When you create a "perturbation" through the foot the whole system needs to react and the force needs to be distributed through the whole limb and up into the trunk.

At the end of the day, you want to feel an isometric contraction and, if in doubt, increase pressure slowly and wait for the isometric contraction to occur. Then a little bit more and repeat. An isometric contraction is an isometric contraction. The patient should be able to hold the isometric contraction and have a brief conversation with you.

Posterior knee stability test

This is an important test that I see so many people struggle with who have done all the strength training and "traditional" approaches and yet have knee, back or groin pain – to name a few issues. This test is stressing the ability of the soleus, the hamstrings, the gastrocnemius and the quadriceps to all co-contract and allow the hip joint to do work.

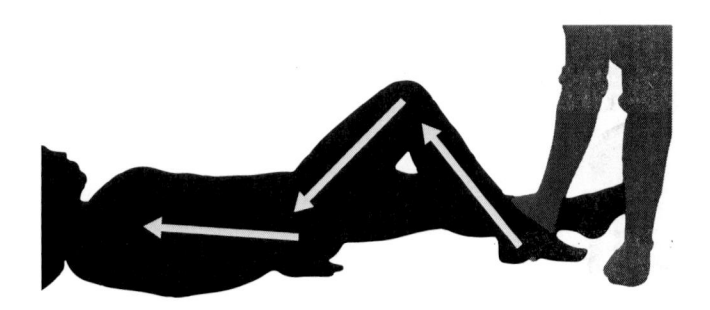

Start by having the patient lie on their back and their opposite leg straight.

Bend the knee to an angle greater than 90 degrees, but ensure the foot is flat on the bed and the ankle joint is not overstretched into plantar flexion.

Place your hand under the foot so your index finger is under the ball of the big toe.

Ask the patient to push down and "squash an orange" into your hand. Allow the patient to build tension into your hand first, give it a couple of seconds.

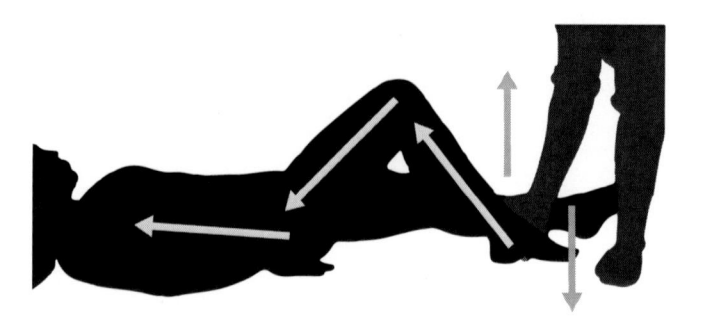

Ensure you build tension through your fingertips first and foremost and NOT the midhand. This will allow you to "feel" the isometric contraction. Then increase your pressure slowly to 40–50 per cent of your maximal effort.

If the patient lifts their lower back in an attempt to push down, correct the patient and retest. Usually this is a motor adaptation/movement strategy, where the patient uses the low back instead of intent from the midfoot.

Once the patient initiates intent from the foot, the uniarticular muscles will contract and reach isometric conditions first (soleus) while the biarticular muscles (hamstrings and gastrocnemius) take time to reach isometric conditions. Once the biarticular muscles reach an isometric state usually the patient will "feel" the hip joint muscles working as the energy transfers through the hamstrings into the hip.

If the patient does not want to push down through the foot and you feel very little force into your hand even before you begin to build your pressure (and there is no history of an ankle injury), then consider protective tone around the pelvic floor and hip joint higher up

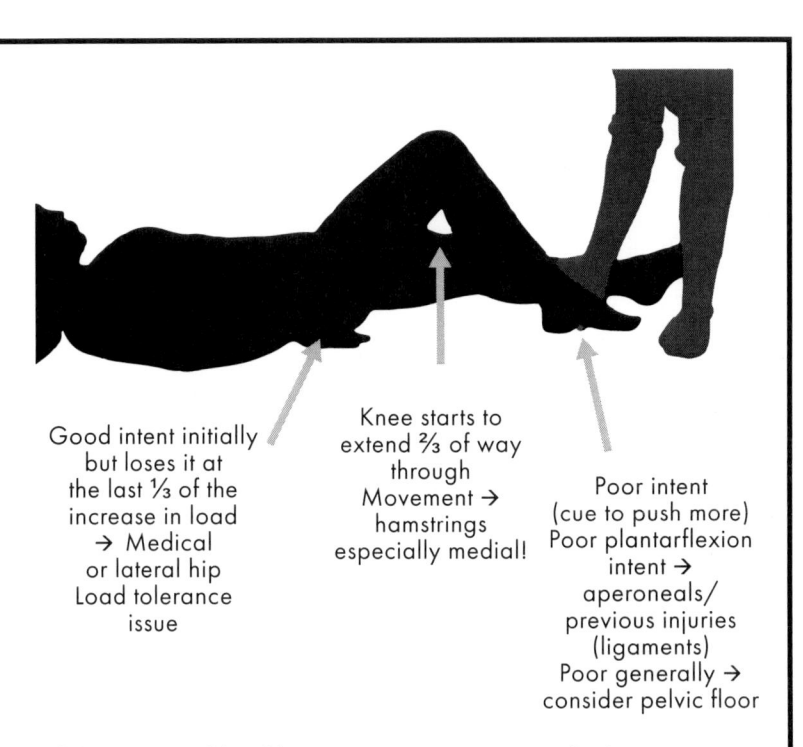

Good intent initially but loses it at the last ⅓ of the increase in load → Medical or lateral hip Load tolerance issue

Knee starts to extend ⅔ of way through Movement → hamstrings especially medial!

Poor intent (cue to push more) Poor plantarflexion intent → aperoneals/ previous injuries (ligaments) Poor generally → consider pelvic floor

If there is an old ankle injury, you may want to look more closely at the ligaments and the peroneus tertius, desensitise and retest after you've completed the full assessment.

If the patient pushes down, is unable to match your pressure and breaks at the knee – and you notice the knee joint extending – then consider the medial hamstrings as the main culprit. Of course, there may be other tissues involved and, as always, the answer will lie in the injury history and the patient's story.

If the patient is unable to match your force towards the end of the test yet the knee joint stays flexed but they "give" at the hip joint then consider the hip muscles' attachment at the greater trochanter or the pelvic floor. Usually if the patient is building tension well but loses it at the end of the test, it'll be the hip rotators. However, it is important to intervene and retest quickly to see if your KPI improves after your assessment is complete.

If the sole of the foot cramps, consider an inability of the soleus to tolerate load. If this is the case, you may need to consider desensitising these tissues or tissues around the ankle. The quadratus plantae may be doing too much work, hence the "cramping" sensation.

If the soleus cramps, then consider an inability of the hamstrings to tolerate load. The nervous system may not want to tolerate load higher up so it "stays" below the knee. Consider desensitising the medial hamstrings and anything in the injury history.

If the hamstrings cramp then I would still consider this an inability to tolerate "load" through the hamstrings and consider desensitising the medial hamstrings and anything in the injury history. Always retest after treating no more than one tissue so you gain an insight into what tissues will need to be taken through a graded exposure program.

Performing some hands-on treatment at the relevant tissue and retesting can often make significant differences to the patient's symptoms. It is important to note, however, that you have only solved the load tolerance problem for the nervous system at this level of the graded exposure ladder.

A new level of load tolerance, a new problem for the nervous system to solve. This is why it is critical to take the patient up the graded exposure ladder after "correcting this" otherwise the changes will only be short term.

By understanding the key principles of force steadiness testing, you can now put a "load" in any direction in the body and see how the nervous system self organises and reacts. This can then allow you to finally accept or reject your working hypothesis that there is a perceived threat around loading certain tissues that you believe are not doing enough work.

Force steadiness testing can be invaluable for finding issues that have not been addressed in patients who have failed traditional approaches. When matched with the patient's story, using second order thinking principles can help you finally give many patients long-lasting relief.

Putting it all together

Now that you have built a working hypothesis and confirmed it with your force steadiness testing, it is time to put it all together and design a value-based treatment plan that gets long-lasting results for your patient while allowing you to work smarter not harder.

The three-layer objective assessment in action

Here's how I applied the three-layer objective assessment to a professional golfer. The patient came to see me with a right-sided meniscal tear that was stable and he was managing OK until the end of the season. In his history, he only ever mentioned his right side (an old ankle sprain) and denied any issues with his left leg.

There was no known mechanism for the left knee pain and it came on gradually so I was really struggling to make sense of why this happened. My presumption was that it may be down to adaptations laid down by the previous ankle injury. As we headed for the objective assessment, I didn't feel as though I had made sense of his story, but we proceeded anyway.

In the objective assessment, he was subconsciously very protective of his LEFT leg, which didn't make sense with his story. I kept probing him for any indication that something had happened to his left leg, but he continued to deny ever suffering an injury on this side.

The next layer, the passive assessment, gave me a better clue about the symptoms and range of motion on both sides, but still there was nothing remarkable.

It was only when I put him on his side for the final part of the objective assessment that I noticed an old scar on the side of his LEFT knee. I asked him about this and he said when he was about eight he fell backwards through his patio doors in his living room, leaving the scar.

The final layer of the assessment then revealed that he really struggled to coordinate and generate force submaximally in certain directions on his left leg. Now this was starting to make sense! It also correlated nicely with what he felt was happening in his golf swing and what his golf coach was trying to achieve with him.

By this stage I was a lot happier that I had made sense of the story and could therefore work on a hypothesis that there was a protective response or "perceived threat" still present from the nervous system with regard to tolerating loads in certain directions on the LEFT leg.

The treatment plan was also a lot clearer for both of us, with some hands-on treatment to desensitise the right knee (20 per cent of my attention). However, the majority of my attention (80 per cent) and the rehab would focus on helping the patient reassure his nervous system that it was not only safe to tolerate load at low levels on his left knee, but also high loads at high speeds, which we will discuss in further chapters.

Chapter 7:
Designing a Long-Term Strategy for Success

In order to design a value-based treatment plan that gets long-lasting results, you must go back to principles. I will again borrow some great questions from Keith Cunningham and adapt them to our situation below.

In order to design a long-lasting, value-based treatment plan you must have identified:

1. Exactly where the patient is currently (point A).

2. Exactly where the patient wants to get back to (point B).

3. What the obstacle or root problem is that is preventing the patient from moving from where they are now to where they want to be.

When you just focus on a diagnosis, we completely miss point three. As Keith Cunningham says, there are few things worse than running in the wrong direction enthusiastically. Said another way, there are few things worse than both you and your patient spending time, energy and money working on a treatment plan that is solving a problem that isn't a problem in the first place but a symptom.

To bring this back to principles, it is critical to separate the problem from the symptom before designing your treatment plan. Once you have done this, there will be a few critical principles that you will need to understand and build into your treatment plan to ensure you achieve the dream outcome for the patient.

They are:

1. Understanding the difference between top-down and bottom-up rehab.

2. How to bridge the gap from low to high-level rehab.

3. Building tripwires into your graded exposure treatment plan.

Top-down versus bottom-up

If you were to ask your patient to define success as a result of their experience with you, the majority of patients would say to "do X without a second thought". Nobody's definition of success is to be "pain free" but to have to move consciously and carefully. That is just exhausting.

Louis Gifford, to the best of my knowledge, coined the term "thoughtless, fearless movement" in his classic book set *Aches and Pains*[7]. It is important to understand that this is what we are really optimising our value-based treatment plans for. Helping a patient to become "pain free", but only when they constantly "think about moving" and "worry about the problem coming back again", is of very little value, in my opinion.

---

[7] Gifford L., (2021), *Aches and Pains Book One: Aches and Pains Sections 1-14, Aches and Pains Book Two: Aches and Pains Sections 15-20, Nerve Root Sections, Aches and Pains Book Three: Graded Exposure Sections 1-4 Case Histories Sections 1-4*, Philippa Tindle

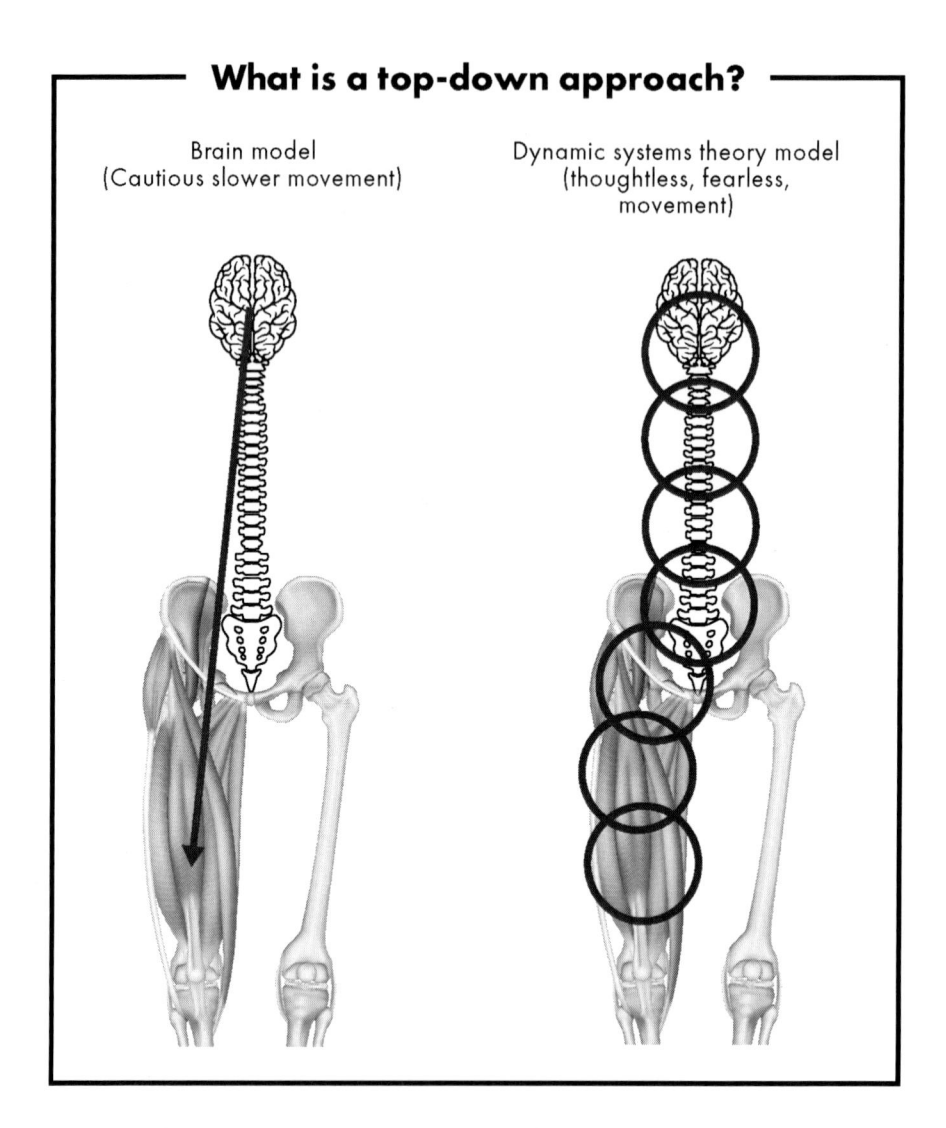

What is a top-down approach?

Brain model
(Cautious slower movement)

Dynamic systems theory model
(thoughtless, fearless, movement)

Have you ever had an acute back pain patient come into your clinic, moving really slowly and cautiously? You could see they literally had to plan every single small movement. When you asked them to bend forward, they moved slowly and cautiously. This is someone using a predominantly top-down approach, where the brain is consciously worrying about every little movement. This is energy expensive and exhausting as it consumes all your attention.

As the pain settles and the patient improves, you'll notice when you ask them to bend forward again, their speed of movement increases and they do the movement "without a second thought". This is more of a bottom-up approach, whereby the brain controls the intention to move and the peripheral tissues work with the spinal cord to "figure out the rest".

Bottom-up is how we are designed to operate. The perfect example of the bottom-up approach is when you go for a run on a trail, your foot suddenly hits an uneven surface and you nearly roll your ankle, but your body adjusts to keep its balance. This demonstrates that the peripheral tissues reacted to the perturbation placed upon your body, communicated quickly to the spinal cord and dealt with the situation. If you had relied on all that information going all the way up to the higher centres, it would have taken too long and you would have fallen over.

Our muscles have physiological properties built into them called preflexes, reflexes and pre-programmed reactions to help us "survive" the real world. Therefore the aim of the value-based treatment plan is to ultimately expose the patient to situations whereby these physiological properties have an opportunity to work exclusively with the spinal cord outside of higher centre control. This allows these tissues to "update" their resting thresholds and, most importantly, show the higher centres they can trust these tissues to work with the spinal cord without the need to control everything. In other words, you want to decrease the "perceived threat" status for these tissues.

This is the EXACT point where a patient rebuilds confidence and self-belief. This is where "thoughtless, fearless movement" is built in the treatment plan. This is where the TRUE VALUE is delivered to the patient.

Unfortunately, most patients are never taken to this level for a number of reasons. The most common reason is that most therapists don't have the know-how to take patients there. It is not their fault. Our training in university focuses on low-level, top-down rehab to prepare us to work in hospital settings with very little attention given to sports injuries or private practice.

I have been fortunate to have been exposed to these situations from working in professional sport and I have probably made every mistake there is to be made when progressing patients early in my career. This is good news for you, as I can teach you how to avoid making these mistakes too so you can save yourself the embarrassment I had to suffer in front of the patients and head coaches!

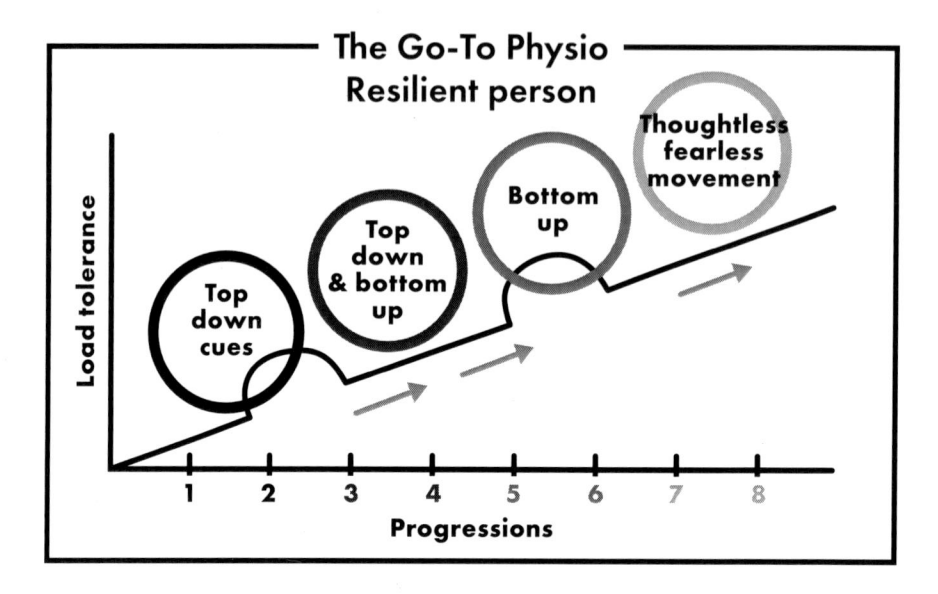

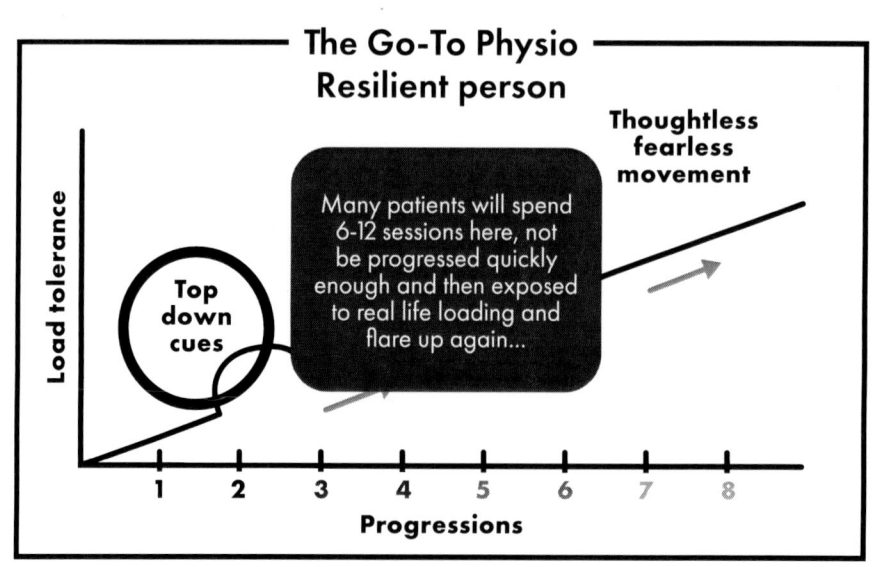

The Go-To Physio — Resilient person

Load tolerance vs Progressions (1–8):
- Top down cues
- Top down & bottom up
- Bottom up
- Thoughtless fearless movement

The Go-To Physio — Resilient person

- Top down cues
- Thoughtless fearless movement

Many patients will spend 6-12 sessions here, not be progressed quickly enough and then exposed to real life loading and flare up again...

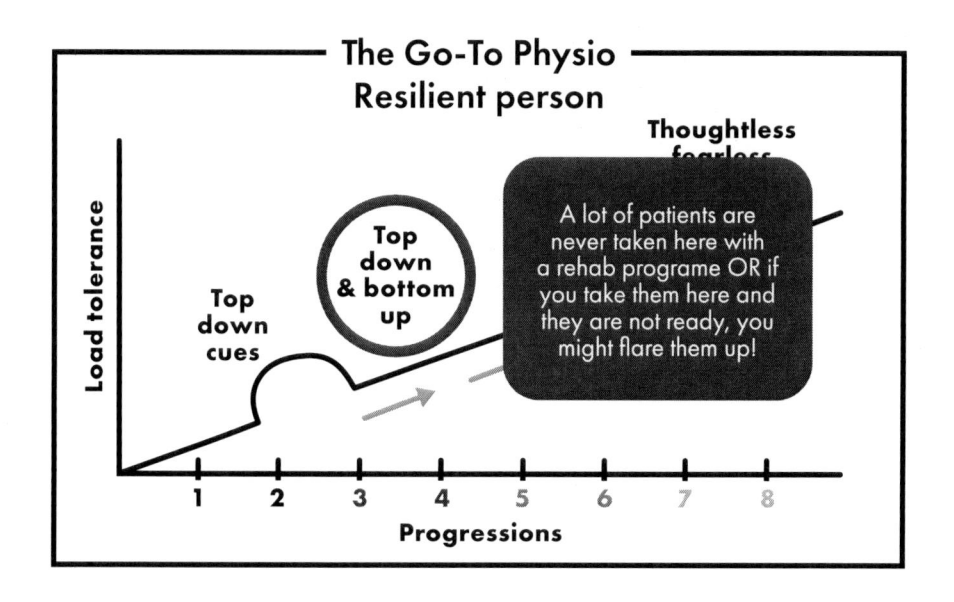

The Go-To Physio — Resilient person

Load tolerance vs **Progressions** (1–8)

- Top down cues
- Top down & bottom up
- Thoughtless fearless

A lot of patients are never taken here with a rehab programme OR if you take them here and they are not ready, you might flare them up!

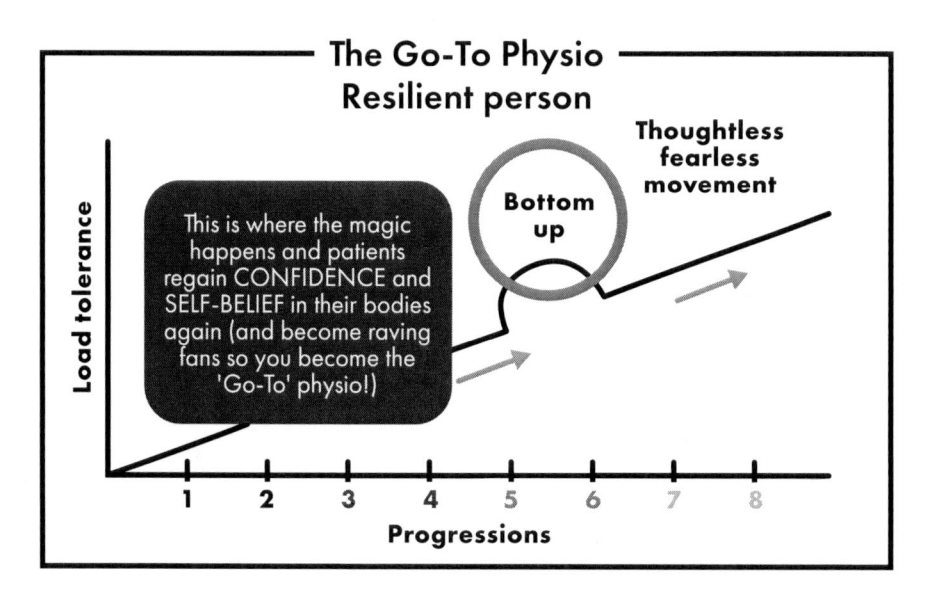

The Go-To Physio — Resilient person

Load tolerance vs **Progressions** (1–8)

- Bottom up
- Thoughtless fearless movement

This is where the magic happens and patients regain CONFIDENCE and SELF-BELIEF in their bodies again (and become raving fans so you become the 'Go-To' physio!)

How to bridge the gap from low to high-level rehab

Now that we have covered bottom-up and top-down approaches, the question is: how do we bridge the gap from top-down to bottom-up or from low-level rehab to high-level rehab? To understand this, we will review our model borrowed from Frans Bosch, which he shared in a lecture to my mentorship group in 2016.

We know that "intention" is really important for movement.

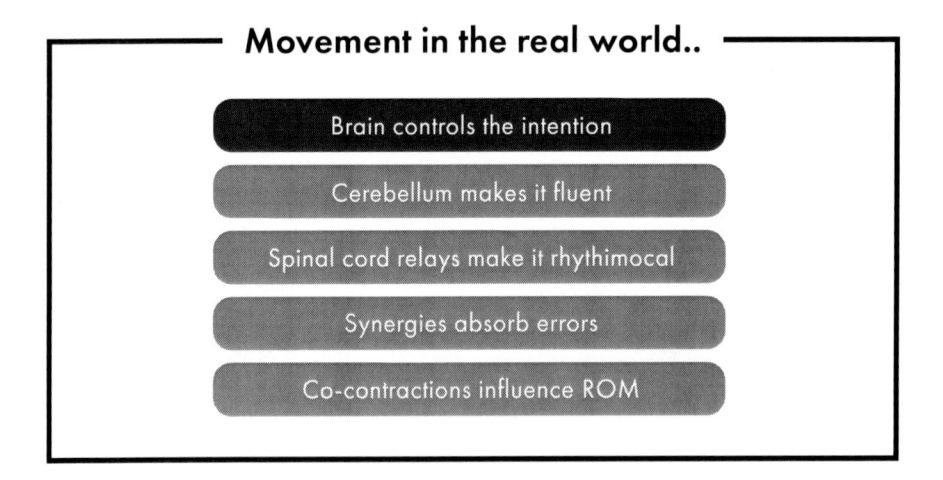

Movement in the real world..

- Brain controls the intention
- Cerebellum makes it fluent
- Spinal cord relays make it rhythimocal
- Synergies absorb errors
- Co-contractions influence ROM

With top-down exercises, the "intention" is usually focused on the body internally (squeeze your glutes) or even externally (squash an orange into the floor). Personally, I only ever tend to use externally-focused cues such as "squash an orange" or "push the ground away". While the literature suggests these are better than internally-focused cues for performance, these still require the patient to consciously think about moving certain body parts.

The ultimate aim is to have the patient focus on the outcome, object or end point, such as standing up. Therefore, for the first one to two sessions I will focus on external cues such as "squash an orange" to attempt to override the motor adaptation strategies and use pure "intent" to force these muscles to do more work.

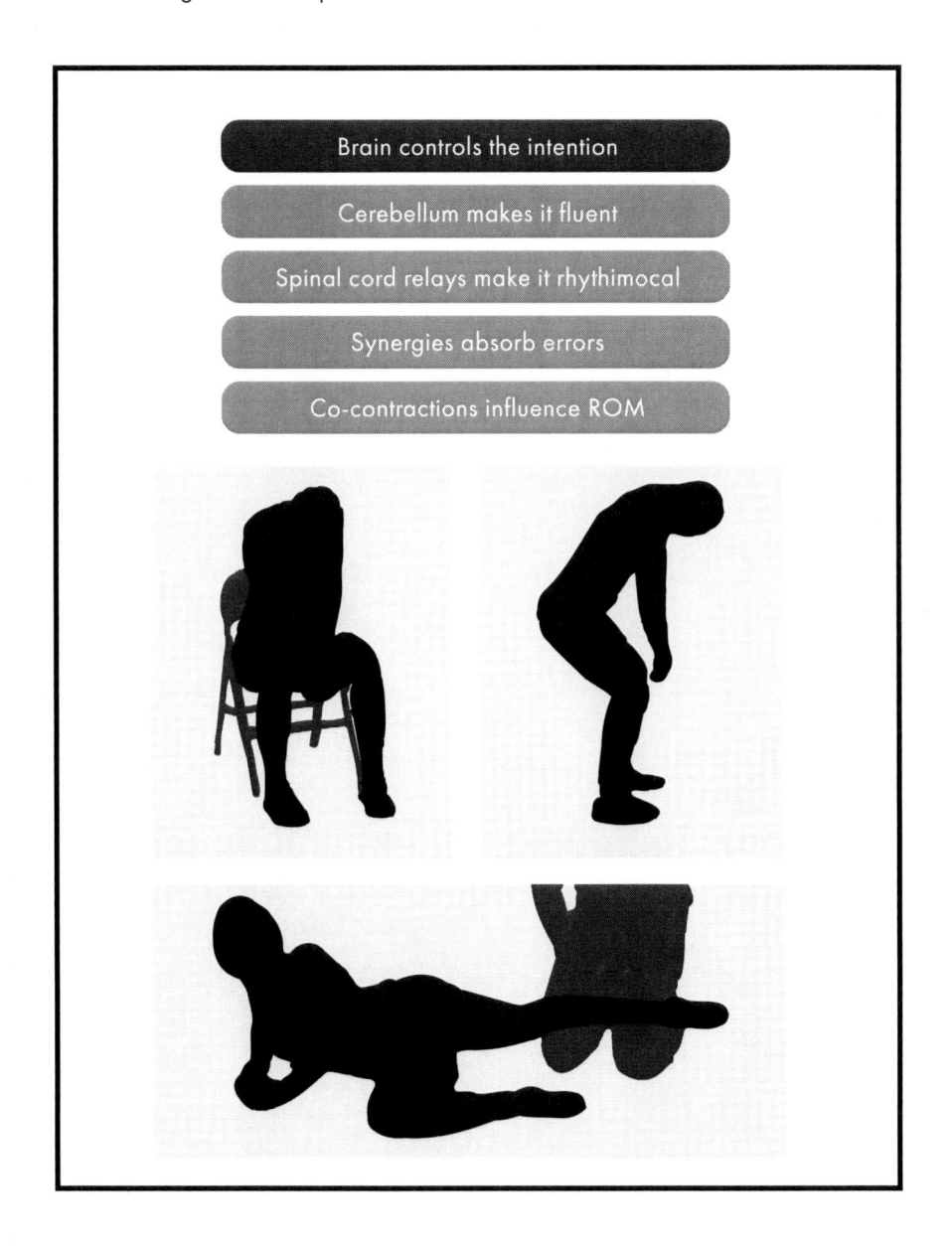

- Brain controls the intention
- Cerebellum makes it fluent
- Spinal cord relays make it rhythimocal
- Synergies absorb errors
- Co-contractions influence ROM

A sit-to-stand exercise or a glute bridge exercise where you ask the patient to "squash an orange" would be an example of this top-down approach. This is obviously time consuming, requires additional energy and conscious thought.

As you progress up the graded exposure ladder, you take advantage of the principle of "challenging the base of support" and put the nervous system into positions statically where there is no choice but to tolerate load through certain tissues.

In this scenario, there is a lot going on and you are allowing the patient's nervous system to "self-organise" some components of the movement at a spinal cord level outside of conscious control. You may still use top-down cues in these types of exercises, for example by cueing "squash the orange" through the foot.

- Brain controls the intention
- Cerebellum makes it fluent
- Spinal cord relays make it rhythimocal
- Synergies absorb errors
- Co-contractions influence ROM

Exercises above such as the "soleus slouch" and "anterior hip loading" exercises will still be cued with a conscious intention to "squash an orange" through the midfoot or laces of the shoes, but there will be other things happening outside of conscious control during these movements. Therefore these types of exercises would combine both top-down and bottom-up approaches. This is where you are really starting to bridge the gap between low – and high-level rehab.

Speed of movement will be an important indicator here to notify you when the patient is ready to fully transition to bottom-up exercises. The initial few reps or sessions will be slow and controlled. However, as the nervous system tends to self-organise, you will notice the patient will increase the speed of movement and the exercises "become easier" as the system becomes more energy efficient.

While the top-down approach will focus on the patient's own body for intention to move, the bottom-up approach will focus exclusively on external objects or tasks. An example of this would be asking the patient to reach for the wall or the floor while taking a small step.

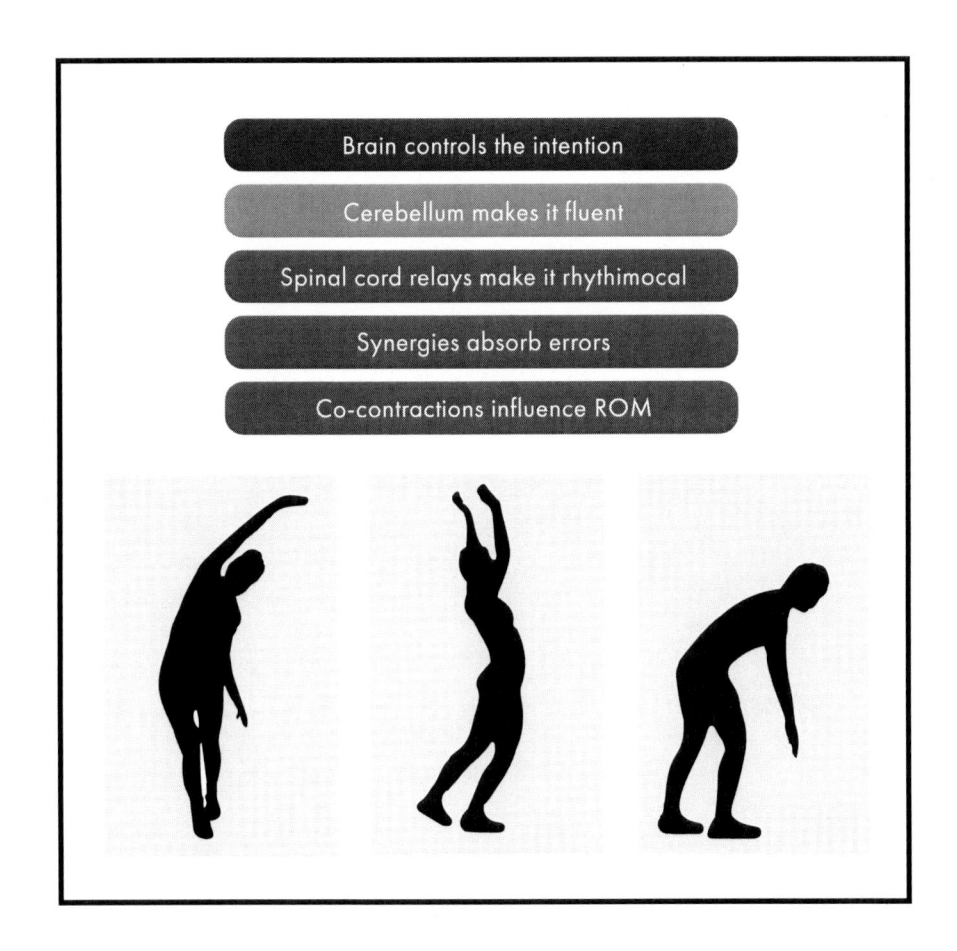

- Brain controls the intention
- Cerebellum makes it fluent
- Spinal cord relays make it rhythimocal
- Synergies absorb errors
- Co-contractions influence ROM

Exercises such as the 3D lunge matrix, first coined by physical therapist Gary Gray, are a great option to use bottom-up exercises to put load in specific directions at this point of the graded exposure program. The sole focus is on the task – i.e. reaching for a wall or object – while the nervous system self-organises and the muscles "figure it out" between themselves without conscious intent.

This is the holy grail and what you should be striving for with every patient's rehab. As you will see in the next section, however, it is not good enough to just use lunges, and for most patients you will need to go further up the graded exposure ladder.

Building tripwires into your graded exposure treatment plan

While progressing patients from top-down to bottom-up can seem straightforward, usually the reality is very different for private practice therapists. Progressing patients that are paying money at the end of sessions in private practice can feel very pressured at times. This can cause you to make decisions based on emotions rather than logic and progress patients too quickly.

Indeed, when I first started out in pro sport, I am ashamed to say I took stupid risks due to getting caught up in the emotions of the situation. I allowed athletes to progress and run too quickly based on emotion rather than logic. Sometimes it came back to bite me hard with the athlete breaking down again or flaring up. It was no fun at all having to walk upstairs and tell the coach that the athlete would take three to four weeks longer to get back to full fitness because I took a wild guess and got it wrong.

One of the biggest benefits of developing a step-by-step system is that it allowed me to take the emotion out of the decision-making process. This meant I was able to take fewer and fewer risks, make fewer mistakes and cause fewer and fewer patients to flare up.

One of the best ways to avoid embarrassing yourself like I did by making decisions based on emotion rather than logic is to build a step-by-step system with in-built tripwires.

Tripwires are devices that catch things early before big problems occur. In our world, tripwires allow you to catch potential problems and show you there is more work to be done at a particular level of the graded exposure ladder before progressing your patient too quickly and flaring them up in the process.

The two most common places for things to go wrong with patients are when progressing the patient from the bed to standing, and also when returning the patient to the highest-level loading activities such as running. This is where I have built-in tripwire "screens" (or movements) that I always ask the patient to perform prior to progressing to the next level.

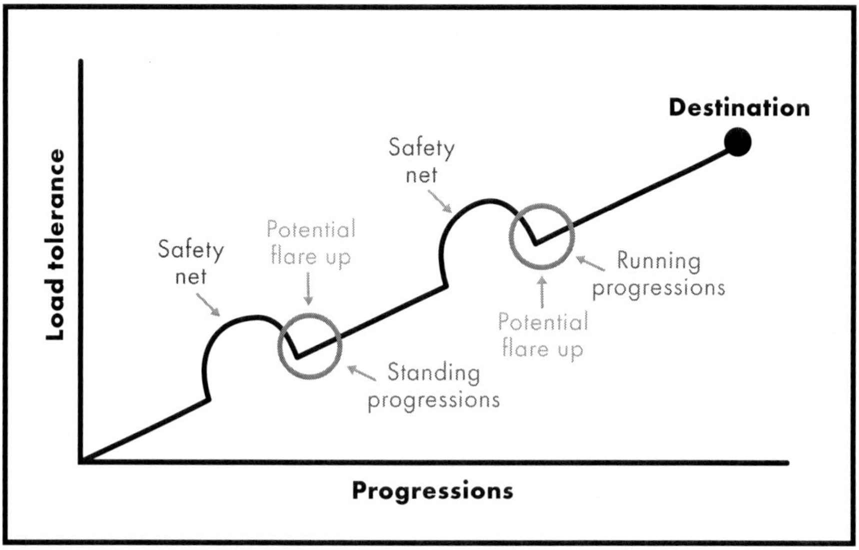
Destination
Safety
net
Potential
flare up
Safety
net
Running
progressions
Potential
flare up
Standing
progressions
Load tolerance
Progressions

For example, before progressing a patient to standing-based exercises (and only after clearing a lot of the submaximal load tolerance issues), I ask the patient to perform a midfoot bridge hold for 30 seconds on each leg.

- The patient lies on their back with their feet flat on the bed.

- Straighten their knees just enough that they can still lift their heel slightly off the bed.

- Now lift the right leg off the bed and ask the patient to push through the left midfoot to bridge up just an inch off the bed.

- Ensure the patient just lifts enough to slide a credit card under their bum. This ensures we keep the load going through the lower limb and not the lower back.

- Hold this position for 30 seconds and ensure there is no weight going through the heel.

- Repeat the test on the other side.

- If there is any cramping in the sole of the foot, the calf or the hamstrings on either leg, this can alert you that the nervous system is still perceiving a load tolerance threat and there is more work to be done before increasing the load in standing.

- Revert back to your assessment and address these issues before progressing to standing progressions.

This is a simple example that has saved me time and time again. This test stresses the soleus and hamstrings far more than they will need to be stressed in the initial standing exercises. If they can tolerate this level of loading here, I can be confident that they will be successful in the standing progressions.

If the patient is cramping in the midfoot bridge and I progress them to an exercise such as the "soleus slouch" as described in later chapters, the patient will be unable to maintain a co-contraction of the knee joint and won't get the desired effect of the exercise. This would cause me to "over cue" and usually become frustrated that the patient is not doing the exercise correctly.

In this scenario, the truth is that the nervous system is not ready for this level of load tolerance and simply puts in motor adaptation strategies to take load away from the tissues that it wanted to protect. With the midfoot bridge type movements above, there is nowhere to hide for the nervous system and so, if there is cramping taking place, this lets you know there is more work to be done. Cleaning up issues at this level of the graded exposure ladder allows you to progress patients easily in later sessions and work smarter not harder.

Another example of a tripwire would be hopping progressions used prior to running. I love hopping progressions as these will again supersede the amount of force the tissues have to tolerate in the early running sessions, but in a more controlled manner and with less volume.

[8] Scarfe, Amy C1; Li, Franois-Xavier1,; Reddin, Dave B2; Bridge, Matthew W3.
A New Progression Scale for Common Lower-Limb Rehabilitation Tasks. *Journal of Strength and Conditioning Research: March 2011 – Volume 25 – Issue 3* – p 612-619, doi: 10.1519/JSC.0b013e3181c7bb0b

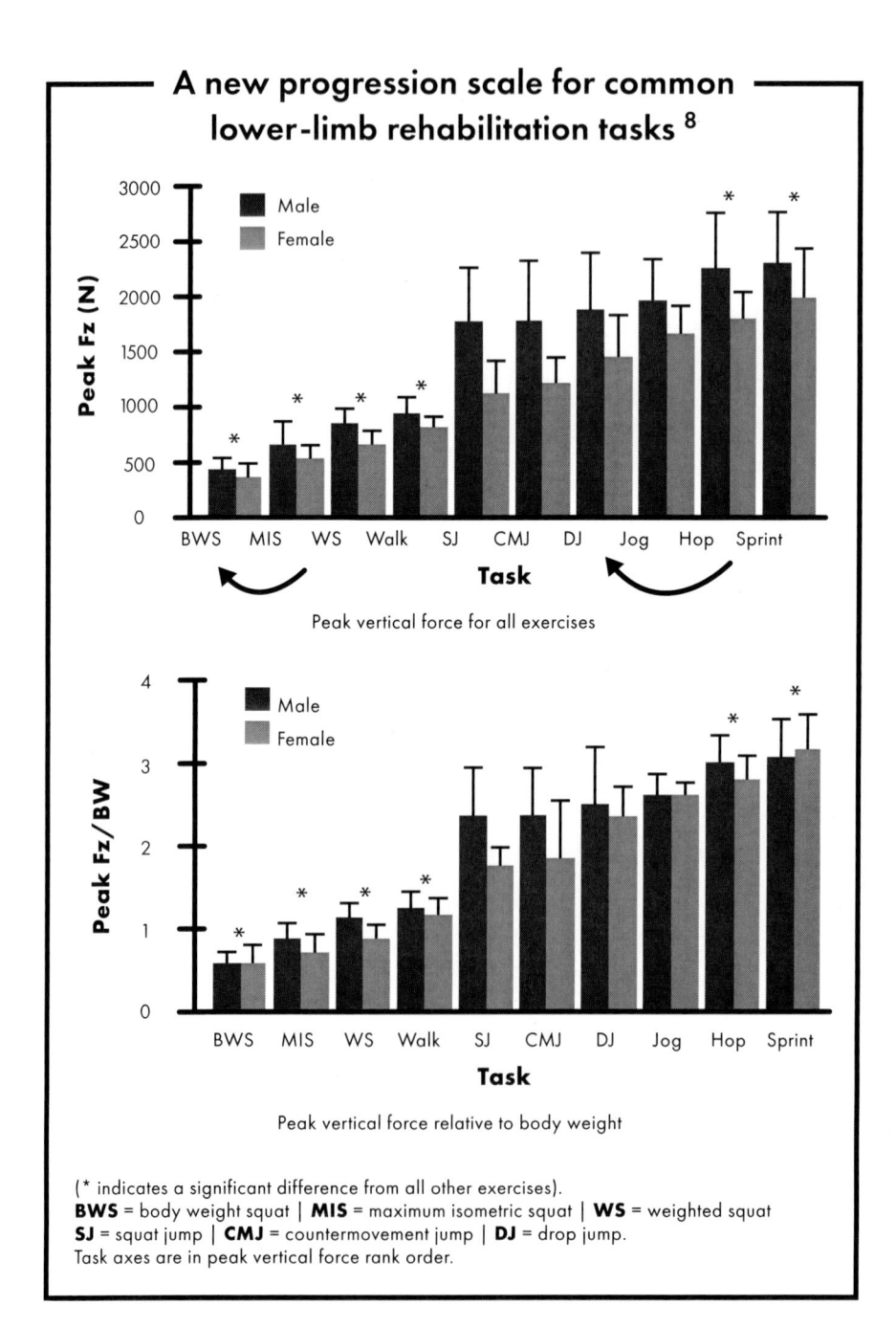

A new progression scale for common lower-limb rehabilitation tasks [8]

Peak vertical force for all exercises

Peak vertical force relative to body weight

(* indicates a significant difference from all other exercises).
BWS = body weight squat | **MIS** = maximum isometric squat | **WS** = weighted squat
SJ = squat jump | **CMJ** = countermovement jump | **DJ** = drop jump.
Task axes are in peak vertical force rank order.

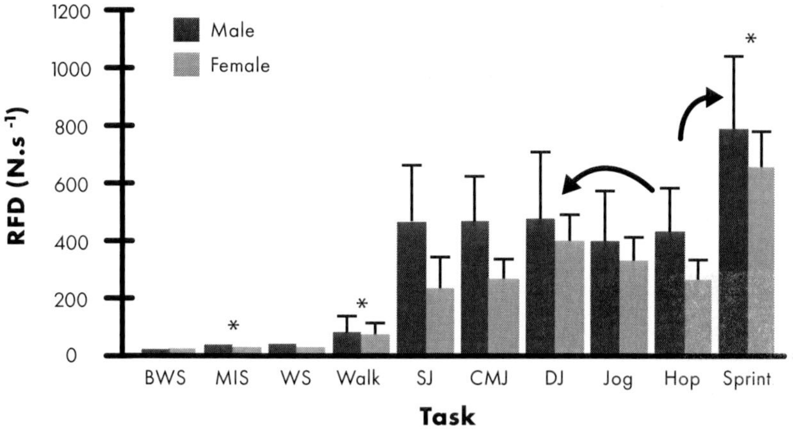

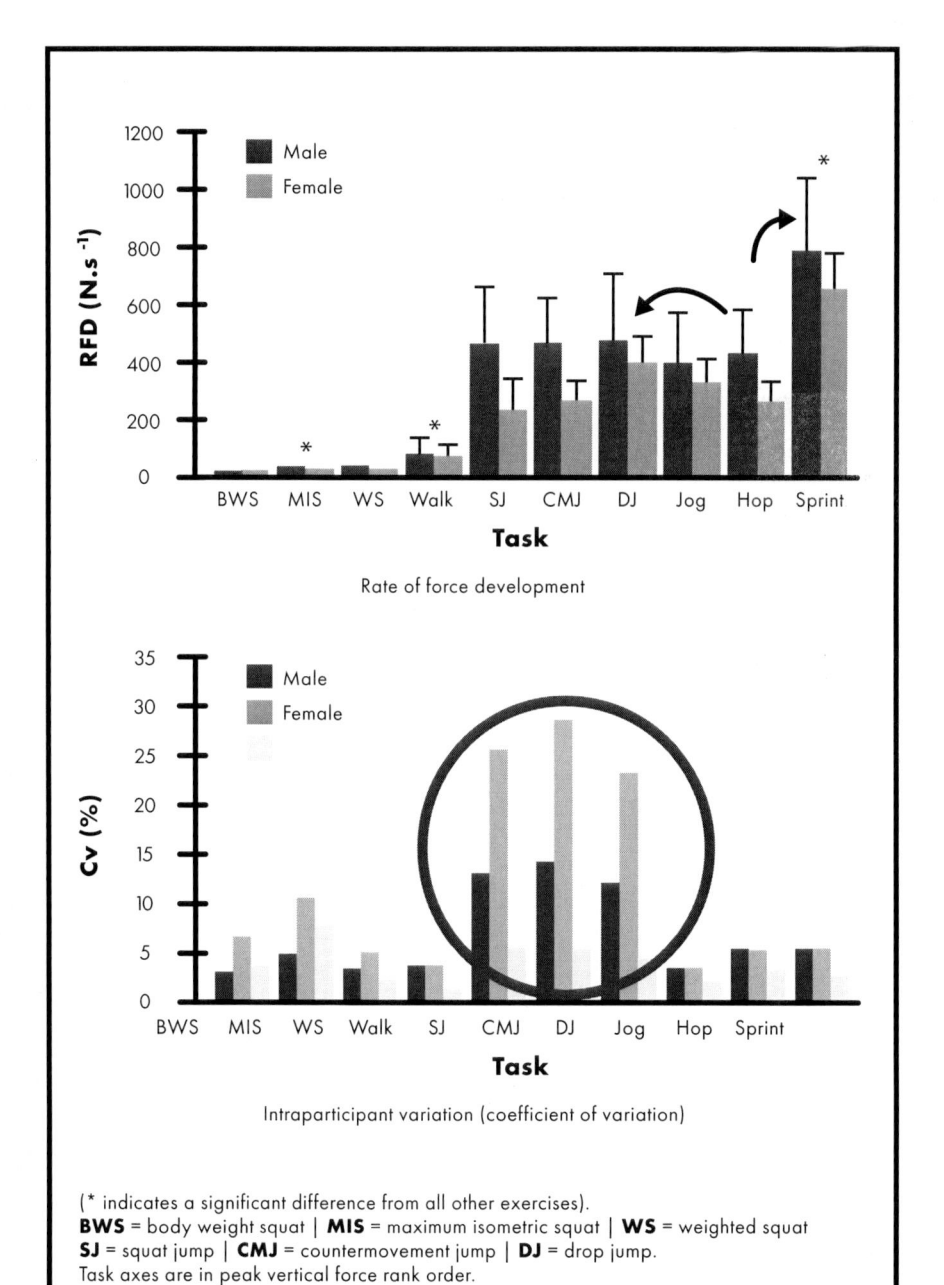

Rate of force development

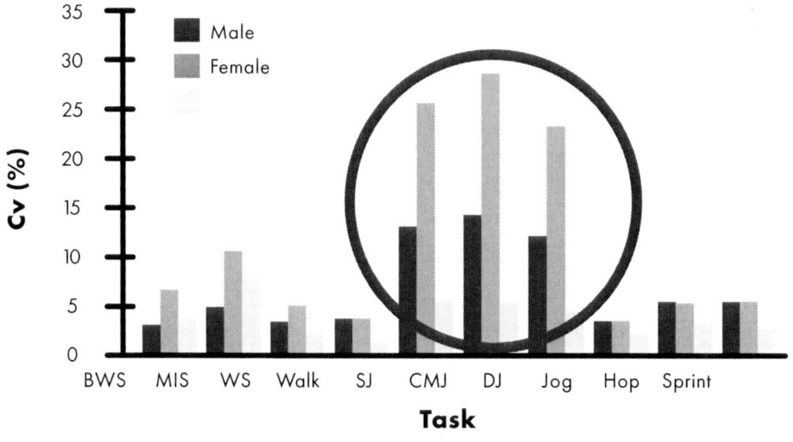

Intraparticipant variation (coefficient of variation)

(* indicates a significant difference from all other exercises).
BWS = body weight squat | **MIS** = maximum isometric squat | **WS** = weighted squat
SJ = squat jump | **CMJ** = countermovement jump | **DJ** = drop jump.
Task axes are in peak vertical force rank order.

In this image, you can see that there are greater ground reaction forces tolerated in hopping than jogging. This is useful information and, again, can be used to your advantage to eliminate the guesswork.

This information allows you to place high loads through certain tissues in small amounts and see if the nervous system can handle them. You can check the ability of the knee to co-contract and whether the patient can use the hip well, among many other things. You can see the one big limitation is that the rate of force development is different, which is why you need to use single-leg continuous hops as you progress in order to solve this problem. If the patient can perform these movements and suffers no reactions then you can be confident they will be able to tolerate similar loads when performing running activities.

A lot of my colleagues in pro sport may return athletes to running faster than I do, yet I will spend a lot more time at this phase of the graded exposure ladder. I find this is where true confidence and self-belief is built and, again, you can put the body in positions where there is no place to hide.

Exercises such as the midfoot bridge and hopping progressions are just some simple examples of tripwires that are really easy to implement yet extremely powerful for giving you confidence and clarity that the patient is either ready to progress or that there is more work to do.

Now that you understand the key principles needed to build successful treatment plans, let's look at how to communicate the plan to your patient in a simple and effective way that gets buy-in and adherence, and stops them from stagnating, cancelling or dropping off.

Part Three:
Patient Adherence and Buy In

This next section will show you how to easily communicate what the issue is to patients and how best to treat it. This will help if you sometimes find yourself struggling to get patients to buy-in to your treatment plan or if you can't get your patients to see the bigger picture of how these exercises will help them and what we are trying to achieve.

If you've ever found yourself in the situation where your patients don't do the exercises at home hence every time they come in for a session it feels like you are starting from the same point, the strategies in this section will solve this issue for you.

These are simple strategies, yet they have the potential to ensure you have a fully booked diary of happy progressing patients. These strategies will ensure your patients keep coming back after three to four sessions if there is more work to do and see it all the way through to the final session so you don't have to constantly worry about having to find new patients.

Chapter 8:
Designing a World-Class Customer Experience

By far and away the most common mistake private practice therapists make is having no genuine strategy or plan in place to get the patient to their ideal destination. I've seen it all too often and I've honestly lost count of how many therapists I've come across who have made this error.

The therapist does the assessment, pops the patient on the bed, spends 90 per cent of the session doing hands-on treatment and gives two to three exercises in the last five minutes before rushing the patient out of the door. In complete transparency, that was me too during the first few years of working in my own private practice.

Rossettini and colleagues[9] have found that improving only the clinical outcomes (e.g. range of motion) or meeting a singular contextual factor are both useful but not sufficient to fully affect patient satisfaction. Patient satisfaction is multidimensional. O'Keeffe and colleagues[10] found that a mix of interpersonal, clinical, and organisational factors are perceived to influence patient-therapist interactions positively.

Patients believed it was vital that physical therapists possessed excellent technical ability and skills such as communication. Patients felt enhanced patient-therapist interaction when the therapist was able to provide a simple, clear explanation.

---

[9] Rossettini, Giacomo et al. "Determinants of patient satisfaction in outpatient musculoskeletal physiotherapy: a systematic, qualitative meta-summary, and meta-synthesis." *Disability and Rehabilitation* 42 (2018): 460 – 472.

[10] O'Keeffe M, Cullinane P, Hurley J, Leahy I, Bunzli S, O'Sullivan PB, O'Sullivan K. What Influences Patient-Therapist Interactions in Musculoskeletal Physical Therapy? Qualitative Systematic Review and Meta-Synthesis. Phys Ther. 2016 May;96(5):609-22. doi: 10.2522/ptj.20150240. Epub 2015 Oct 1. PMID: 26427530.

Patients valued an easy explanation of what their problem was, how the physical therapist could help them, and why the therapist was prescribing certain exercises. Patients felt more comfortable when they knew what their treatment plan was and felt interaction with their therapist was enhanced as a result.

On the other hand, patients did not like it when the education given to them was technical and felt that this factor had a negative impact on the patient-therapist relationship. Other key points from that paper highlight the importance of patient-centred care.

For example, patients reported that they felt a stronger bond with their therapist when their treatment was individualised and related specifically to their presentation. Patients also appreciated it when their therapist made an effort to adjust the treatment when they experienced problems and made it easier for them. Patients who did not receive individual care and reported being treated like just another patient felt they did not have a positive interaction.

Finally, taking patient opinion and preference into consideration is also important and doing so encourages the patient to take an active role in their rehabilitation. The points raised in the O'Keeffe paper certainly back up what I have also witnessed in private practice. Indeed, here is the power of this in action in the real world where a therapist under my mentorship explained the problem, solution and plan in a simple way to the patient.

The bottom line is that a patient trusts a therapist with a plan. A patient wants a simple plan. Think of it another way, you get onto a crowded bus and you have no idea how long the journey is going to be, or when the first stop is, so you keep wondering if you should ask the bus to stop so that you can get off and get your bearings. This is the same as taking it session by session with your patients, with no real plan in place.

The next thing we need to discuss is exercise compliance. This is a skill that you must master if you want the best shot of getting results with patients. We know exercise compliance is not very common (Campbell et al, 2001) and therefore need to work smarter not harder.

From the research, it appears that patients will do their exercises initially out of loyalty to the therapist, but as time goes on will only do the exercises that appear to give them the most benefit or are easiest to fit into their daily lives. The key thing to understand here is that patients will never be as motivated as they are in the first session and even first week. Therefore, you need a different approach to exercise adherence as the sessions progress and motivation naturally begins to drop.

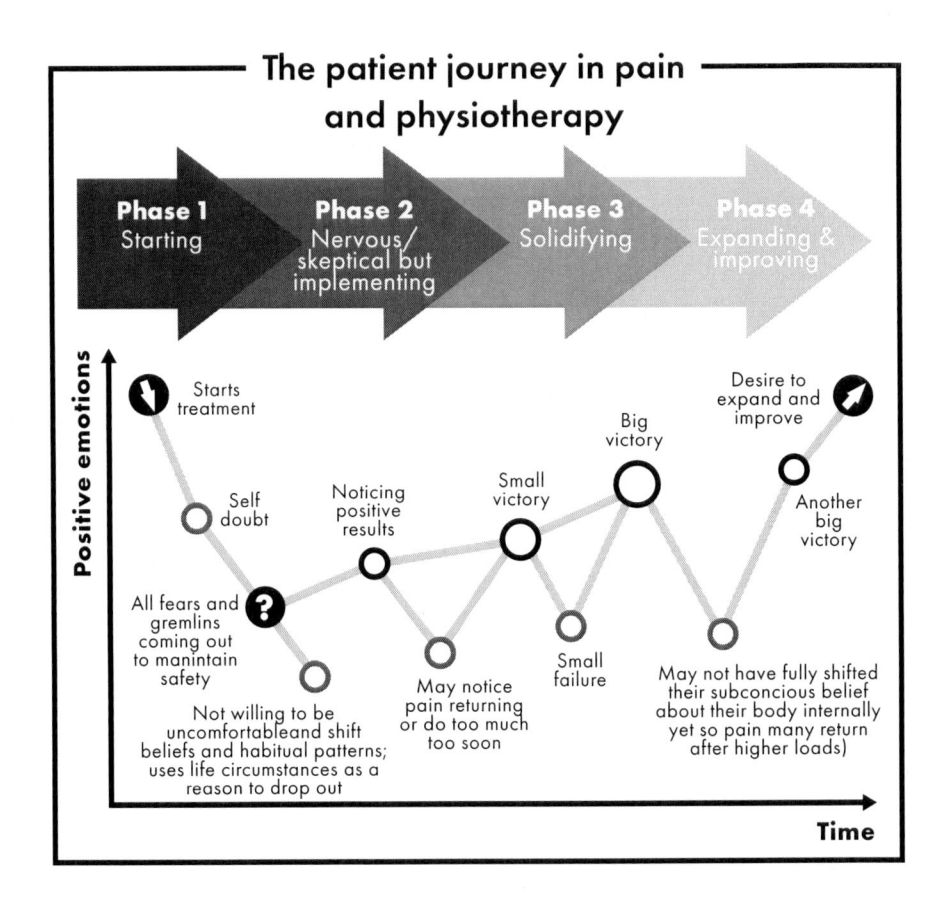

The patient journey in pain and physiotherapy

Phase 1 Starting

Phase 2 Nervous/skeptical but implementing

Phase 3 Solidifying

Phase 4 Expanding & improving

Positive emotions

- Starts treatment
- Self doubt
- Noticing positive results
- Small victory
- Big victory
- Small failure
- Desire to expand and improve
- Another big victory

All fears and gremlins coming out to manintain safety

Not willing to be uncomfortable and shift beliefs and habitual patterns; uses life circumstances as a reason to drop out

May notice pain returning or do too much too soon

May not have fully shifted their subconcious belief about their body internally yet so pain many return after higher loads)

Time

Another important point is that the patient must be able to feel the difference after doing the exercise and these exercises must be easy to accommodate into their everyday lives.

Ultimately though, what is the best way to keep motivation as high as possible? The answer is to ensure that the patient can see the progress made in each session by hitting key milestones in the treatment plan that you have designed together. This again highlights the importance of a clear, simple plan with milestones at each stage of the graded exposure path.

Using the pro sport approach to put it all together to ensure patient adherence and buy-in

Let's revisit our grade two hamstring injury from Chapter 4 in a little more depth to help you gain the clarity to ensure every patient adheres to and completely buys into your treatment plan.

Let's look at a basic timeline for a grade two hamstring injury below.

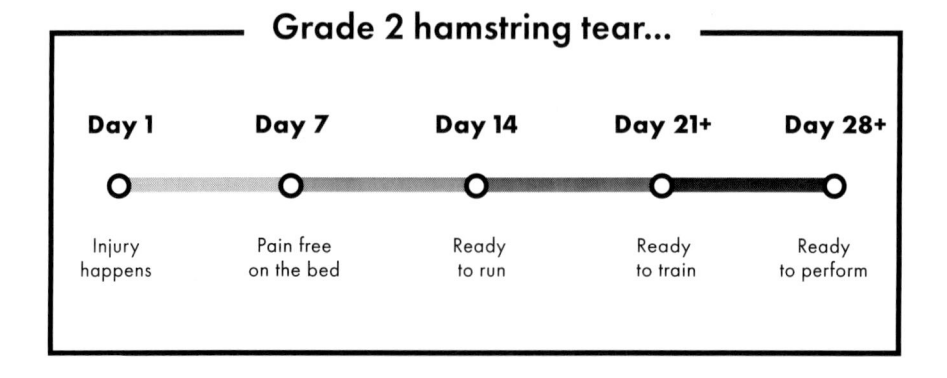

Grade 2 hamstring tear...

Day 1	Day 7	Day 14	Day 21+	Day 28+
Injury happens	Pain free on the bed	Ready to run	Ready to train	Ready to perform

After ten days or so, the patient may be pain free with all their clinical tests on the bed, but realistically it will usually take around four to six weeks to get the patient back to "thoughtless, fearless movement" from this injury. The key point here is that just because a patient is free from pain, it does not mean they have the confidence to go back to the activities they expressed in the subjective assessment, or that their body is ready for that.

At around day seven to ten, when the athlete may be pain free on the bed, they may attempt to train or even play because the pain has eased, which can have devastating consequences. This is why it's so important to set the expectations of the player and the coach.

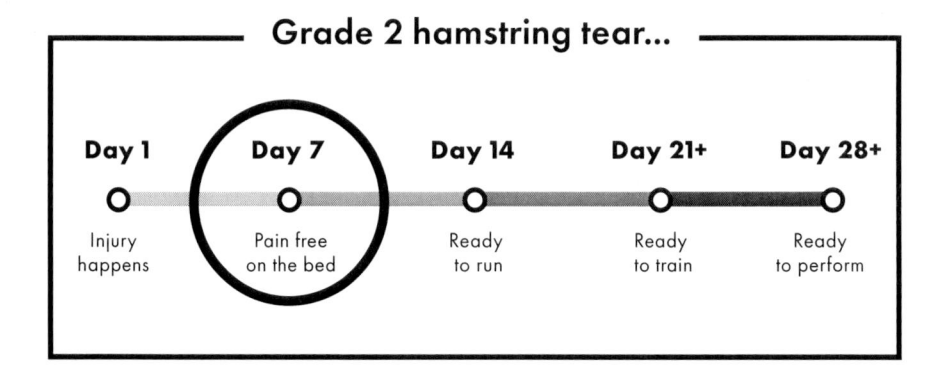

Grade 2 hamstring tear...

Day 1	Day 7	Day 14	Day 21+	Day 28+
Injury happens	Pain free on the bed	Ready to run	Ready to train	Ready to perform

Likewise, if I, as the therapist, let the athlete return to training or playing just because the pain has eased and without first knowing whether it is safe for them to return, I would not last in the job long and my reputation would probably be ruined.

Is it safe to return to the highest level of load tolerance just because the patient is pain free?

Day 1 — Injury happens

Day 7-10 — Pain free on the bed

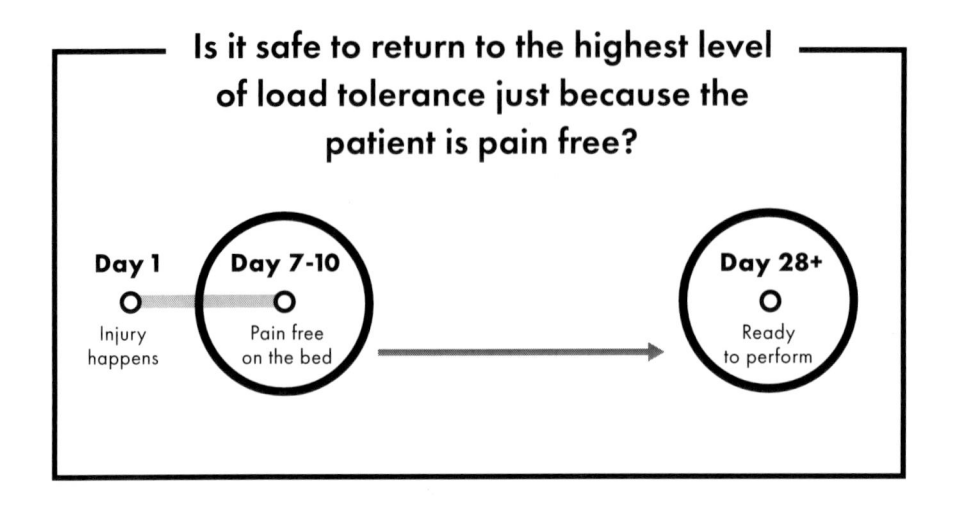

Day 28+ — Ready to perform

So, why does this scenario happen in private practice every single day?

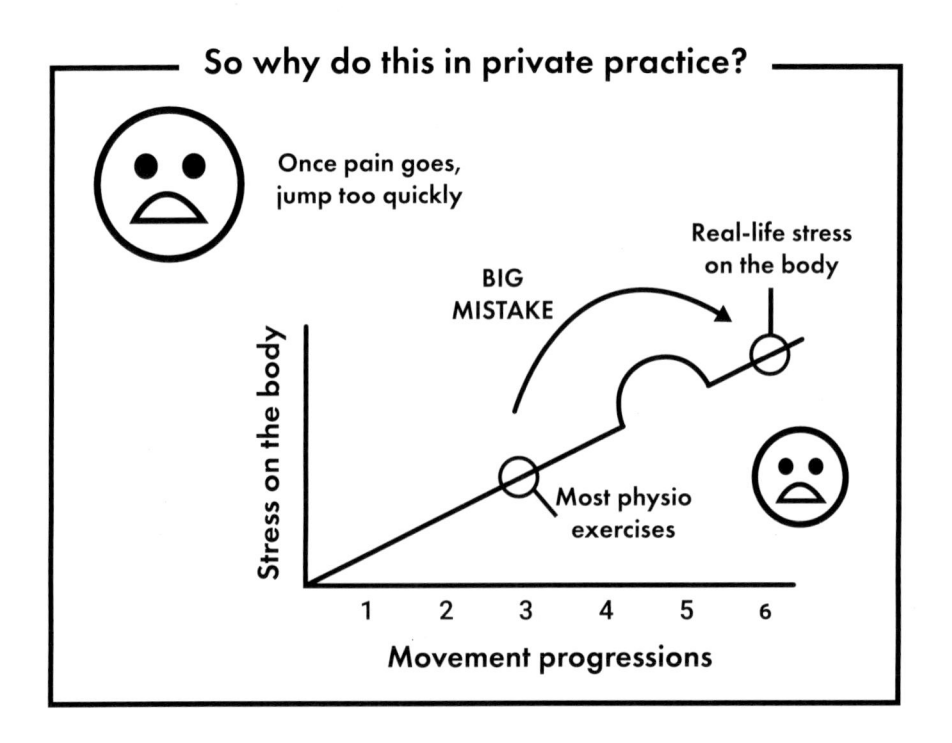

So why do this in private practice?

Once pain goes, jump too quickly

BIG MISTAKE

Real-life stress on the body

Most physio exercises

Stress on the body (y-axis)

Movement progressions: 1, 2, 3, 4, 5, 6

The answer is that expectations are not set at the outset of treatment. You therefore need to set expectations in the first session and devise a step-by-step graded exposure treatment plan so you can take the emotion out of the decision making and make decisions based on logic where the patient has earned the right to progress to the next milestone.

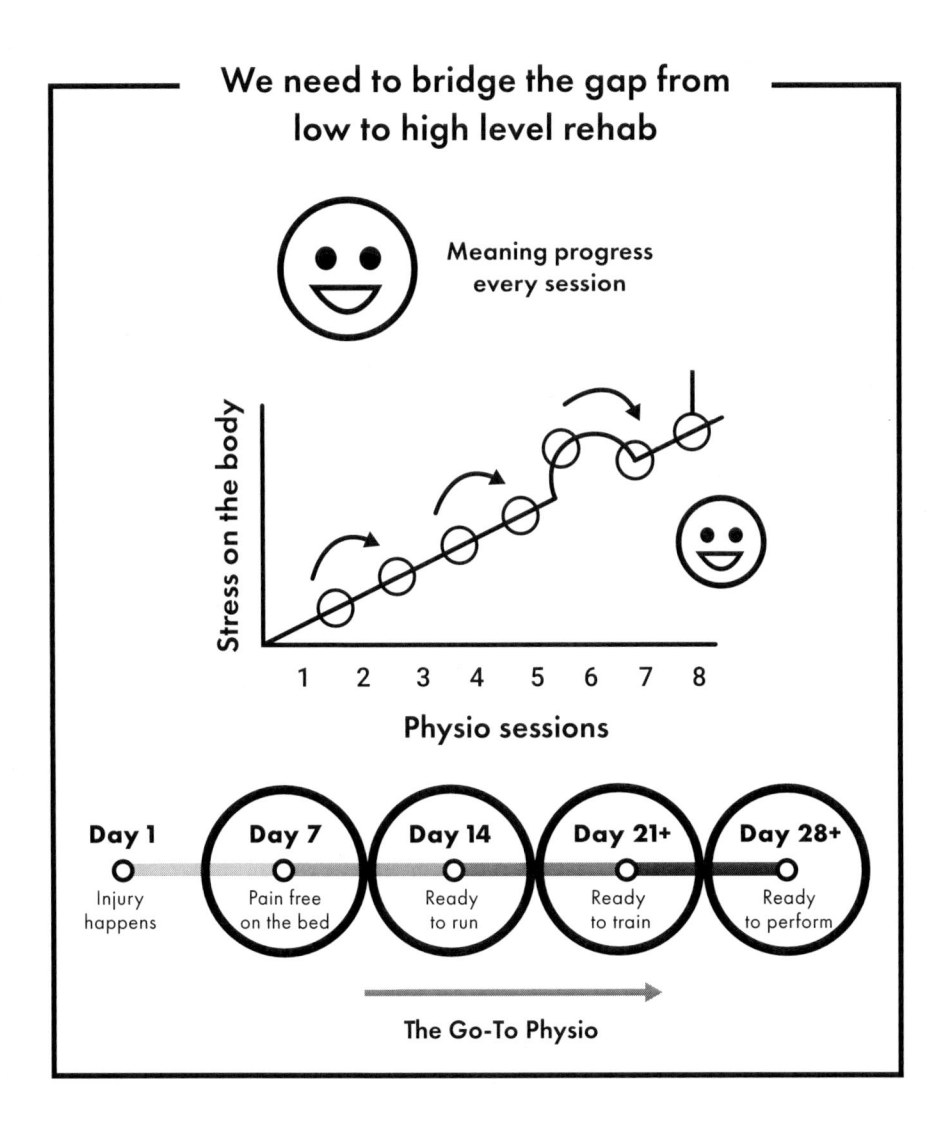

We need to bridge the gap from low to high level rehab

Meaning progress every session

Stress on the body vs **Physio sessions** (1–8)

Day 1	Day 7	Day 14	Day 21+	Day 28+
Injury happens	Pain free on the bed	Ready to run	Ready to train	Ready to perform

The Go-To Physio

Very often, even if your patients are pain free in the treatment room this does not mean they are comfortable performing the awkward movements and situations that they need to in real life. Therefore relying only on clinical tests in the treatment room and finishing with the patient at this point is a massive mistake. Remember the internal motivators of the patient and bridge the gap to get them back to these activities. This is where you can offer far more value than you take in payment, which will help drive your results, reviews and referrals.

Just remind yourself that the patient doesn't really care about a "strong core" or "strong glutes". They care about the internal motivators and what having a strong core or glutes allows them to do throughout the day.

Patients EXPECT pain relief. Therefore you need to focus your treatment plan on what they are doing for the six to ten hours a day when they're not working on their rehab, rather than the six to ten reps. When you do this, the patient can FEEL THE DIFFERENCE throughout the day and SEE THE VALUE of your input.

The patient needs to see the progress (milestones) in each session and there must also be a clear next step at the end of each session. Once you focus on making meaningful impacts on your patients and their six to ten hours a day rather than the six to ten reps of an exercise, your clarity and focus will change along with your results, reviews and referrals.

As the loading increases, it is not uncommon for patients to feel "tightness" or other "symptoms" and even to begin to doubt themselves as the loading progresses. This is where the therapist's confidence and clarity is non-negotiable. You, as their therapist, must have a clear plan and trust the process.

You will need very different skills to deal with the patient when progress slows and motivation levels drop (usually in sessions four onwards) than you will in the initial few sessions. This is why we have developed the 8 Pillars of the 'Go-To' Therapist. In reality you need all 8 Pillars if you want to thrive as a private practice 'Go-To' Therapist who can get predictable results, reviews and referrals with even your most complex patients.

Confidence & clarity

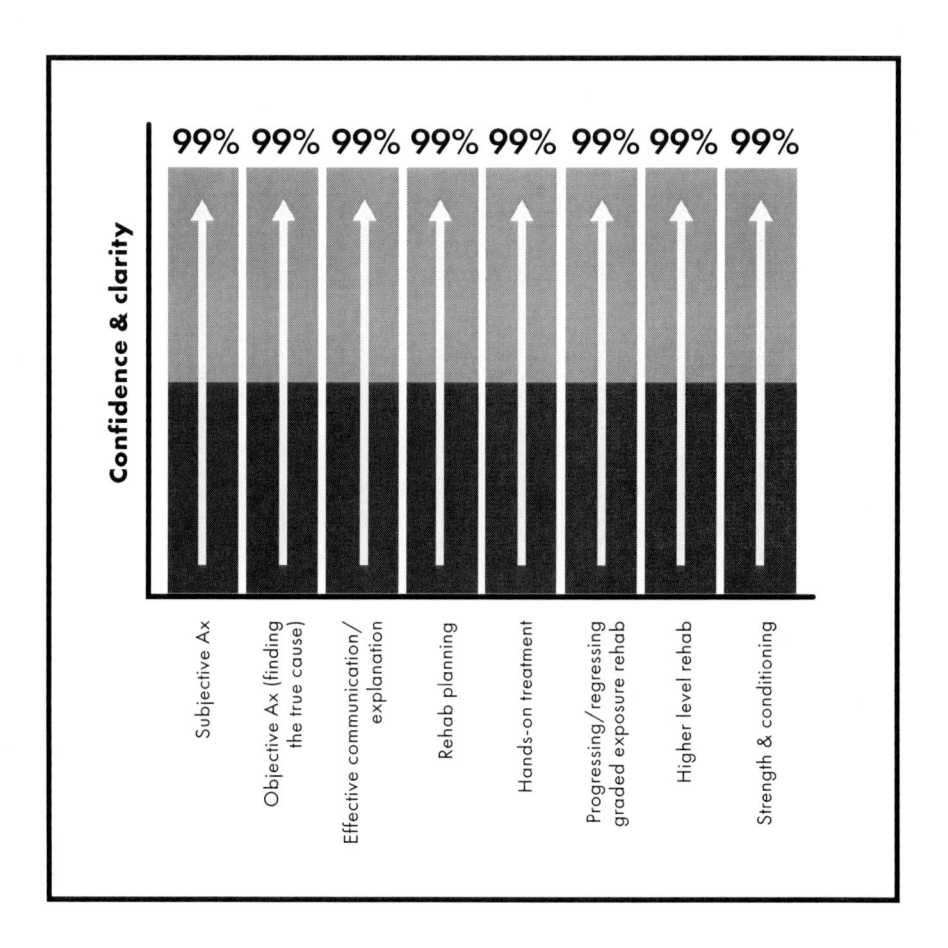

99% 99% 99% 99% 99% 99% 99% 99%

- Subjective Ax
- Objective Ax (finding the true cause)
- Effective communication/explanation
- Rehab planning
- Hands-on treatment
- Progressing/regressing graded exposure rehab
- Higher level rehab
- Strength & conditioning

When you focus on what the patient needs to be able to do throughout the day, you can focus your treatment and rehab approach specifically on making the patient successful and help them "FEEL" the difference FAST! All this requires from you as the therapist is a little "focus".

The Fogg Behaviour Model[11] is useful to help you focus and shows that three elements must converge at the same moment for a behaviour to occur: Motivation, Ability, and a Prompt, or B=MAP!

[11] Stanford University, Behavior Design Lab, https://behaviordesign.stanford.edu/resources/fogg-behavior-model

When a behaviour does not occur, at least one of those three elements is missing. Therefore by focusing on the internal motivator, you can create specific exercises that fit into the context of the patient's "wants" and "needs" at an appropriate level of the graded exposure level so the patient can "feel the difference" after doing the exercises, which will further increase their motivation for doing the exercises. This focuses on coordination exercises rather than just "strengthening" exercises in order to "feel the difference" immediately, which we will discuss in later chapters.

The final element of the Fogg Behaviour Model is Prompt. This needs to be a "trigger" for the patient that is easily accessible throughout the day. For example, a trigger for the patient to do an exercise could be going up the stairs. Every time they do this, in the early stages of their rehab you may get them to "squash an orange through the midfoot" to encourage the ankle joint, soleus and hamstring muscles to do more work to co-contract at the knee joint and take less load off the anterior knee and quadriceps to decrease the pain experience and help the patient be successful throughout the day. The patient "feels the difference" the exercise makes and so is motivated to keep doing it. The exercise is also convenient to do and the trigger/prompt is visible throughout the patient's daily life, which gives them an opportunity to practice.

If you can get your patients to do their homework/exercises, then you are giving yourself and the patient the best shot at getting long lasting results. Let's now look at how we design treatment plans that get results, raving fans and referrals.

Chapter 9:
How to Design a Treatment Plan that Gives Massive Value to You and Your Patient

---

Over the past few weeks, I've been doing this 45-minute outdoor running HIIT session. I have a specific loop I do, and each week I have a target of a specific electrical box at the bottom of a hill. I need to finish within 45 minutes.

Anyway, as I've listened to the same session in my headphones over the last few weeks I've developed "checkpoints" that I need to be at during various stages of the run, where the girl says certain phrases. Last week I noticed I was slightly behind on my "checkpoints" and it gave me a bit of a wake up call. I had to go outside my comfort zone and up the pace and catch up to where I should have been.

Now, not only did I hit that electrical box but I ended up surpassing it and finished halfway up the hill.

Now, let me tell you what happened on my most recent run…

As I was running I noticed I was actually ahead of my usual "checkpoints" through the first part of the run and this really motivated me to "push on" even more. Long story short, not only did I make it up the hill today but I went another 100 metres beyond the hill and hit a PB!

So, what's the point of this story and how will it make you and me better therapists and help us design better treatment plans? Well there are a few points actually…

First up is the power of knowing the outcome and checkpoints in your treatment plan! You see, that "fast start" I made where I could see some good results motivated me to keep going. Remember that the thing our patients buy is the long-term value, aka their "dream outcome", but the thing that makes them stay long enough to get it is the short-term experience. These are little milestones a patient sees along the way that shows them they are on the right path. That first checkpoint on my most recent run showed me I was on "track"!

I got a big emotional response when I found out I had hit that first milestone and you want patients to have a big emotional win early and hit milestones fast. We call this a "fast start" in the 'Go-To' Therapist Mentorship. This gives them emotional buy-in and momentum to "see it through" to their ultimate goal without dropping off, cancelling or not showing up at all.

Now, to bring this back to your treatment plan design, it must have a clear outcome and checkpoints built-in. These checkpoints or milestones need to be designed to make "fast starts" and get emotional buy-in from your patients. Designing these plans not only benefits your patients but also keeps you super clear on how to always ensure you are giving more in value than you are taking in payment! Not only that, but they also allow you to see if you are off track and need to change your treatment approach to deliver the ultimate result for the patient. This is all super powerful if your goal is to give your patients great value for their money!

So, how do you actually design these outcomes and milestones within the 80/20 rule?

Designing treatment plans using the 80/20 rule

At this point, you have now completed your analysis after performing your subjective and objective assessment. It is now time to design your 80/20 'Go-To' Physio high-value treatment plan to turn your patient into a raving fan who refers their friends and family to your clinic. This means 20 per cent of your time (six minutes in a 30-minute session, or 12 minutes in an hour session) will be dedicated to desensitising the tissues contributing directly to the pain experience. This may include the tissues that you identified with the question, "What is happening that, if it wasn't happening, would cause the symptoms to resolve?". For a knee pain example, you may choose to desensitise the vastus lateralis with some hands-on treatment to decrease the knee pain experience.

It is still important to settle the symptoms down and sometimes, depending on the patient's irritability, this may consume the majority of the first session, so use the times as a guide and not a definite. This time can also include your eccentrics, isometrics – whatever you need to do to settle the pain experience if you do not use hands-on treatment.

The remaining 80 per cent of your time (24 minutes out of a 30-minute session, or 48 minutes out of an hour session) will be given to WHY these tissues have overloaded or become sensitised in the first place. Your focus will be guided by the answer to the question, "What isn't happening that, if it was happening, would cause the symptoms to disappear?". Returning to the knee pain example, you may choose to do some hands-on treatment, focused on the medial hamstrings, soleus or hip – depending on your subjective and objective assessment findings – and a graded exposure load tolerance program targeted at said tissues. How do you get this out of your head and communicate this to your patient? You use the power of inversion.

Using inversion to design world-class treatment plans

Inversion is the principle of looking at a problem in reverse in order to make it easier to solve. Inversion comes originally from algebra, where an equation is oftentimes easier to solve if you invert it – but it also works for non-maths problems, including designing treatment plans.

The patient is currently at point A and wants to get to point B (destination).

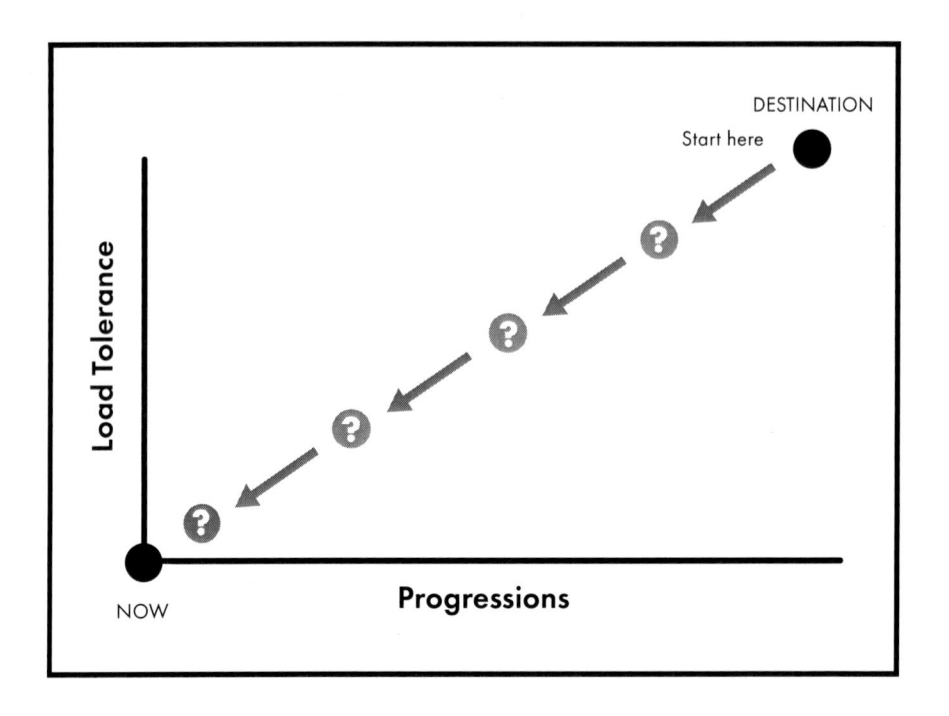

[Figure: Graph with "Load Tolerance" on y-axis and "Progressions" on x-axis. A dashed arrow progresses from "NOW" at the origin upward through a series of question mark milestones to "DESTINATION / Start here" at the top right.]

Asking the patient a simple question such as, "What needs to happen before you are confident to do [insert dream outcome]?" is a powerful way to gain an insight into the patient's expectations while allowing them to contribute to ensure a patient-centred approach in the treatment plan design.

For example, what needs to happen prior to you getting back running at a 10K PB? Then list all the things/activities/milestones that the patient says on the side of your whiteboard. If the patient is missing anything from the list, you may help them and prompt/guide them to these additional steps. In the knee pain example, a patient may say they need to be pain free walking up and down stairs and then they can run. You may then redirect the patient and help them understand it is important that they can hop pain free before running, as running is a series of hops, and add that activity/milestone to the list.

This process also helps you, as the therapist, to focus and get clear on the plan by asking the questions, and allowing time for your brain to process the information and come up with solutions. Very often the patient will say one or two things that you would otherwise have completely overlooked in the treatment plan design. In other cases, you may have recognised an activity, but not realised how important this was to the patient in day-to-day life.

You can then begin to fill in the 10,000 foot overview of the plan for the patient, using simple language with basic milestone labels at each level of the graded exposure path. Things may change as the sessions progress, therefore it is important to get a high-level overview rather than getting into the weeds of the plan. The plan communicated to the patient will be in simple milestones, even though your internal plan may be focused more on muscle strengthening etc.

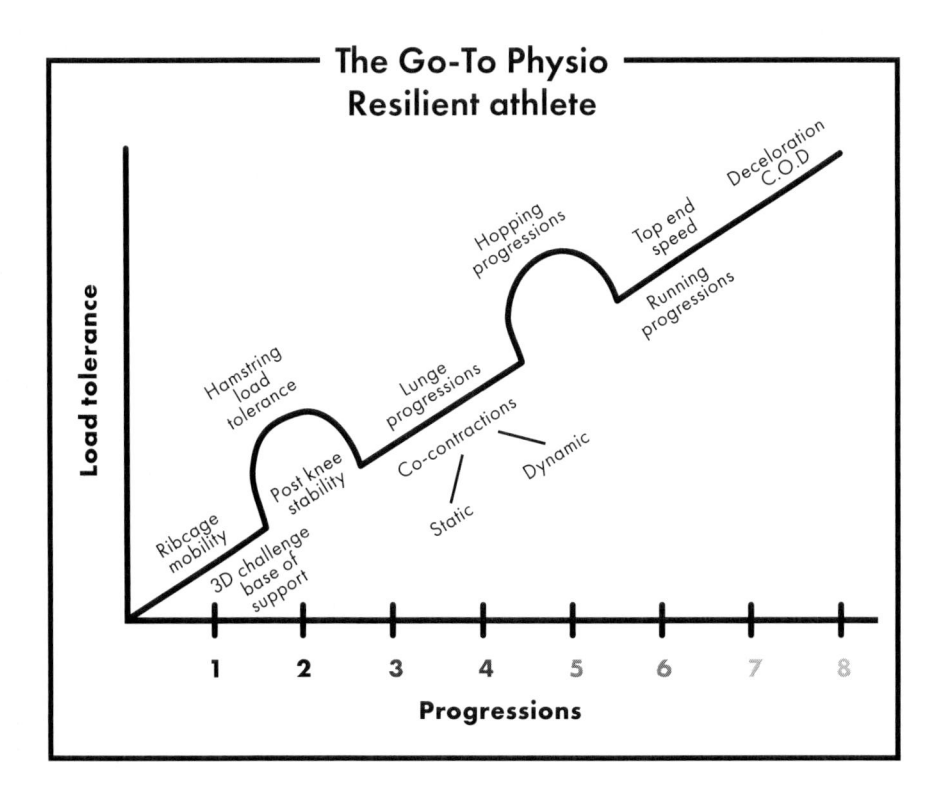

The Go-To Physio — Resilient athlete

The Go-To Physio
Resilient person

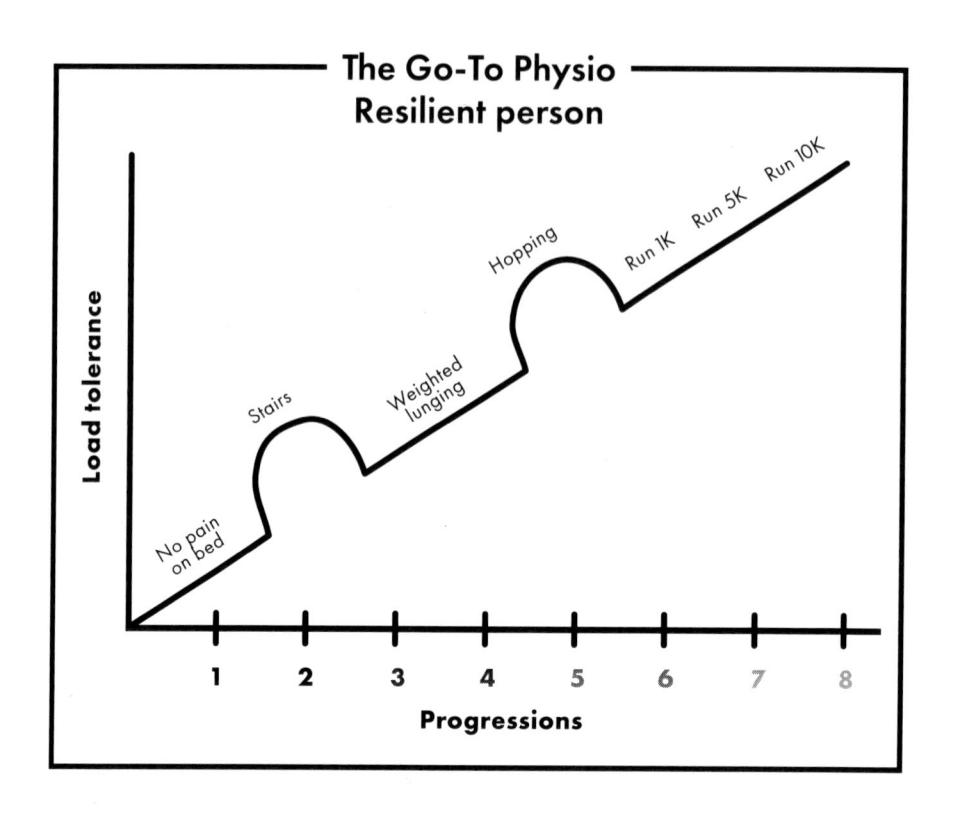

A graph showing Load tolerance vs Progressions (1-8), with an upward trajectory marked with milestones: No pain on bed, Stairs, Weighted lunging, Hopping, Run 1K, Run 5K, Run 10K.

The importance of making a fast start in your treatment plan

With the 10,000 foot overview filled in, the main thing you need to get right in the first session is ensuring you make a fast start so the patient can feel the difference quickly. This will be the focus for the remainder of the session with regards not only to hands-on treatment, but also the rehab exercises you prescribe the patient.

Load tolerance (y-axis) / **Progressions** (x-axis)

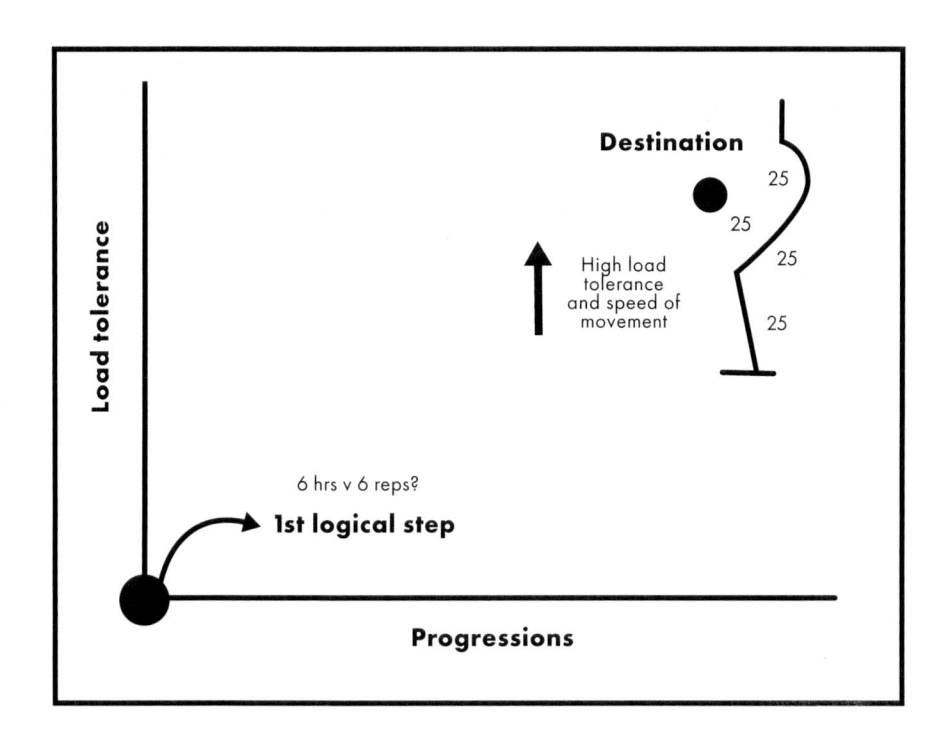

- 1st logical step — 6 hrs v 6 reps?
- Destination — High load tolerance and speed of movement
- 25, 25, 25, 25

Your exercises should focus on helping the patient be successful in hitting the first milestone or working towards getting them their first "big emotional win". This will give you the best chance of buy-in and the patient staying the course of treatment all the way to their dream outcome.

With every exercise you prescribe, the patient should identify the "prompt" or "trigger" that will allow them to take action throughout their day. It should adhere to the Fogg's behaviour model and have a clear motivation (working towards a key milestone); the patient should have the ability to do the exercise without pain (and feel the difference afterwards); and there should be a clear prompt or trigger for when they will do this exercise throughout the day. Using this model will ensure you stay focused on always delivering high-value treatment plans and give you the best chance of creating raving fans who refer.

Using top-down cues to start fast

In an ideal world the patient would only do activities that resemble the graded exposure load tolerance that they are currently at in the treatment plan. However, this is unrealistic in the real world. This is where top-down cues can be extremely effective for helping the patient get "quick wins" and "feel the difference" throughout the day. For example with our knee pain patient, you may be at the bottom of the graded exposure ladder in session one and helping the patient decrease the pain experience, restore range of motion and increase load tolerance through the hamstrings with your bed assessment.

The problem is that the patient may need to tackle stairs throughout their day and this is also a key milestone. Going up and down stairs is clearly of greater load tolerance than the bed activities, however that doesn't mean you can't help the patient be successful. This is where you would use a top-down cue, such as "squash an orange through the midfoot" on the way up the stairs. Teaching the patient correct foot pressure distribution on the way down the stairs can help them be successful and notice a decrease in their pain experience in the first few sessions. Although this is an energy-expensive strategy and requires conscious thought, it does allow you to gain a "quick win" for the patient in the first few sessions and can tide you over until you can progress them to this level with bottom-up progressions where they no longer need to think about "squashing an orange". This demonstrates the power of top-down cues initially to buy you time to get the patient to "thoughtless, fearless movement".

Now you understand how to design a high-value based treatment plan, let's look at how you put all of this together for a patient.

Chapter 10:
How to Get Complete Patient Adherence and Buy-In

According to the dictionary, an explanation is a statement or account that makes something clear. The reality, in private practice, is that most patient explanations are filled with anatomical words and terminology. This is essentially a "different language" for patients and when you use such terminology to tell patients about the problem and solution, you are essentially talking "double Dutch". Is it any wonder most patients do not adhere, drop off or cancel once the pain eases?

According to a recent study by O'Keeffe et al (2015) entitled *What Influences Patient-Therapist Interactions in Musculoskeletal Physical Therapy? Qualitative Systematic Review and Meta-Synthesis*[12] patients felt patient-therapist interaction was enhanced when the therapist had the ability to provide a simple, clear explanation. Patients valued an easy explanation of what their problem was, how the physical therapist could help them, and why the therapist was prescribing certain exercises. Patients felt more comfortable when they knew what their treatment plan was and felt interaction with their therapist was enhanced as a result.

On the other hand, patients did not like it when the education given to them was technical and they therefore felt that this had a negative impact on the patient-therapist relationship.

---

[12] O'Keeffe M, Cullinane P, Hurley J, Leahy I, Bunzli S, O'Sullivan PB, O'Sullivan K. What Influences Patient-Therapist Interactions in Musculoskeletal Physical Therapy? Qualitative Systematic Review and Meta-Synthesis. Phys Ther. 2016 May;96(5):609-22. doi: 10.2522/ptj.20150240. Epub 2015 Oct 1. PMID: 26427530.

In 2017, I was on a family holiday to Turkey and brought a book with me on making your marketing message simple. It was called *The Art Of Explanation*[13] by Lee LeFever. Truth be told, I brought the book with me to help me figure out how I could finally get a fully booked clinic and it helped me do just that, but not the way I was expecting!

You see, the whole principle of the book was that your explanation needs to be simple. If the person you are talking to doesn't understand some of the words you say, they lose confidence in understanding and you lose their attention. Think about when you open up a really "technically heavy" research paper or text book. As you read a paragraph and don't understand some of the big, fancy words, you will naturally find yourself losing confidence in your understanding and more than likely will put the book or paper down. Said another way, it is consuming too much of your brain's calories and we naturally want to switch off and allow our brains to wander!

This got me thinking about pain science explanations and how many of us spend time trying to drag the patient up to our level. I had spent the last couple of years outlining the problem and plan to the patient, but I wasn't adhering to the basic principles in this book. When I finished the book, I got to work figuring out how to make this work in my clinic.

After a few Turkish beers by the pool, I drafted the first round of what I then called "Effective Explanation". I got back to the clinic and implemented it right away. Truth be told, it took me a few goes to smooth it out, yet it worked better than expected. It has continued to evolve over the years and it's my secret weapon to having a fully booked clinic with happy, progressing patients. Now, more than 850 therapists all over the world use it too, after completing the subjective and objective assessment, to get patient buy-in, adherence and momentum to see their treatment all the way through to the final sessions that they ethically need.

---

[13] LeFever, L. (2012). The Art of Explanation: Making Your Ideas, Products, and Services Easier to Understand. Wiley.

It communicates three critical things to the patient in the most simple terms:

1. The problem

2. The solution

3. The plan

Most importantly, it sets expectations in the initial assessment for your patient so you don't need to feel stressed or anxious after session two to three or book the patient in for more sessions than they ethically need. You and your patient will be clear on the plan and exactly what needs to be done in the next session to keep them progressing.

So, why does it work so well? Well, firstly when you confuse someone you lose. Effective explanation takes the confusion and complexity out of your patient's situation. That is a high-value skill in itself. If they are confused about why they are doing an exercise, or why they need to come back again, they will not take action and you will lose them. Secondly, you give someone a plan. You will always trust someone who has a plan more than someone who doesn't. Think about it from your patient's point of view: would you rather work with a therapist who gives you a clear road map to success, or work with someone who has no real plan and is just going session to session?

Which therapist will the patient have more confidence in?

Which therapist is the patient more likely to rebook in with?

Which therapist are you?

Finally, your plan is aspirational and not just focused on the site of pain. We are hardwired to survive and thrive. Treatment plans that focus on the patient's aspirations in life and becoming a better version of themselves win every time! Effective explanation does just that. Rather than designing treatment plans focused on just strengthening muscles, we build high-value treatment plans that help them not only survive but thrive!

Effective explanation is non-negotiable for a fully-booked diary of happy, progressing patients. So, how do you apply this in private and overcome the final mistake by coming down to the patient's level? You use simple items that nearly every patient knows and understands... numbers, stickmen and letters.

Implementing effective explanation

Let's illustrate this with a quick example of a knee-pain patient who is overloading their knee joint and not using their soleus, hamstring and hip enough due to an old ankle injury.

Before we proceed, it's important to note that with effective explanation you will need to sacrifice a little accuracy for understanding. This does not mean you "lie" or "deceive" the patient, far from it. However, you need to simplify the terms you use and the level of detail you provide about the workings of the knee joint to make it as simple as possible for them to understand that the knee joint is doing too much work and the other muscles that you will be targeting with your rehab are not doing enough work.

In the following example, the soleus will be doing a bit more work than the hamstrings and hip at lower levels of functional activities, yet adding another level of complexity risks adding confusion. Remember to keep this as simple as humanly possible so the patient understands what you really need them to understand.

The final point before we get started is not to copy this example for every knee-pain patient. You must be ethical and base your explanation on the findings in your assessment. For some knee-pain patients, the soleus, hamstring and hip might be doing a great job and it might be something completely different. As you will see in the example, at all times be honest and "show don't tell" your patient. With that said, let's get started.

Remember, in order to design a long-lasting, value-based treatment plan you must have identified:

1. Exactly where the patient is currently (point A).

2. Exactly where the patient wants to get back to (point B).

3. What obstacle or root problem is preventing the patient from moving from where they are not to where they want to be.

With effective explanation, I usually like to **demonstrate Point B first.** Demonstrate in simple terms what should be happening, specific to the patient's wants and needs. This is where the patient wants to get back to.

This image demonstrates, in simple terms, what should be happening for the leg when the foot hits the floor for a runner (we sacrifice a little accuracy for understanding). The soleus, quads, hamstrings and glutes are all doing their jobs – 25 per cent each on this occasion.

Next, demonstrate point A – in simple terms what is currently happening, specific to the patient's situation.

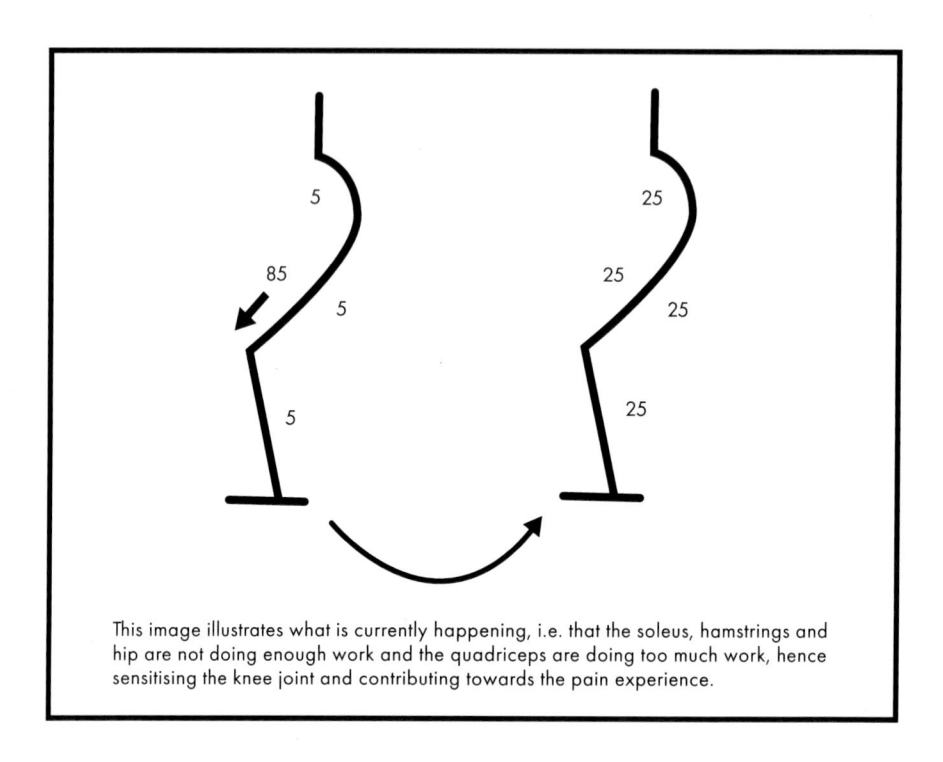

[Diagram showing two leg outlines with numerical values: Left leg labeled with 5, 85, 5, 5; Right leg labeled with 25, 25, 25, 25, 25. A curved arrow connects the bottom of the left leg to the bottom of the right leg.]

This image illustrates what is currently happening, i.e. that the soleus, hamstrings and hip are not doing enough work and the quadriceps are doing too much work, hence sensitising the knee joint and contributing towards the pain experience.

As you can see, we have defined point A, where the patient is currently, and point B, where the patient wants to get back to. The diagram also shows, in a simple way, that the soleus, hamstring and hip muscles not doing enough work (due to an old ankle injury, in this instance) is the root problem, with the arrow illustrating the gap or obstacle.

Now that we have identified and explained the root problem to the patient – specific to their story and providing proof of why we think this by highlighting our findings in the objective assessment – we must communicate the "plan" to the patient. In order to do this effectively, we will use the 5 Step 'Go-To' Physio Patient-Retention Method.

The 5 Step 'Go-To' Physio Patient-Retention Method

The 5 Step 'Go-To' Physio Patient-Retention Method incorporates the five main "must haves" to ensure the patient will stay the course of treatment. The five "non negotiables" to patient retention are:

1. Knowing your result/benefit.

2. Mapping out milestones/progress.

3. Pre-framing.

4. Have a clear next step.

5. Get them great results.

Step 1:
Know your result/benefit to the patient

Most therapists focus on getting rid of the pain for patients. Remember, the pain (back, knee, shoulder etc) is an EXTERNAL MOTIVATOR for the patient. The reason the patient has come to see you is because that external pain is causing them a problem in their life and there are consequences to that problem. This is the INTERNAL MOTIVATOR for the patient.

The result or benefit to the patient is resolving this problem, NOT to get rid of their back, knee, shoulder pain. Yet so many therapists focus all their program design, communication and energy on the EXTERNAL pain. This is a COMMUNICATION MISMATCH and it is like you communicating in double Dutch while your patient is speaking English. You need to understand what results the patient is looking for in the REAL WORLD! In the effective explanation, you clearly demonstrate the end result to the patient.

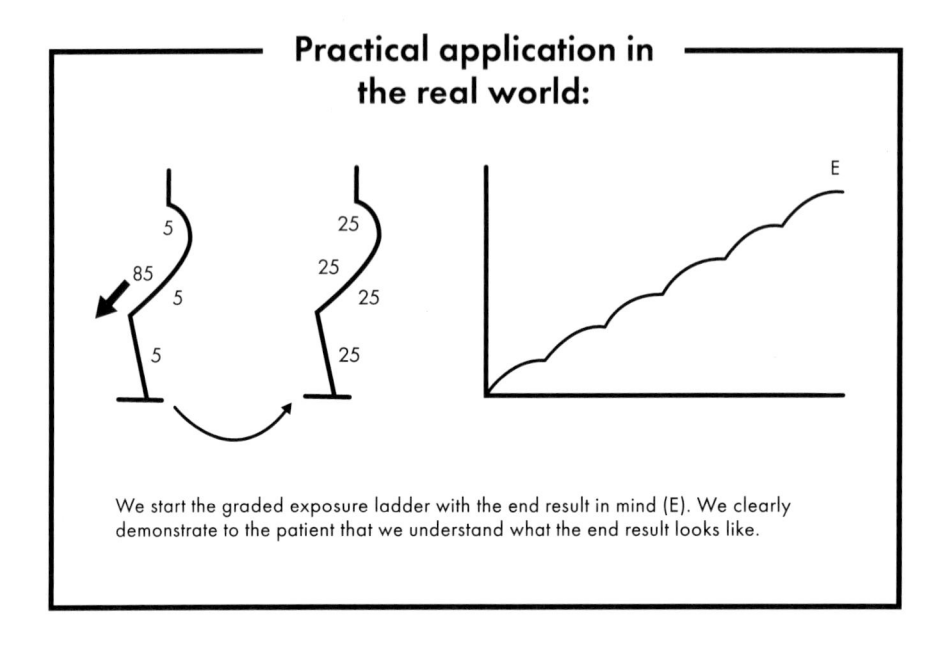

Practical application in the real world:

We start the graded exposure ladder with the end result in mind (E). We clearly demonstrate to the patient that we understand what the end result looks like.

Step 2:
Map out milestones/progress

Patients may initially come to you for the dream outcome and this may take time to achieve. Remember, the thing that makes patients stay around long enough to achieve these outcomes is the short-term experience.

The patient needs to see small milestones along the way being achieved to know they are on the right track to achieving their dream outcome. This also gives you as the therapist a massive amount of focus each session on what you are working towards instead of trying to do everything in the same session.

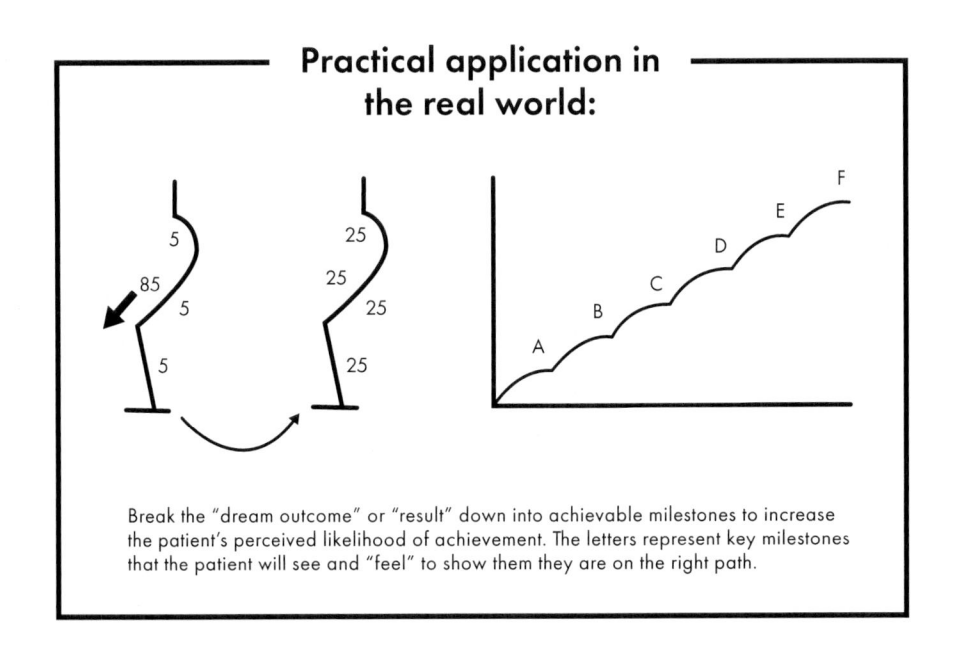

> ## Practical application in the real world:
>
> Break the "dream outcome" or "result" down into achievable milestones to increase the patient's perceived likelihood of achievement. The letters represent key milestones that the patient will see and "feel" to show them they are on the right path.

Step 3:
Pre-framing

Your patient will never be as motivated as they are when leaving the first session. Then reality sets in and they have to actually do the work. You also know the common objections that you will run into in sessions three to four, usually when the pain is easing and the patient may want to go back to running, for example.

It is a lot harder to overcome the patient's objection when it comes into their mind than it is to manage it before the thought even appears. There is also a major shift in control and authority if you pre-frame. If the patient goes against your advice, runs and experiences a "flare up", your expertise and authority is enforced and usually the patient comes back with their tail between their legs.

The patient journey in pain and physiotherapy

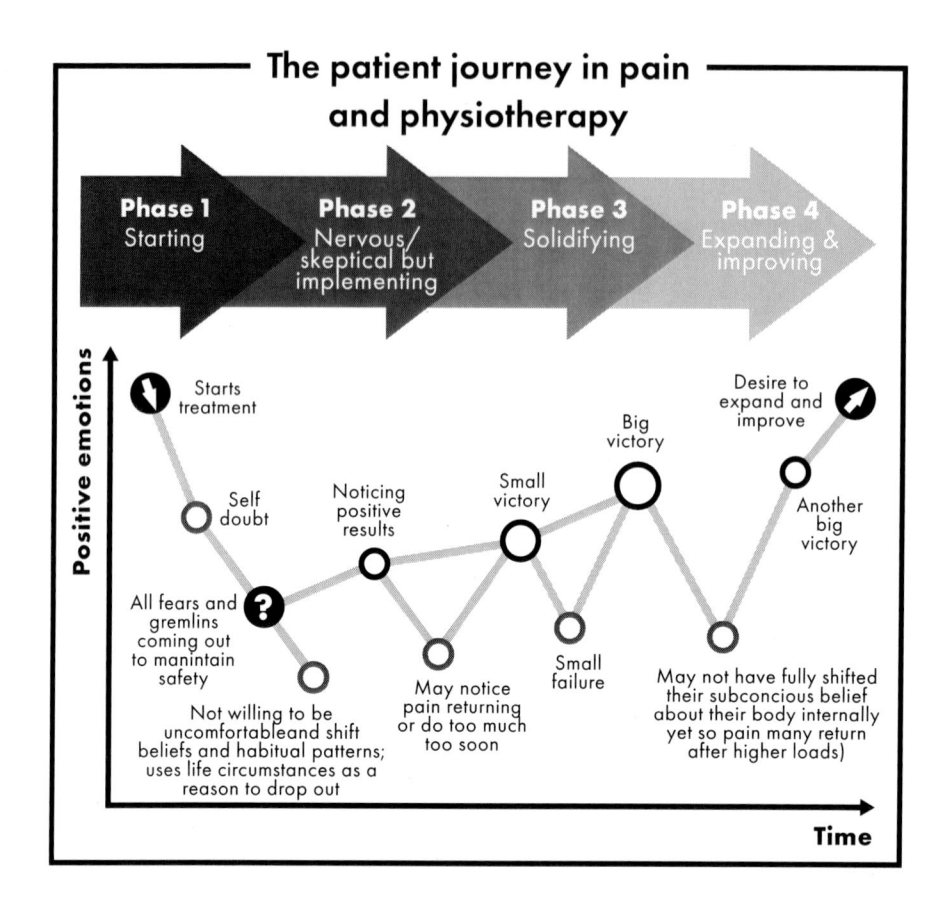

Phase 1 Starting
Phase 2 Nervous/skeptical but implementing
Phase 3 Solidifying
Phase 4 Expanding & improving

Positive emotions ↑

- Starts treatment
- Self doubt
- All fears and gremlins coming out to manintain safety
- Not willing to be uncomfortable and shift beliefs and habitual patterns; uses life circumstances as a reason to drop out
- Noticing positive results
- May notice pain returning or do too much too soon
- Small victory
- Small failure
- Big victory
- May not have fully shifted their subconcious belief about their body internally yet so pain many return after higher loads)
- Another big victory
- Desire to expand and improve

→ Time

If you do not pre-frame and they "try" a run too early and experience a "flare-up", often the patient can come back upset, angry or they may not come back at all, as they don't feel they are making any progress. This highlights two very different patient responses based on making (or not making) one simple intervention in the initial assessment.

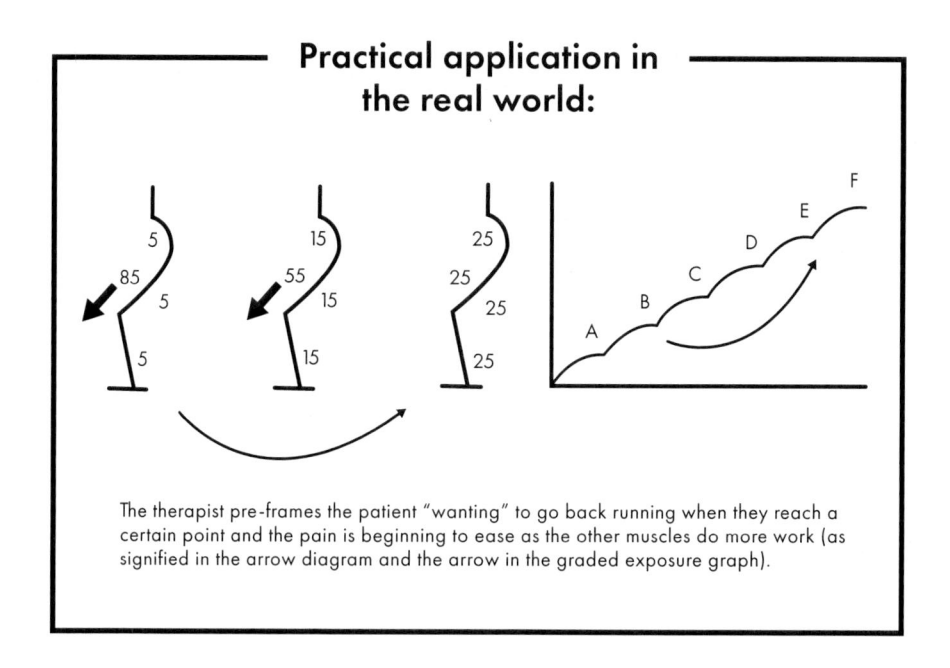

> ## Practical application in the real world:
>
> The therapist pre-frames the patient "wanting" to go back running when they reach a certain point and the pain is beginning to ease as the other muscles do more work (as signified in the arrow diagram and the arrow in the graded exposure graph).

The middle diagram symbolises that the pain has eased, yet the patient can see there is still more work to be done with the illustration of the quadriceps still doing more work than the soleus, hamstring and hip muscles.

Prognosis and number of sessions

After you have explained the process, you then proceed to give the patient a realistic time frame and number of sessions this will take. By this stage, the patient has seen the process and work involved and they can therefore logically justify why it may take six to eight sessions as opposed to the therapist just randomly saying a number without the patient understanding the reasoning behind it.

Step 4:
Have a clear next step

There is limited value in drawing out the treatment plan in the first session and hoping the patient remembers the plan. Once they leave your clinic, life gets in the way and they naturally forget.

In my experience of mentoring over 850 therapists all over the world, one of the biggest mistakes they make is to assume the patient knows the plan while the therapist keeps the plan "in their head". This is why, at the start and end of every session, I draw out the graded exposure graph to remind and focus the patient on where they are now and where they are going next.

This is powerful as it allows the patient to see that they have made progress and there is more progress yet to be made, all the while keeping the dream outcome or internal motivator top of mind.

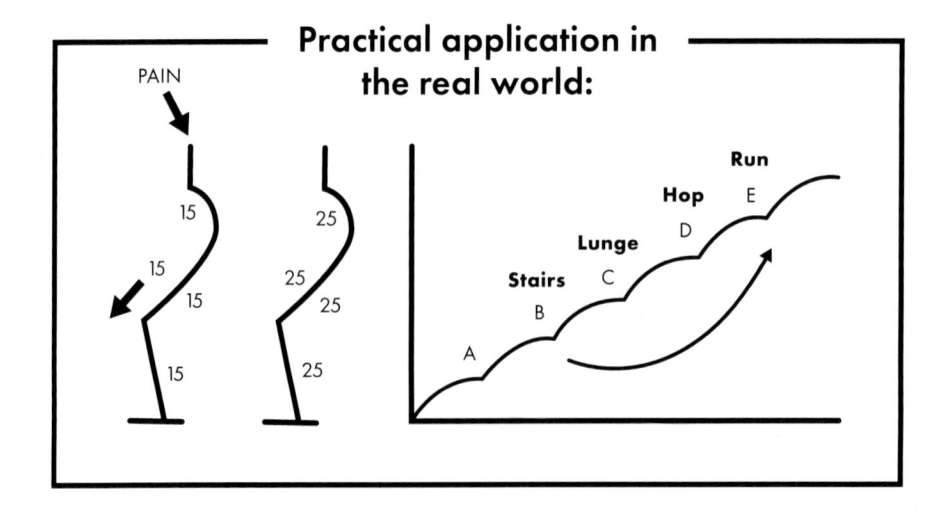

Practical application in the real world:

Step 5:
Start fast and get them great results

This needs to be a given, yet so many therapists fall at the first hurdle. Having the dream outcome or internal motivator front of mind not only helps the patient but also helps the therapist to focus. Make the patient successful and "FEEL" the difference FAST! All this requires from the therapist is a little "focus".

The effective explanation is the 10,000 foot overview

The biggest mistakes therapists make when implementing the effective explanation is that they get too granular in the details. This is more like the 10,000 foot overview of the plan. If you zoom out the GPS in a car, you can see the high-level view and the direction you are going in. You do not need to be at a street level with this explanation. Remember, it communicates three critical things to the patient in the most simple terms:

1. The problem
2. The solution
3. The plan

A patient trusts a therapist with a plan far more than a therapist who just takes it session to session. Now that you have a plan, let's walk the talk and execute that plan to have a massive impact on every patient's life by delivering world-class results.

THE GO-TO PHYSIO MENTORSHIP

Discover Dave O'Sullivan's step-by-step method to rapidly improve patient adherence and progress — while skyrocketing confidence in your clinical care!

❝ The Go-To Physio Mentorship is one of the most comprehensive, forward-thinking personal development programs available to physical therapists.

Dave and his team are phenomenal. I went from struggling to feeling confident in my abilities virtually overnight. This also took my client numbers from 10-15 a week to 15-20 to 20-30 in the first 3 months — I now struggle to fit them all in the diary!

I would recommend The Go-To Physio Mentorship to any therapist who is willing to go that extra mile to succeed. ❞

TONI STANTON

Scan the QR code now to find out more about how The Go-To Physio Mentorship can help you and your business grow!

Part Four:
Delivering World-Class Results

Now that the plan is in place, it is time to take action to ensure all your patients have incredible results where they actively spread positive word of mouth and generate referrals without you having to ask.

This section will show you how to start fast with your patients to ensure you maintain your authority and the patient's confidence in you as the therapist who will help them achieve their dream outcome.

It will show you how to use hands-on treatment safely and responsibly and how to design rehab exercises that get results fast. Finally, you will discover how to gain the "know how" to bridge the gap from low to high-level rehab and progress your patients all the way to the final session.

Once you have these skills, you will naturally enhance your confidence and reputation for handling complex issues in your clinic with ease and help people who have failed with traditional approaches. This will ensure you become the 'Go-To' Physio who builds a 'Go-To' Clinic that has patients travelling from all over to see you.

Chapter 11:
Curing Symptoms with Hands-On Treatment

When I first started out in professional sport, I took a hands-on course that led me to believe I was breaking up "adhesions" and scar tissue. For the first two years of my career I used to go home at night with aching hands and be genuinely worried about how I would survive a career in this industry over the next 40 years. The problem was that the hands-on techniques were changing range of motion and helping people feel better, albeit only in the short-term for some.

The hands-on technique I was taught was not the problem, rather it was my intention behind the hands-on technique. I had a belief and intention to break up the scar tissue and this led me to work far harder than I needed to. I had an intention of physically trying to break something up. I would use pin and stretch, trigger point and deep tissue massage to name but a few types of techniques.

It was only a few years later when I came across the likes of Greg Lehman and Diane Jacobs that I started to consider alternative reasons for my results with hands-on treatment. It made a lot of sense that it was more of a nervous system response as opposed to an actual "breaking up" of scar tissue, especially in relation to the concept of just getting short-term changes. This led me to change my own "intention" and I was able to replicate the same results with less effort, as I was now doing my best to work with the nervous system rather than against it.

Initially, I was going as deep and quick as possible, with some of my patients naturally "tightening up" which led me to go even deeper, I am embarrassed to say. I was young and thought I was doing the right thing. I would use the results I usually achieved by the end of the session to justify to myself that I was on the right track.

Nowadays I focus more on a "load tolerance" approach to the nervous system. I do my best to work with the nervous system rather than against it for long-lasting results. Because, let's face it, in a battle between myself and the patient's nervous system, there is only ever going to be one winner and it will not be me!

I very much see the hands-on treatment intent is to simply show the nervous system it is safe to restore the ability to absorb load through these soft tissues in this area of the body and work coherently with its synergists and antagonists.

The importance of respecting peripheral tissues

While we appreciate that the responses to hands-on treatment may be "non-specific", I still believe we need to be "specific" with our hands-on treatment. More precisely, by appreciating the importance of the peripheral tissues' role in communicating with the nervous system in order to achieve "thoughtless, fearless, movement".

Smooth force generation (coordination) is highly dependent on the sense of force, which is part of proprioception. Golgi tendon organs, muscle spindles and pressure-sensitive skin receptors are all important contributors to the sense of force. All of these important elements detect mechanical tissue changes and transmit action potentials to the central nervous system (CNS). Simply put, the skin, fascia, nerves, ligaments and muscles all have an important role in coordination and helping the person be successful. I believe too many people have gone too far the other way and think it is all about the higher centres and that is all there is to it.

The load tolerance locally of the tissues (skin, fascia, nerves, muscles) is the starting point of the graded exposure in restoring the ability to tolerate load in the particular direction identified through your assessment. A better term than load tolerance may be the ability to tolerate tension. We want these tissues to tolerate tension. This is important for movement efficiency and coordination because when these tissues tension or lengthen, their receptors will be stimulated, giving important sensory information to the spinal cord and higher centres. This is a key piece of the puzzle in achieving "thoughtless, fearless movement".

A higher-level strategy for the 'Go-To' Physio is to simply restore full physiological joint range of motion and the ability to tolerate load through these tissues in every direction. Essentially you give the nervous system access to as close to full sensory information as possible and then put the body in positions with our rehab that allow it to "self-organise" and figure it out.

Helping these tissues to mobilise and put some local load through them appears to help their load tolerance, from my own personal experience. I believe it may, on some level, update the "resting threshold" or "belief system" of the communication between the peripheral tissues and the spinal cord level. The work of Mick Thacker and predictive processing's role in hands-on treatment interests me greatly, although in the interests of full disclosure, I am not clear yet on the "how".

In saying all this, it is important to also point out that the exact mechanism of why this works is still unclear. I am very comfortable in not knowing the exact mechanism and resisting the urge to make up "far-fetched" explanations to the patient. Remember at all times, YOU are the GUIDE and NOT the HERO in this story. The patient is the HERO. If new research emerges to explain the reasoning behind such improvements that you see clinically, then I am fine with changing my beliefs and explanations. I am not emotionally attached to the possible reasons I have outlined above.

Therefore my explanation is a very simple one that informs the patient that I am just helping them to tolerate some load going through these tissues again and helping them update their nervous system's belief so that it understands it is now safe to use these tissues again.

The problem with hands-on treatment that causes the fourth session patient progress slump

The novel stimulus applied by your hands with your first treatment session will usually create some kind of nervous system response/adaptation. This can be a tripwire for therapists and patients, where the patient leaves the session feeling great but then the pain comes back again shortly after.

The trap some therapists can fall into is to repeat the same hands-on treatment process. What they commonly find is that in the second session, there is some relief in symptoms but it is not as great as in the first session, which can be puzzling for both the therapist and the patient. However, the problem, in my opinion, is that this hands-on treatment is a little less novel now and so the reaction from the nervous system is not as great.

By the fourth session, in my experience, repeating those same hands-on techniques usually has little to no benefit and the patient's progress plateaus. This highlights the importance of the graded exposure program for both the patient's nervous system to "keep these changes" and for the therapist's ability to keep the patient progressing.

This, therefore, is why I believe you truly need to have that step-by-step graded exposure plan in place to keep the gains between sessions, to ensure the pain or loss in range of motion does not return and to get the patient capable of tolerating these loads at both high loads and high speeds, specific to their needs to be able to enjoy their life with thoughtless, fearless movement. Repeating the same hands-on techniques in session four as you did in session one is simply working at a tactical level.

Hands-on treatment is working at a tactical level

The 'Go-To' Physio should not be interested in the tactic or technique first and foremost, rather they should always be coming back to principles. As the saying from Harrington Emerson, a renowned business theorist, goes: "As to methods, there may be a million and then some, but principles are few. The man who grasps principles can successfully select his own methods. The man who tries methods, ignoring principles, is sure to have trouble."

This also holds true for hands-on techniques. The principle is the most important thing to understand and then the tactic becomes almost irrelevant. Pin and stretch, deep tissue massage, and dry needling are all tactics deployed to help the patient get from point A to point B. However, you must first understand what points A and B are, and what the obstacle stopping the patient from getting from point A to B is. In order to do this, second order consequences become critical.

Always consider second order consequences before performing hands-on treatment

In 2015, in my last year with the Huddersfield Giants, I broke one of my cardinal rules: never just treat the site of pain. A player came in five minutes before our final training session, the day before a game, and asked me to quickly "release" his glute. It felt tight overnight and just needed a "quick elbow", he informed me.

Against my better judgement I obliged and "freed up" his glute. Long story short, five minutes into the session, he was bent over in agony. His lower back had "locked up". He could barely straighten up. Sh%t! I thought!

No one was going to join the dots of his glute and back, but I knew straight away I had f*%ked up and should have quickly assessed the player and given his nervous system and subconscious mind what it needed, rather than what the player and his conscious mind wanted. This was a classic example of me taking away his nervous system's own protective strategy and leaving him, presumably, feeling too "loosey goosey"! There was only ever going to be one winner, his nervous system!

I then went on a dry needling course, during which the course instructor informed us that everyone with back pain was to get a dry needle in the gluteus medius! EVERYONE!! The point is, cookie-cutter approaches are dangerous. If you just treat the symptoms without considering the second order consequences, you are setting yourself up for failure, and I speak from my own personal experience.

Think twice, treat once – use your hands-on treatment like a sniper rifle rather than a bazooka

I can't remember where I heard this story, to give full credit, but someone once told me about some chiropractor proudly exclaiming that his hands were like a sniper rifle: one shot, one kill! While I am sceptical that it is this easy with every patient, I really like the analogy to illustrate the concept of "think twice, treat once".

This also ties into the concept of second order thinking or second order consequences, which may be a better term on this occasion. Failing to consider second order consequences doesn't help anyone, although I'll admit I've done this a few times in my career. Picture the scene: the patient is improving and I perform a hands-on treatment technique only for them to get off the bed feeling worse! Sh%t again! Will I ever learn?! Thankfully, considering second order consequences before applying a hands-on treatment technique nowadays means I do it less and less.

Soft tissue techniques are simply tactics that help you get from point A to point B

When you "reframe" soft tissue or hands-on treatment as a method that allows you to simply help "reassure" the patient's nervous system that it is safe to tolerate load, you are empowered with so many more options, including now being able to use this tool alongside your non-manual therapy techniques such as exercise.

There will be times when hands-on treatment may not be appropriate – or even work – to help get the patient to the next level of the graded exposure program. However, having the mindset that you are simply helping get the patient to the next level of the graded exposure program now gives you more options, such as using static holds with breathing, isometrics and other "tactics" to achieve the same result. With a simple refocus on what you are trying to achieve, you are no longer a "slave" to having to use your hands.

If a change is going to happen, it is going to happen within the first 60 seconds (usually)

A real benefit of changing your focus from any physical structural changes taking place to the tissues to an actual nervous system response is that, usually, if a change is going to happen, it is going to happen within the first 60 seconds of your hands-on treatment. This is great news for the 'Go-To' Physio who does not want to spend the whole session performing hands-on treatment. However, this then begs the question, how do you know when you have done enough soft tissue treatment to get the changes you want?

The answer is you use key performance indicators (KPIs) to gain an insight into the patient's nervous system.

Using KPIs to mitigate risk and give you unshakeable confidence

A KPI is a measurable value that demonstrates how effectively an action or set of actions is achieving its objectives. A 'Go-To' Physio will use KPIs to evaluate success at reaching targets. A high-level KPI may be the overall goal for the patient or even getting them to the next step of the graded exposure ladder, while a low-level KPI might be a small step in the longer process of getting a patient to the next level of the graded exposure ladder.

A KPI can be any subjective or objective marker that can measure whether your inputs are helping deliver the desired output. It may include things like decreased pain, increased range of motion or increased load tolerance etc.

Using KPIs prior to and after your hands-on treatment is a powerful strategy to gain confidence quickly that you are on the right track with your patient. Before any hands-on treatment technique, I always use a KPI to check my work. For example, a low-level KPI may be improving the load tolerance ability of the soleus, hamstrings and quadriceps to co-contract using a coordinate test from my objective assessment as a KPI. A higher-level KPI may be performing a lunge pain free (a higher level of the graded exposure ladder). I would then assess the patient's ability to perform these actions.

Next, I would aim to "desensitise" the load tolerance ability of the medial hamstrings and then recheck my low-level KPI first and foremost. I would then get one of three scenarios:

1. The KPI does not improve and therefore either my hands-on technique is not effective or I am not at the root of this issue. I may then choose to re-evaluate my actions.

2. The KPI improves but it is not at the desired level yet and so I perform another round of hands-on treatment and/or superset with some exercise-based intervention to achieve the same desired output.

3. The KPI improves to the desired output and I then check the high-level KPI to see if this also has improved or if there is more work to be done on further increasing load tolerance in the form of some exercise-based intervention.

After every input, such as hands-on treatment or exercise I prescribe to the patient, I always re-check the KPI I am using at this time. If option two or three is happening, I am confident I am on the right track. If option one has happened and there is no improvement of my KPI, then I know I have more thinking time ahead, but also that I have not wasted a full session performing hands-on treatment that is not getting me or the patient closer to their desired outcome.

Another way of thinking about this is simply assess, intervene, reassess. However, I would like you to move away from "assess" and work towards "performance indicators" to keep you focused on ensuring your KPI is not just some random assessment, but rather is always getting you closer to the patient's dream outcome. A small shift in terminology, yet a huge shift in focus for a 'Go To' Physio.

Decrease co-contractions centrally by improving co-contractions peripherally

At a 'Go-To' Physio Mentorship Refresher course recently, I had a therapist who had ongoing persistent back pain. The mechanism of injury was a forward reach and twist while getting her child out of the car seat. The symptoms were all around the lower and mid-back area now, especially when she went to touch her toes and twist. Her movement was slow, cautious and a typical top-down movement strategy.

Through the story and objective assessment, I was able to see that the patient had a poor load tolerance through her left hamstring. This coincided with a previous knee injury prior to the original episode of back pain. My first instinct was to "free up" the lower back and settle the symptoms. However, when I examined the second order consequences, I was able to spot that I would be leaving the patient feeling "loosey goosey" when I rechecked the toe touch, which I was using as the main KPI.

So, I delayed gratification and went to work restoring some load tolerance through the hamstring. After improving the KPI that I was using on the bed, I then got the patient to stand up and recheck her toe touch. There was a marked improvement in her low back symptoms and she was moving away from a slow, cautious top-down strategy to more of a smooth, bottom-up strategy.

The hands-on treatment probably took me less than 60 seconds, but it was the KPIs that told me I was on the right track and going in the right direction. If the KPIs hadn't improved, then I would have gone to the next thing on my list from the patient's story and assessment findings. I wouldn't have spent a full session doing hands-on treatment, only to find it made no difference. This is the beauty of using KPIs before and after hands-on treatment. It gives you unwavering confidence that you are on the right track and helps you then set the patient up for success with the appropriate rehab graded exposure exercises to take home so they will feel the difference and continue to make progress between sessions.

Integrating hands-on treatment into a step-by-step system

There is no doubt hands-on treatment helps some people and has its benefits. The problems arise when patients become passive and reliant on it. The effective explanation combined with the coordinative exercise focus covered in the coming chapters will help combat this issue too. This graph is a visual representation of how I encourage therapists to think about the use of hands-on treatment in private practice.

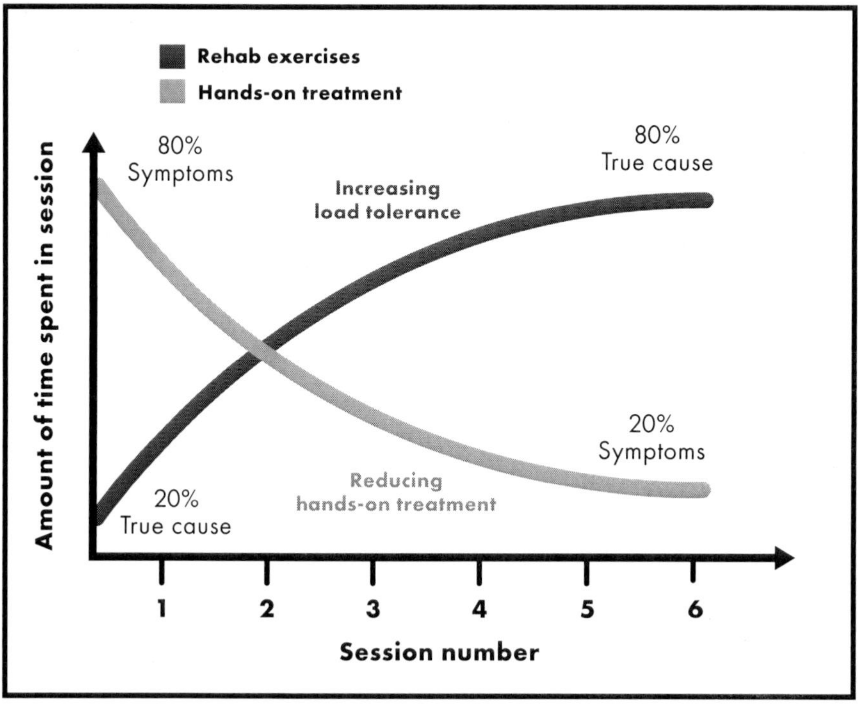
Rehab exercises
Hands-on treatment
Amount of time spent in session
80%
Symptoms
80%
True cause
Increasing
load tolerance
20%
Symptoms
20%
True cause
Reducing
hands-on treatment
1
2
3
4
5
6
Session number

In the first session, you may find yourself using more hands-on treatment to settle the symptoms (20 per cent) while also targeting the peripheral tissues that you want to "desensitise" and to show the patient's nervous system it is safe to do more (80 per cent). You will do this using KPIs and a Goldilocks approach of not too much, not too little, just the right amount. With irritable patients, you may find yourself spending more time on the symptoms in the first session to get this under control. Every patient will be slightly different and therefore a common sense approach is required at all times.

After every hands-on treatment, you may choose to quickly check your KPI and you may also be supersetting this with a coordinative load tolerance exercise, again rechecking the KPI afterwards. Once the KPI improves or is going in the right direction, you may choose to only check the KPI at the end of the coordinative load tolerance exercise instead.

You may perform a five-minute block where the patient is on the bed for 60–90 seconds receiving hands-on treatment, followed by a coordinative load tolerance exercise and a quick check of the KPI. This process may be repeated two to three times. This means the patient is very active in the session and not just lying on the bed "receiving" hands-on treatment for 20–30 minutes with no active input. The patient is working hard and the pace is fast. In my experience, this stops the patient becoming reliant on hands-on treatment while also keeping the "changes" for long-lasting relief.

As the sessions progress, the symptoms will have settled if you have addressed the root problem and you'll find yourself using less and less hands-on treatment. The majority of your hands-on treatment at this point will be a quick "once over" aimed exclusively at the root problem tissues (80 per cent). More and more time will be spent on the rehab exercises at this point.

As you progress up the graded exposure ladder, old injuries may now start to come into play where previously the load tolerance was not enough to expose their motor adaptations. Therefore, in later sessions, it is not unusual to be treating old injuries with hands-on treatment to again "desensitise" and increase the load tolerance of these particular tissues.

A final word on using KPIs

As your sessions progress, your KPIs do not always have to be improving. A KPI can also stay the same or, said another way, not regress. This is a good sign, especially if you have increased the load tolerance on the nervous system and the peripheral tissues and there have been no negative consequences as you progress up the graded exposure ladder.

Chapter 12:
Lower-Level Rehab That Gets You Instant Results

In the first weekend of June in the summer of 2017 I attended my first ever live Peter O'Sullivan course in London. I had always admired Peter's work yet this seminar gave me an opportunity to give him my unfocused attention for two out of the three days (I had to miss the final day due to other commitments).

The first day was focused on the "theory" and he spent the next day "treating" some complex cases on stage. It was a joy to watch Peter work and I certainly model myself on his approach of "walking the walk", as well as being able to "talk the talk".

Peter was working with a couple of patients on day two and he made a significant difference to these people's pain levels and mobility. They came in with top-down, guarded movement behaviours and left well on their way to bottom-up, relaxed movement. It was interesting to read the Twitter feeds of delegates at this conference, and their "reasoning" as to why he was able to make all of these changes. The majority of therapists were focusing on higher centre changes and "beliefs" about the patient which I've no doubt contributed greatly to the results.

When I saw the difference in results with the patients, I dismissed my initial "superficial thoughts" and challenged myself to think on a deeper level, asking myself one simple question:

"What are all the possible reasons that may have contributed to these results?"

On the way home on the train, I made a list of all the possibilities that may have helped the patients that day, in addition to the higher centre changes and beliefs. I replayed the types of movements/actions that Peter had the patients do and the types of cues he used over and over in my mind. In addition to challenging and potentially updating the patient's beliefs, he also did a number of other things that day in the process either consciously or subconsciously:

- He allowed the patient to relax the ribcage and lengthen the diaphragm, which helped the low back muscles to relax.

- He got the patient to relax the neck and just breathe, which facilitated the ribcage's ability to depress and retract and allow the low back muscles to "dampen down".

- He got the patient to take more load through the midfoot by getting them to relax their backs when they were standing.

- He got the patients to continue to take more load through the midfoot and lower limb when bending down to pick things up.

- He used the breath to help the patient be successful.

- He cued the patient to exhale on the way down as the diaphragm was lengthening and got them to inhale on the way up as the diaphragm was shortening.

- He was training co-contractions around the knee joint, which helped the glutes do more work on the way up by delaying knee extension until the hip joints also had a chance to do more work. This ultimately meant the low back did not have to do too much work.

- He had each patient's full attention and they were working "hard" doing these simple movements.

More than likely Peter was not too worried about all these things happening and was focusing more on the patient, yet all these things were happening as well. As you know by now, I am a massive fan of working smarter not harder and this approach to rehab certainly resonated with me. More importantly I then went on to ask myself the question: "How can I take the principles of this approach and use it also for lower and upper limb issues?"

This led me to reexamine my own rehab approach at this point and I got to work testing this new approach in my own clinic and with the pro sport teams I was working with at the time. The results were amazing and the biggest difference I noticed was that the changes were almost instantaneous in some scenarios. What surprised me most was that the patients were "feeling the difference" straight away and behaving just like they did when they had hands-on treatment.

They felt "different", they felt "lighter" and more "springy" after doing these types of exercises. This led me to further think about why this occurred, which I'll explain in more detail in the coming chapters, but the exciting thing was that I finally had a way to recreate the hands-on treatment feeling without needing to do hands-on treatment itself.

Strategy vs. tactics when designing rehabilitation exercises

One of the biggest things that concerns me these days in the age of YouTube and Instagram is that more and more therapists are priding themselves on coming up with more and more exercise variations and "new exercises". I am concerned that this leads to more and more overwhelm, which ultimately leads to a lack of clarity and hence confidence suffers.

As I progress my career and continue to "critically think" first and foremost, I find I use fewer and fewer exercise variations, and instead just do the basics extraordinarily well. Finding an exercise on YouTube or Instagram and then "trying" it with your patient the next day is simply a "tactical" move. I'll put my hand up and admit I've done this earlier in my career and even flared some patients up using exercises I had just seen on the web. This is also one of the most dangerous things you can do as a therapist without considering the second order consequences.

Nowadays, when I see an exercise variation that intrigues me on YouTube or Instagram, the first thing I ask is whether this exercise adheres to my rehab principles. The second question I then ask myself is how/if I can make this exercise better by adhering to my rehab principles? Another question I ask myself is where this exercise variation would sit in my graded exposure approach. Which exercise progression does it sit before and after? What would a progression or regression of this exercise be?

The final question then would be: "Have I got an exercise already that is loading these tissues in a more simple and direct way for the patient and is easier for me to teach?" If I answer no to this question, then I will consider using this variation at the right time of the graded exposure program for the patient.

Coordinative load tolerance exercises

While strengthening focused exercises have their place and there is no denying the evidence base, a big frustration for me both in professional sport and private practice was that they were very hit and miss with patients. Some patients responded well and some didn't respond as expected. In high-pressure environments such as pro sport or private practice, you need to get results quickly. The truth is strength training takes time.

The other problem that I have observed with strength training is that the patient's nervous system can be extremely clever in avoiding loading tissues even when strength training. These subtle "things" that a person does during the exercises such as arching their back, shrugging their shoulder slightly or lifting their big toe slightly off the floor as the weight goes back to the heels are all subtle "motor adaptations" that can take load away from certain tissues and cause other tissues to do more work. This means that the tissues you are targeting may not be getting the desired results as it is so easy for the nervous system to take load away from areas that may still have a "perceived threat" present.

I needed a different solution, a solution that would allow me to put the patient's nervous system in a position where they had no choice but to tolerate the load so that it presented an opportunity for their nervous system to update its own belief system. This led me to rethink my approach further and come up with a more "coordinative load tolerance" approach with my exercise prescription rather than just strengthening. Seeing Peter O'Sullivan in action was the final piece of the jigsaw puzzle that I needed to bring it all together.

The term "coordinative load tolerance" is not an attempt to come up with yet another three-word "technique". Rather, my aim is to focus the therapist on what we are trying to achieve with our exercise prescription.

The reason the patient can feel "different", "lighter", or more "springy" straight away is more than likely not due to strength changes. These would take considerably more time to kick in. Therefore the changes "felt" must be due to a "self-organisation" of the patient's nervous system and a more energy-efficient strategy. Energy efficiency to me is using the right amount of energy to do the task at hand, no more, no less. Remember the motor adaptation strategies that a patient uses? Well, we are simply "undoing" these strategies and helping their nervous system to remember the previous strategies where everything was doing its job, no more, no less. Therefore, there needs to be a big emphasis on coordination rather than strength with your rehabilitation exercises if you are to get changes that the patient can "feel" quickly.

If you recall from our patient adherence section, patients are more likely to do exercises that allow them to "feel" the difference. Therefore coordination-focused exercises are much more powerful at first in private practice than strength-focused exercises, in my experience. It also helps the patient become less reliant on hands-on treatment because they have something they can do to give them the same "feeling".

When I make sure the patient is not using motor adaptation strategies before I switch to strength-focused exercises, I see a much better and quicker carry over once I introduce strength-focused exercises to their rehab.

In addition to focusing on coordination, you also need to consider load tolerance because this is an important aspect to also consider when designing exercises.

Load tolerance refers both to the physical and mental aspects of the patient's body and nervous system. Just like stretching gains are more than likely due to stretch tolerance rather than physical changes in the muscle's ability to lengthen, the same concept can be applied here with these coordinative load tolerance exercises. You will see patients start with a very slow guarded top-down approach and quickly move towards a smooth, faster bottom-up approach as their nervous system tolerates the physical and mental load placed upon the body. The beauty about the nervous system is that it can change very quickly when given the right stimulus (and also negatively if given the wrong stimulus), so progress can happen very quickly for patients, often within a session.

The load tolerance will therefore need to continue to increase as you progress the patient. It is not just about designing an exercise that gets all the synergies and antagonists to work well together but also to work well together tolerating more and more load, as you progress the patient's nervous system up the graded exposure ladder towards the dream outcome. So, with all of that said, what are the principles of coordinative load tolerance exercises?

Principles of coordinative load tolerance exercise prescription

These principles can act as a guide for you so that you no longer have to learn exercises and give them to every patient. Instead these principles can empower you to design exercises that solve a specific problem for the patient in front of you.

The principles of coordinative load tolerance exercises are as follows:

1. Identify point A, where the patient is currently, and point B, where you want to get them to.

2. Identify which tissues are not tolerating load well through your assessment.

3. Clarify how these tissues must function as "synergies" and "antagonists" in the real world in order for the patient to be successful with a whole body approach.

4. Have a KPI that you can check pre and post intervention to gain an insight into whether the patient's nervous system is interpreting this

stimulus as a positive or negative that shows you that you are on the right path and making progress towards point B.

5. Put the patient's body in a position at the appropriate point of the graded exposure ladder where the identified tissues have no choice but to tolerate load.

6. Challenge the patient's base of support appropriately to command the subconscious mind's attention and allow the patient to experience "deliberate practice" of the exercise at hand.

7. Remove any potential opportunities for the nervous system to "cheat" by putting these potential tissues into their end range of motion to disadvantage the tissues' length-tension relationships (think relaxing the neck and low back so the lower limb has to do more work).

8. Have instant feedback for both the patient and therapist to allow them both to clearly see whether the patient's nervous system is using a motor adaptation strategy.

9. Allow the patient's nervous system an opportunity to "self-organise" and "figure it out" with plenty of repetitions at the appropriate speed of movement.

10. Recheck the KPIs and ensure the exercise is having a positive influence on the patient's ability to move towards point B.

Commanding the subconscious mind's attention

With the influx of social media and other triggers in this day and age, it has never been so difficult to command your patient's conscious attention let alone their subconscious mind. Your attention, or should I say your patient's attention, is the new most important currency for private practice therapists.

In order for these coordinative exercises to get quick and long-lasting results, you must command the attention of the patient's subconscious mind. The human body sends 11 million bits per second to the brain for processing, yet the conscious mind seems to be able to process only 50 bits[14].

To command the subconscious mind's attention you can do a few things. The first thing I like to do is to challenge the patient's base of support. This immediately causes a "threat" to the person's safety and forces the subconscious mind to "react". You'll notice that the majority of the exercises I create put the patient in a position where they have no choice but to tolerate the load through the tissues I want them to (and if they don't, they will fall over!). This ensures I command the attention of the patient's attention both consciously and subconsciously. The second thing I do is to ensure that all my exercises adhere to deliberate practice principles.

Six steps to design exercises that allow for deliberate practice

According to James Clear, author of *Atomic Habits*, "Deliberate practice refers to a special type of practice that is purposeful and systematic. While regular practice might include mindless repetitions, deliberate practice requires focused attention and is conducted with the specific goal of improving performance."[15]

This is exactly what you must do with our private practice patients for every single rep. No repetition must be mindless or not work towards the ultimate goal of improving the patient's performance in life.

The six steps are as follows:

---

[14] Britannica, available at: https://www.britannica.com/science/information-theory/Physiology
[15] Clear J., (2018), *Atomic Habits: An Easy & Proven Way to Build Good Habits & Break Bad Ones*, Random House Business, 1st edition

Step 1. The exercise is ultimately designed to improve the performance of the person in the real world or a piece of the process towards reaching the dream outcome. This ensures you train the muscles appropriately and give them an opportunity to function and communicate with the nervous system as they are designed to do.

Step 2. It is repeated a lot. If Step 1 is adhered to then this step will allow the patient plenty of opportunities to practice throughout the day naturally as it is working towards their dream outcome. This is important as coordination requires repetition rather than just three sets of ten.

Step 3. Feedback on results is available immediately. This can be in the form of pain or the absence of pain and/or other things such as not falling over!

Step 4. It's highly demanding mentally. This links to commanding the patient's conscious and subconscious attention in order to attempt to update the belief systems internally. It also ensures you have an appropriate "load tolerance" mentally for the patient's nervous system to adapt and overcome.

Step 5. It's hard for the patient. This also links with commanding the patient's complete attention. It should be noted that the exercise is hard yet achievable. If it is too difficult then motivation will drop, naturally. This highlights the critical importance of prescribing the right exercise at the right time on the graded exposure ladder.

Step 6. It requires good goals to be able to help towards the ultimate outcome. This ensures that the exercise designed is part of the process working towards the dream outcome. The soleus slouch example that follows is an example of taking the ultimate outcome of sprinting or walking pain free and breaking it down to focus on the co-contraction ability of the knee joint while also stimulating all the tissues in the appropriate manner as they are designed to function.

Examples of lower limb coordinative load tolerance exercises

Midfoot bridge

The aim of this exercise is to present the patient's nervous system with an opportunity to use all the muscles of the lower limb in a manner that happens when the patient extends their hips in real life.

As the hip extends during gait, the weight transfers from the heel to the midfoot. Therefore, you want the weight to be exclusively on the midfoot. This ensures you stimulate the soleus and provide it with an opportunity to work with the biarticular muscles, especially the distal hamstrings, to transfer forces through the hamstring and into the hip joint.

This exercise would be done in the first session or two when the patient's motivation is highest, as it does require them to lie on their back, making opportunities to practise throughout the day more difficult.

It can be performed bilaterally or unilaterally, depending on the level that your patient is able to tolerate. The key here is that intent into the roller is through the midfoot and ball of the big toe. The patient MUST initiate the movement from the foot rather than using the back to lift the hips off the floor.

The patient only lifts the hips slightly off the floor, as the higher they lift the more likely it is that the back muscles will get involved, and in this particular instance you are trying to get more load through the lower limb muscles.

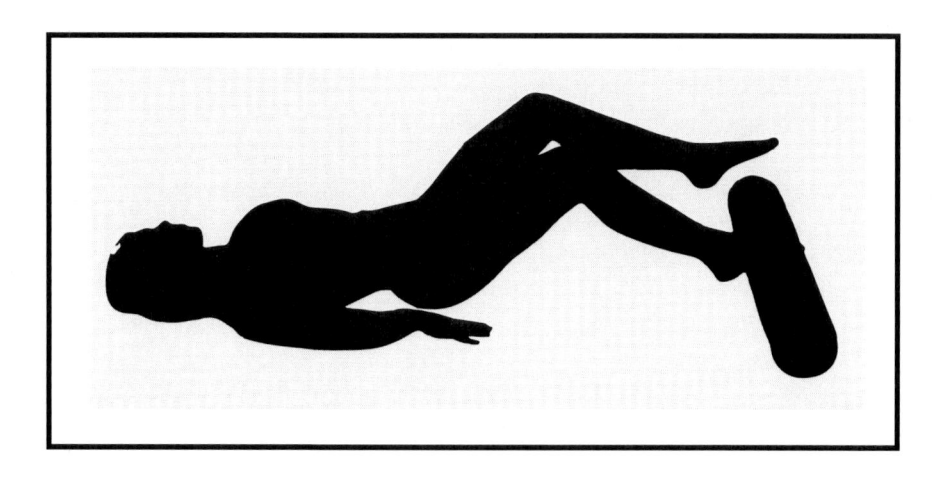

To start with you might ask your patient to hold the position for six seconds and repeat for six reps. The patient will usually have a "novel" conscious experience of the distal hamstrings working hard initially, for example. As they get used to this feeling, they will then feel the glutes working more in this movement as they "tolerate" the hamstring load better.

If the patient struggles with the roller, you can use a softer surface such as a sandbag, or put the roller up against the wall to remove the stability component of the roller.

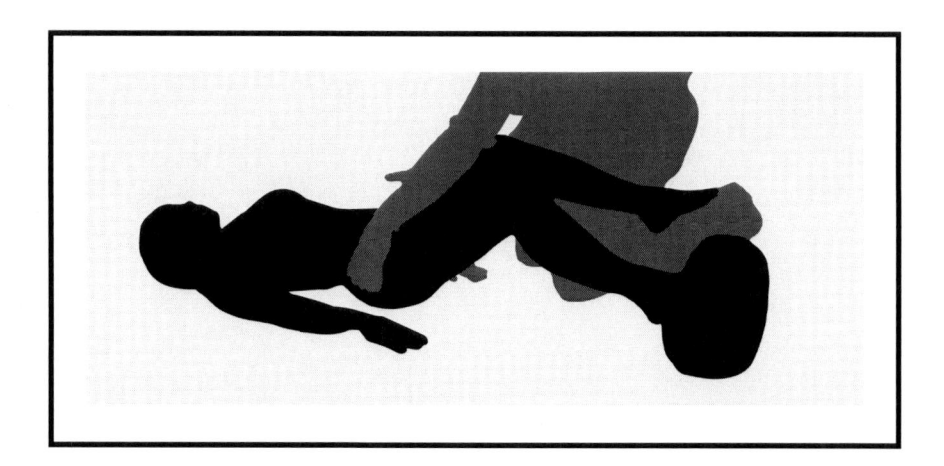

If the patient is cramping in the sole of the foot, the soleus or hamstrings then this exercise progression may be too high a level in the graded exposure ladder and you may choose to either:

- Intervene with hands-on treatment to whichever tissues are not doing enough work
- Regress to a standing midfoot bridge exercise
- Or even just the start position of this exercise where the patient initiates the intent through the midfoot without actually lifting the hips up.

The soleus slouch

This is an exercise I came up with after seeing Peter O'Sullivan do something similar bilaterally with his back pain patients. After experimenting for a few days, I came up with this variation to solve the problem of the quadriceps and/or the lower back muscles doing too much work while the soleus, hamstrings and glutes did not do enough work. The soleus slouch solves this problem and gives the soleus, hamstring and glutes an opportunity to work together without the quadriceps or lower back muscles taking over.

Building tension through the midfoot delays knee extension and allows the hamstring to work isometrically, allowing the force to transfer through it to the glute so that it can actively hip extend at the top of the movement (rather than the knee snapping back, creating "fake" hip extension). The beauty of the neck and low back being relaxed is that the soleus, hamstrings and glutes have no choice but to tolerate load because the back or neck can't cheat.

It is important to note you MUST have cleared the ability to "co-contract" the knee joint on the bed with the coordinative testing example outlined in Chapter 6 and the midfoot bridge test before using this exercise. This ensures the hamstrings have an appropriate level of load tolerance so the patient can be successful with this exercise. If they don't have an adequate load tolerance and you progress the patient too quickly, you will notice the knee will keep snapping back and you will quickly become frustrated at the patient's inability to do the exercise correctly.

No amount of conscious cueing will solve the problem, from my experience. It is simply a case of right exercise at the wrong time for the patient. Presuming it is the right exercise at the right time, let's look at how to get the most out of the exercise.

Step 1. Challenge the patient's base of support and cue the patient to bring their ribs, pelvis and sternum over the midfoot with the leg that you want to load in front and the knee slightly soft (about 10-20 degrees flexed). Ensure they don't hip hinge and the whole body actually comes forward in order to genuinely challenge the base of support and command the subconscious mind's attention. The weight comes forward onto the midfoot with little to no weight through the heel (although the heel does not lift off the floor).

It is also important that the back leg's big toe is in line with the front leg's heel. Often the patient's nervous system will try to "cheat" and increase the base of support by increasing this distance by moving the back leg further away from the front leg and taking some of the load in the process.

Step 2. Once you have the start position, get the patient to relax the neck (chin to chest) and slouch the shoulders. The patient should immediately feel more load now going through the front leg's midfoot and soleus.

This position alone may be enough for some patients initially and you will immediately see the person's conscious mind focus on the exercise like magic. You may also notice their breathing rate changes, indicating that you also have the autonomic nervous system's attention.

Before you go any further it is important to note that the key thing throughout this exercise is that the knee stays forwards and does not snap back. If the patient has poor intent through the midfoot, the knee will likely snap back, and for the first couple of reps you may need to give them some feedback with your hand to keep the knee forwards, or use a top-down cue to keep the knee forwards and really "squash the orange" through the midfoot.

Step 3. Keeping the start position, get the patient to reach their fingertips towards the floor. If the patient is struggling with this level of load tolerance, you may start by only asking them to reach as far as the knee.

If you notice the knee beginning to flex at this point, it may indicate the inability of the ribcage to depress and retract, and the low back muscles to lengthen, which may give clues that this may also need to be addressed.

Don't underestimate how challenging this exercise can be even for professional athletes. For most patients, this will be the first time in a long time that all of these tissues have tolerated this level of load without "cheating".

Step 4. To come back up again, the patient must still keep the chin tucked and the lower back relaxed to avoid "cheating" and doing some work as the intent once again comes from the midfoot to initiate the return to the start position.

Keep a close eye on the knee snapping back. This would indicate that the quadriceps are overpowering the hamstring's inability to delay knee extension. You can continue to cue the patient to "squash an orange" initially to increase the conscious intent for the soleus and hamstrings to do more work.

The first few sets of this exercise will usually be slow, guarded and top-down. However, as the load tolerance improves, the patient will quickly move towards a smooth and faster bottom-up approach.

I usually start with three sets of six repetitions which will all be quite slow. It is often not uncommon for a patient to then progress all the way up to three sets of 20 repetitions within a few days. I inform the patient to start with three sets of six reps and work towards the three sets of 20 reps by the time I see them again. They will often look at you in shock initially, but by the following week will have mastered this key skill of delaying knee extension and allowing the hip an opportunity to do more work without the quadriceps or lower back muscles doing too much.

In the 'Go-To' Physio Mentorship, we can add subtle variations to this powerful exercise to put more or less load on certain muscles/tissues in the frontal and transverse planes as well, depending on the findings of the objective assessment.

Upper limb example: wrist taps

An upper limb example of demanding the subconscious mind's attention is the anterior loading wall drill shared over the following pages. This exercise may be used to restore a load tolerance for the long head of biceps for a range of shoulder symptom issues such as rotator cuff or labral issues. This exercise will be used after you have restored a basic level of load tolerance on the bed with the force steadiness style coordinative testing.

You start with the principles in mind and ensure the patient is again challenging their base of support with their belly button over their shoe laces to ensure the upper limb has no choice but to tolerate load.

The patient's hand is nice and low on the wall (approx 30 degrees of shoulder flexion), fingers pointing down, and weight through the midhand and fingertips (no heel). This intent through the midhand ensures that the forearm flexors are allowed to "coordinate" with the muscles around the shoulder, as has to happen in real life. This ensures the elbow joint maintains a co-contraction and allows the biceps to transfer the forces through the hand, elbow and shoulder successfully.

You can ask your patient to hold the position for a number of breaths, or build tension on an inhale and relax on an exhale, or any variations of sets and reps as you wish. Remember, this is about coordination rather than strength, so little and often is key.

If the patient experiences shoulder pain at this level of the graded exposure ladder, then there is still a perceived threat present and so I would regress to the bed progressions and/or hands-on treatment towards the tissues identified as contributing to the pain experience.

To progress this movement once the patient can perform the exercise pain free, you can add perturbations at the wrist. These rapid perturbations will require the elbow, wrist, and shoulder to react quickly, and will require more bottom-up strategies as the movement will be too quick for top-down control.

To perform the perturbations, get the same start position, then ask the patient to tap their heel nice and fast on and off of the wall for 20 reps. The more "rhythmical" the taps become, the more the movement will happen outside of conscious control and at the spinal cord level.

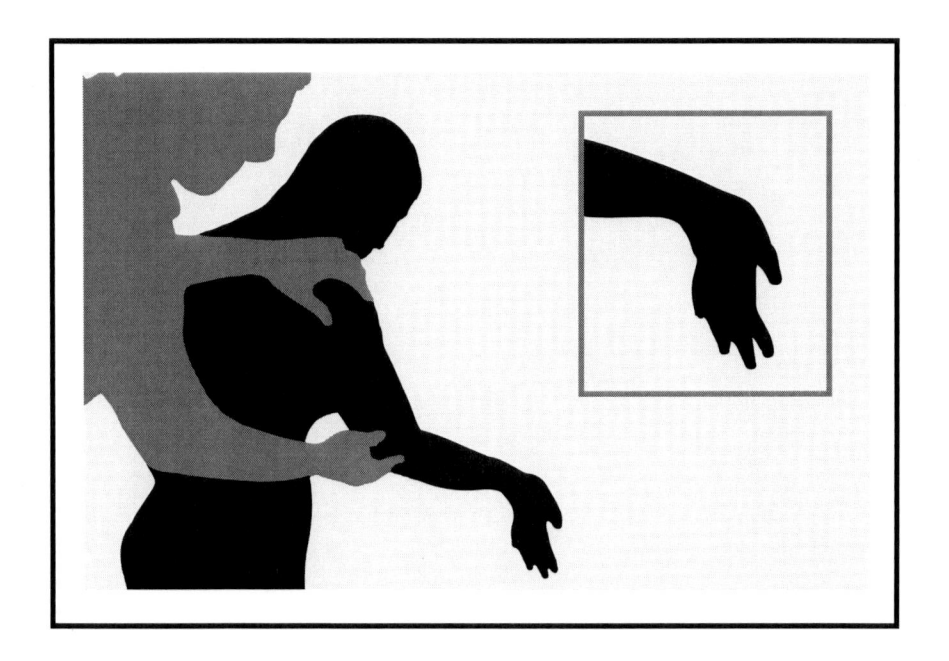

After 20 reps, it is not unusual for even a pro athlete to really feel the forearm, biceps and shoulder all working well together. As always, recheck your KPIs pre and post intervention to ensure the exercise is not causing a negative reaction for the patient's nervous system.

Work smarter not harder

The beauty of these types of exercise is that they require very few cues or work for you, the therapist. It is simply a case of putting the patient in the right position at the right time and letting their nervous system be exposed, adapt, update and overcome.

Once the patient has moved from a predominantly top-down, slow, cautious approach to a more bottom-up, faster, more fluent approach with these types of exercises, it is time to differentiate yourself from every other therapist and bridge the gap between low and high-level rehab.

Chapter 13:
Bridging the Gap from Low to High-Level Rehab

He was fuming at me! "Why did you tell him I was ready?" Sh$t, I could feel my face burning up! Ten minutes earlier I had told the Munster head coach the player would be ready for the weekend.

On paper, the injury had healed... all his tests on the bed were fine. He had ticked all my boxes yet was still complaining of feeling "not quite right". That was the first time I realised there was a big difference between being pain-free in the physio room and being confident to do daily tasks, or perform in real-life situations. There and then I learned a harsh lesson I'll never forget...

Pain-free does not equal confidence!

Truth be told I thought he was being soft! I was under massive pressure by the coach to get him back in the predicted time frame. Once again I had put myself under pressure trying to get the athlete back in the quickest possible time, and this time it had come back to bite me in the ass.

I would have to swallow my medicine. I walked across the University of Limerick basketball courts to the head coach's office and let him know the news. He screamed and shouted at me for a few minutes, and I swore to myself there and then I'd never put myself in this position again. This was on me!

I needed to be better, but first I needed to figure out what I needed to do to get this guy "feeling right". So I did what I always did when I had a problem... ring my mentor and ask for help! He suggested I look at the new research coming out on predictive processing and I went to work. I read everything I could find and flew over to London to attend a Mick Thacker course which I enjoyed!

Things started to finally make sense, on paper at least. Yet I was still struggling to see how to apply this information in the real world. Time solved the athlete's problem and another week later he felt "right" and all was fine again, but I couldn't help feeling I was still missing something.

Why were all the tests on the bed and all the timescales telling me the athlete was ready yet the person in front of me just didn't feel confident enough to perform? How could I prevent this in the future and still get him back to feeling "right" in my predicted timeframe? I would have to wait a couple of years for it all to fall into place when I finally came across the Louis Gifford phrase "thoughtless, fearless, movement" while reading *Aches and Pains*. There and then everything clicked into place!

I was focusing too much on getting my athletes to be pain-free and not enough on preparing them to move with "thoughtless, fearless movement". That simple shift in mindset made all the difference. It also fitted perfectly with the Frans Bosch stuff I was reading at the time and I finally had a simple way to ensure that I could bridge the gap from low to high-level rehab while keeping "thoughtless, fearless, movement" front and centre of everything I did!

I finally knew how to fill in the missing steps in my graded exposure rehab plan. I had clarity on how to progress patients step by step for the first time, and the patients were responding even better than I had hoped. I was still able to cut times off predicted return to play times and they were going back on the pitch even better!

As for my private practice patients, this was the biggest surprise of all. That subtle shift away from getting them pain-free to building confidence took a couple of extra sessions yet they didn't bat an eyelid. The results were better... the patients were more thankful... and the reviews and referrals followed thereafter.

How do you practically bridge the gap to "thoughtless, fearless movement"?

On a very simplistic level, bridging the gap is essentially getting the patient to work all of the targeted muscles outside of their conscious control with "thoughtless, fearless movement". While the intention in the top-down exercises in the previous chapter had very much been focused on the hands or the foot, the intention of the exercises at this level is on an external focus, such as an object. This gives the muscles an opportunity to now communicate to the spinal cord without top-down influence and react to the environment accordingly. This is where true confidence is built through the exposure, adaptation, updating and overcoming of load tolerance for the patient's nervous system.

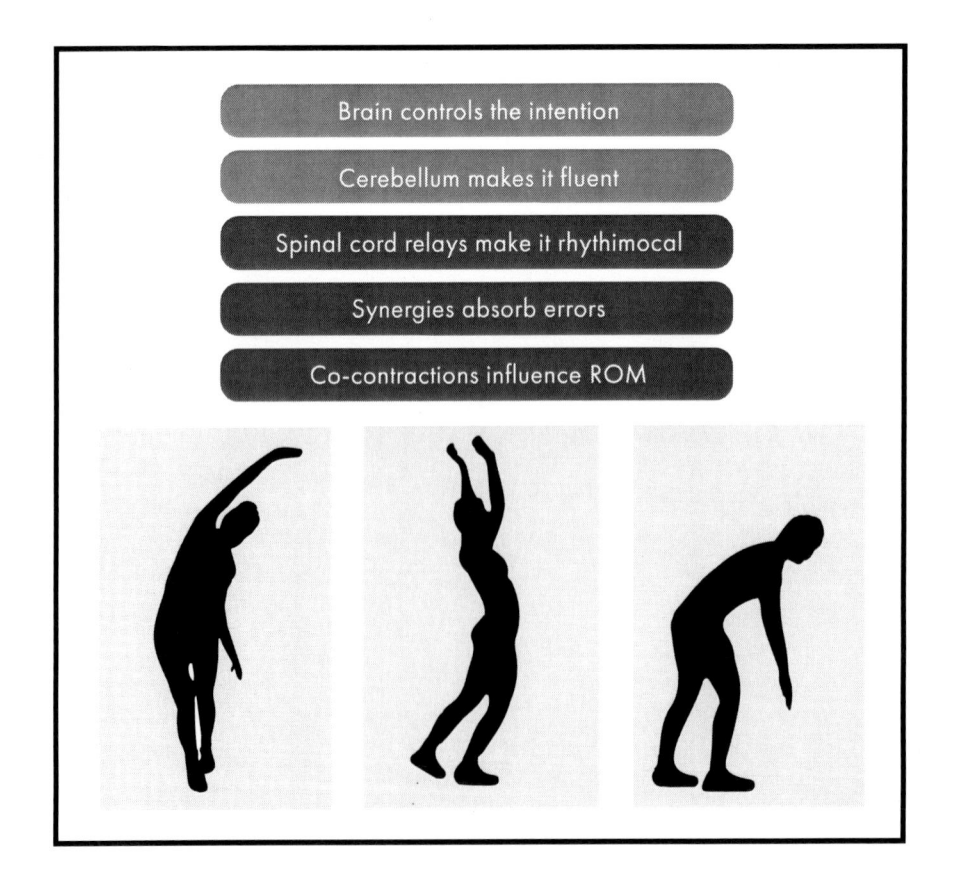

- Brain controls the intention
- Cerebellum makes it fluent
- Spinal cord relays make it rhythimocal
- Synergies absorb errors
- Co-contractions influence ROM

The key rehabilitation principles of the 'Go-To' Physio remain the same:

- We challenge the base of support to demand the subconscious mind's attention.
- We put the body in a position where it has no choice but to tolerate load.
- We make the exercise adhere to the six steps of deliberate practice.

For example, when the patient performs a small step or a lunge, you may focus their intention on reaching their fingertips in a certain direction in order to continue to give certain tissues no choice but to tolerate load.

To give the patient no option but to tolerate load through the specific tissues, you need to not only challenge their base of support, but also consider manipulating length-tension relationships to make it harder for some muscles to kick in and help out. This ensures you put a load in a specific direction and give the patient's nervous system an opportunity to expose, adapt, update and overcome.

A cue you will use often is to ensure the patient has a "small step, big reach". In order to increase the base of support and decrease load on certain muscles, the nervous system can often use a subconscious strategy of increasing the distance between both legs and not wanting to reach very far. Therefore a cue of "small step, big reach" solves this problem.

It is also worth noting that both of these actions need to happen simultaneously to further challenge the nervous system to self-organise. Another "cheat" a patient will use is to step, land and THEN reach. This is a preplanned movement and there is not enough "chaos" to expose the nervous system to adapt, update and overcome. You want the reach to be happening at the same time, if not before, the foot hits the floor in order to ensure you create a genuine perturbation that the peripheral tissues and spinal cord have to deal with.

Examples of manipulating length-tension relationships to increase or decrease load tolerance

The following images provide an example of how the position of the rib cage can alter the length-tension relationship of the hamstrings with a reach forward up and overhead, which will force the soleus and quads to do more work due to the poor glute length-tension relationship. By contrast, a reach forward and down will target the gluteal muscles to produce more force as the hip travels backwards to challenge the base of support with less work being done at the knee joint and ankle as a result.

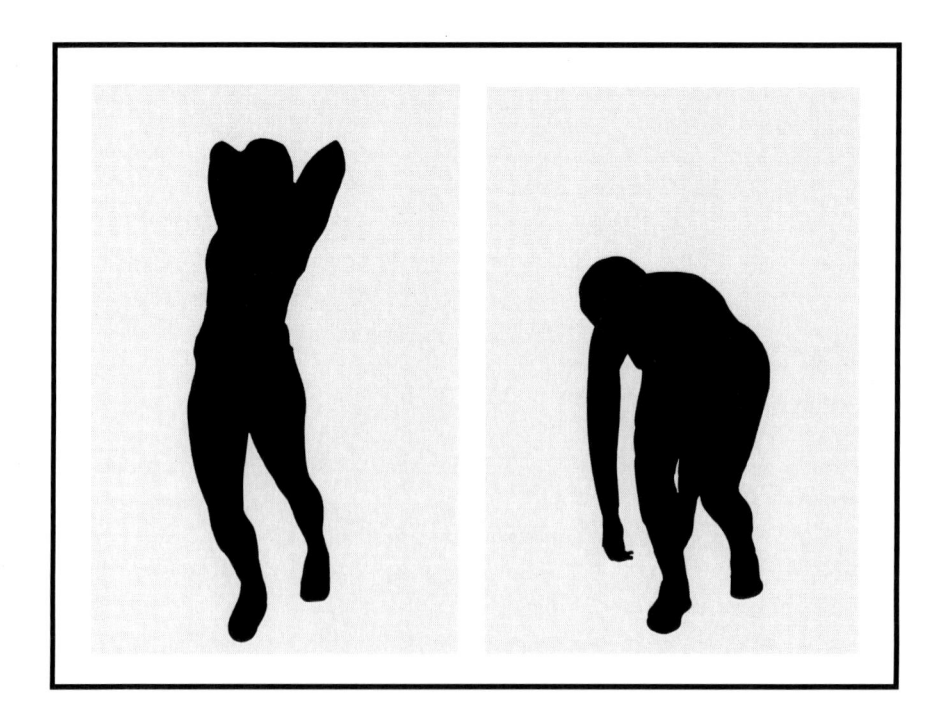

A simple regression or progression for any joint

If you consider the examples I have just shared, a reach overhead will put more load on the ankle. Therefore, if you have an ankle pain patient, the reach overhead would sit as a progression, a reach forward would sit as a regression, and a small step with no reach would sit somewhere in the middle.

If you consider a gluteal tendinopathy or hip injury, the exact same exercises would serve different progressions and regressions. The reach forward and down would put more load on the hip joint; therefore this would be the progression, while the reach overhead would serve as the regression and the step without any reach would also sit somewhere in the middle.

I hope you are beginning to see how powerful this is, as you can now instantly progress or regress your patient's exposure to load tolerance for any muscle or joint in the body.

A final exam to help understand this would be if I wanted to put more load through the lateral hip and less load through the adductor muscles on the right leg. A small step forward with the right leg with a right hand reach to the contralateral side in the frontal plane will challenge the peroneals, lateral hip, QL, and oblique muscles to tolerate load on the ipsilateral side.

As the patient reaches to the opposite side wall, the hip will challenge the base of support and the glutes have no choice but to tolerate the load if the step is small and the reach is big enough.

The intention of the patient throughout these movements is to focus on reaching for an external object, such as a wall, to ensure they maintain a bottom-up strategy throughout the movement.

Restoring "thoughtless, fearless movement" with acceleration-type movements

While these are great examples of how to show the nervous system it is safe to tolerate load in deceleration type movements, the question now is how do you regain confidence to accelerate or really "trust" pushing off a limb again?

This is where the "slouch to box" progressions become invaluable. The "slouch to box" can be performed in any plane to target any tissue, but the following example will cover the sagittal plane.

This exercise once again adheres to our principles of putting the body in a position where it has no choice but to tolerate load and gives the person's nervous system an opportunity to be exposed, adapt, update and overcome the load tolerance while building confidence consciously for the patient.

- Start at the bottom of the slouched split squat position and hold at the bottom position for a couple of seconds to take out the eccentric component.

- Ensure the patient's neck is completely relaxed and the low back muscles are also relaxed.

- Ask the patient to "aggressively" push off the midfoot while keeping the neck and back relaxed for as long as possible throughout the movement until the opposite foot lands on a box.

- You will need to keep an eye on the knee joint of the leg initiating the intent and ensure the knee maintains a co-contraction (no snap back) throughout, with the knee extension happening after the hip extension.

The beauty of this exercise is that by relaxing the neck and low back, the patient and their nervous system have no choice but to load the limb. It is not uncommon for the first few reps to feel "slow" and "clunky", before soon progressing to "powerful" and "smooth" as the patient's nervous system updates its belief system and the patient's confidence soars.

This phase ensures you successfully bridge the gap from low-level to high loads through the limb and successfully bridge the gap before performing acceleration-type drills for ankle, knee or muscle strain-type conditions.

As you progress through the rehab process, you can then start to integrate the low back and neck muscles back into the equation once you are confident the nervous system is happy to tolerate load through the limb.

Frans Bosch uses exercises like this where the patient performs a single leg 'Romanian Deadlift' before finishing the movement with the free leg on a box. This would be one such exercise you could then use to progress to which would allow the low back muscles to contribute more to the movement, now you are happy that the lower limb is doing enough work.

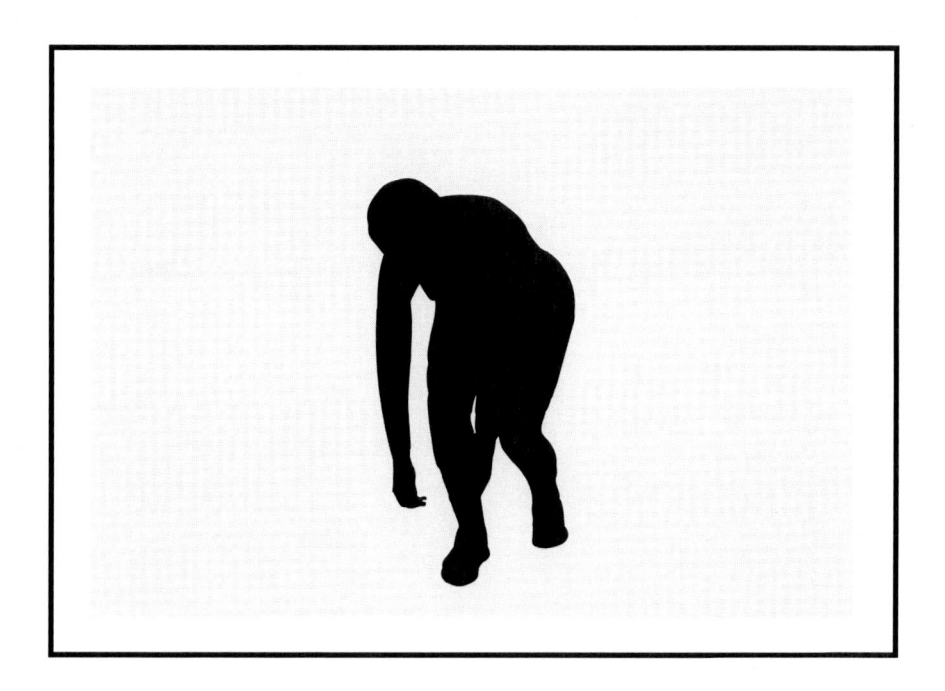

If a motor adaptation is present, you will typically see a patient snap the knee back and overextend their lumbar spine to achieve the outcome. If you see this happening, you know there is more work to be done on a subconscious level and the "slouch to box" or even regressions prior to this may be needed.

A word of warning when working at this level of the graded exposure ladder

At this stage of the graded exposure ladder, you need to consider the patient's injury history and have previous injuries top of mind. A lot of the assessments up to this point have been pretty low level, so you may not see old injuries and motor adaptations show up as the level of load has not been challenging enough.

With these higher-level movements and increased speed of movements, you may now start to see movement strategies/adaptations kick in, in the form of subtle shifts of the body, or turning in or out of the foot for example, to avoid loading certain tissues. The nervous system is a master of "cheating" and finding ways to avoid loading certain tissues, so keep your eyes peeled!

As you move through this process in the treatment plan and the patient's confidence is noticeably increasing, they will no doubt ask you the dreaded question: "Am I ready to run again now?" This is a question that many therapists fear and essentially "guess" at, taking silly risks in the process. In the next chapter we will cover how to take the emotion out of the decision-making process and have unshakeable confidence when allowing your patients to return to running or other higher-level activities without flaring up or taking silly risks.

Chapter 14:
How to Know Exactly When the Patient is Ready to Return to Running or Other High-Load Activities

I could feel my heart thumping inside my chest as I took the stairs up to the coach's office at Kirkstall Training Ground in Leeds. I was about to tell the Leeds Rhinos head coach that our star player, who was supposed to be back playing next week, would be out for another four to six weeks.

The player had just "broken down" again and felt his hamstring "go". Clinically, it looked like he had re-torn the injured area or extended the tear. An MRI would reveal later that he had extended the original tear by a few centimetres.

The coach went "bananas". The question I was dreading finally got asked! "Why did this happen?"

S*%t! Do I cave in and tell him that, in all honesty, I had no f*%king idea if the guy was ready to run or not and felt I had to get him running due to the pressure the head coach was putting on me? Do I tell him I let the athlete run because he was our star player and the one controlling the rehab pace rather than me having authority and control? Do I tell him I took a silly risk and it backfired? Do I tell him I had no genuine way of making these decisions and was making them based on emotion rather than logic?

Nah, f*%k that! "I think it might be coming from his back, we'll need to MRI his lower back to see if there is something there…" That should buy me some time and protect my ego!

The truth is I was guessing. I was taking silly risks because I had no system to make decisions based on logic rather than emotions. Emotions run high in pro sport on a daily basis and also in private practice when patients are handing over their hard-earned money at the end of sessions.

When emotions go up, intellect goes down!

In this chapter we will ensure that we take the emotions out of the decision-making process and ensure the patient is ready to return to higher-level activities without taking silly risks.

The power of our final tripwire

If you recall in Chapter 7, we placed two tripwires into our treatment plan at the points where most issues happen: progressing from the bed to standing and also from standing to higher-level activities such as running.

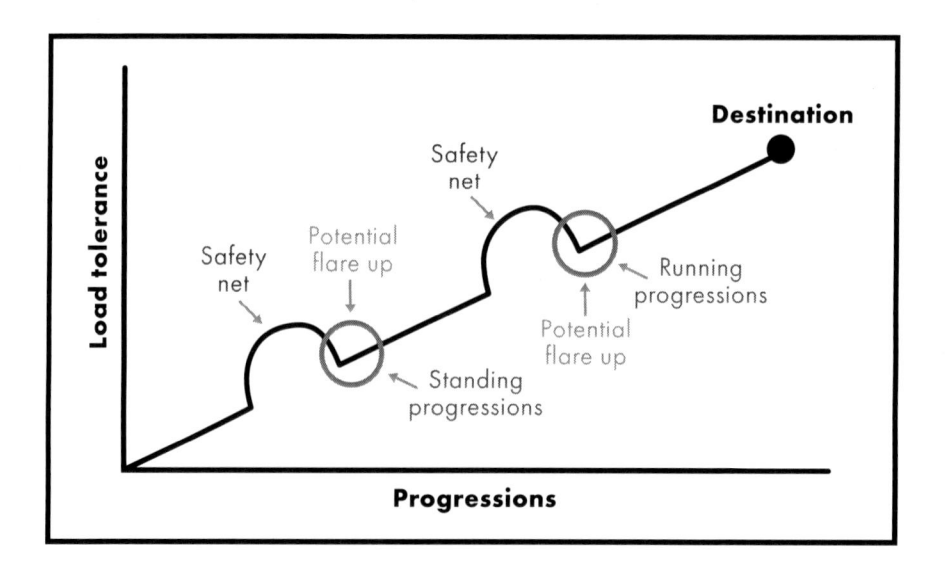

In this chapter, we are going to use hopping progressions as a tripwire to ensure the patient is truly ready to go back to higher-level activities such as running. In the 'Go To' Physio Mentorship we also use "hopping" progressions with the upper limb, so the same principles apply for the upper limbs as those I'll outline here.

I love hopping progressions as these will, again, supersede the amount of force the tissues have to tolerate in the early running sessions but in a more controlled manner and with less volume. As we covered in Chapter 7, there are greater ground reaction forces tolerated in hopping than jogging. Therefore, in theory, if the patient can manage hopping progressions and not regress in their KPIs, then logically you can justify allowing the patient to resume the running graded exposure ladder. This is a simple yet critical step to eliminate the guesswork.

Many of my colleagues and very good professional sports physio friends return athletes to low-level running as soon as possible. With motor adaptations in mind, I delay for as long as possible until the patient has "earned the right" to progress to this stage.

While many of my colleagues may have the athlete running early, I find I spend more time in the hopping phase than them, and this means by the time I get my patient back to higher-level activities, it is usually plain sailing. By this stage, my patient has tolerated the same loads and speeds of movement as running without regressing in their KPIs and, most importantly, shifted from top-down strategies to bottom-up when I have exposed the desired tissues to load and they can tolerate this load. This fills me with confidence when I send my patient back running, because I know they have earned the right to run again.

I also find I can start my patients' running progressions at far greater speeds and progress to high-speed running more quickly than my colleagues (usually) by focusing more on quality than quantity. There is no right or wrong way of doing things, but I usually require the patient to have "earned the right" to progress to this level with "thoughtless, fearless movement" prior to exposing them to the final hurdle.

Hopping progressions

The progressions remain the same with regards to putting loads through certain tissues in either the sagittal, frontal and/or transverse plane. The order I usually prefer to progress with this as follows:

1. Leaps from one leg to the other with a progression of reaching to challenge the base of support and bias certain tissues.

2. Hop and stick on the same leg with a progression of reaching to challenge the base of support and bias certain tissues.

3. Hopping consecutively on the same leg two to three times with a stick and then progressing by using reaches to challenge the base of support and bias certain tissues.

4. Continuous hops over a set distance.

Leaping

The first level of hopping progression would be leaping from one leg and landing on the other. You want your patient to land with their centre of gravity between their base of support. This means they now have movement options when they land and can continue to move forwards, back, sideways, or twist or turn. The good news is you've given the brain an awareness of this position through the graded exposure program by having the patient landing on the midfoot and building tension through the midfoot.

If the patient lands too far back on the heel or too far forward on the toes, they are not in an energy-efficient position for the next step. Landing on the midfoot means everything is doing its job and the nervous system is managing the perturbation efficiently without relying on certain tissues doing too much work.

As in the previous chapter, you can further progress the patient by asking them to reach in a certain direction to place more or less load on tissues and joints just as the patient lands. To self-organise and stabilise their centre of gravity between the base of support, the pelvis and ribcage will need to react and travel while the muscles have to react subconsciously.

Hop and stick

Instead of pushing off one leg and landing on another leg as per the leaping progressions, these hopping progressions require the patient to produce and absorb force on the same limb. As the patient is now hopping off of the same leg they need to land on, there's less time for the body to react. Therefore the patient needs better bottom-up strategies to be able to tolerate this speed of movement.

The landing position is exactly the same as in the previous progression, with the centre of gravity in the middle of the base of support, even if the patient is reaching in a certain direction to bias certain tissues.

Hop, hop, stick

Once the patient has nailed the hop and stick, you can quickly move on to the hop, hop, stick, which is three consecutive hops where they need to maintain stiffness and keep a good co-contraction at the knee during the first two hops with a good landing on the final hop. The concepts are the same, the movement now is just a lot faster so the patient needs even better bottom-up strategies with even less time to consciously plan the landing. You can use your reaches to direct load as needed.

Continuous hops over a set distance

The final hopping progression is an "overload" exercise where you get the patient to perform a series of continuous hops over a set distance, usually 20 to 30 metres. The focus in this progression is again on muscle stiffness, coordination, co-contractions around the knee joint and the ability to produce force continuously over a set period of time and distance.

You can increase the speed of movement at this level to essentially 100 per cent maximal effort and the intent is to replicate as close to the rate of force development as possible for the muscles on one leg. The landing is of less importance in this progression and it is more focused on maximal intent to ensure the patient truly has "thoughtless, fearless movement" before allowing them to return to running.

For higher-level athletes, it is through this level of load tolerance that you will catch the final motor adaptations at play. The patient will usually be doing something "strange" with their hands or torso to attempt to make up for the lack of intent through the limb. It is hard to explain in a book, but it is important to be aware of these types of strategies and ask "why?" specific to the patient's injury history.

If the KPIs have not regressed and the patient is moving with "thoughtless, fearless movement" then you can be very confident the patient is ready to run.

Confidence sets your patient free

If you go through the higher-level hopping progressions and there are no adverse reactions from the nervous system (such as reduced motor outputs upon retesting, reduced range of motion, swelling, or whatever markers you are using), then you can be very confident the patient is ready to start their running progressions as they have proven to you their nervous system can tolerate such loads.

When the patient is back running in the next step, the whole limb will be contributing without having to bias a particular direction like we have been doing, so in actual fact there will be even less load on the tissues that had the original "threat response". This is what gives me complete confidence, because I know the patient can tolerate even higher forces than the ground reaction forces they will need to endure when running.

The hopping progressions can all be progressed in the same session if the patient is ready to do so – it is completely down to the person in front of you. I would then leave them with the highest loading progressions with the highest rate of force development for a week, or a day or so if in a pro sport setting, and reassess for any negative reactions. If all is good, then you progress the patient to the next level.

It is worth mentioning again that at this point in the treatment plan, I quickly screen all planes and directions of loading for any energy inefficiencies that did not show up until this level and speed of loading. It is not uncommon to see a big discrepancy in force absorption or force production at these high levels that were not picked up on with the previous levels of load tolerance, with the patient's injury history again top of mind.

If there are energy inefficiencies present, especially in the highest hopping progressions for an elite athlete, then this may not set you back in terms of prognosis for return to play but rather offer insight into what the athlete needs to be focusing on when they return to team training. Also, this work may actually be integrated into their strength and conditioning programme to ensure they build resilience, which we will talk about in later chapters.

The final point to mention in this chapter is that you may not have to take all your patients through the high-level hopping progressions that are mentioned in this chapter. If you have a patient who wants to just get back to lifting their kids or grandkids, then this step's level of loading may in fact be external weight such as kettlebells or barbells etc., where you have some control of the quantity of loading.

However, I would certainly take the majority of my lower limb patients through the leaping progressions as a minimum, as the majority of people need to be able to run for a bus some day or run after their kids, so I like them to be able to tolerate this level of loading before moving onto the more resilience-based focus of the graded exposure programme. With that said, let's now move on to the highest-level loading such as our running progressions in the next chapter.

Chapter 15:
Return to Running Acceleration and Deceleration Progression

Wednesday 29 November, 2017, Brisbane, Australia

I'm about to leave the hotel and head to Brisbane Broncos' training ground to perform a running session with our captain, three days before the World Cup final. Unfortunately, I already know what the outcome of this running session is going to be, but I need the player to now also know and take the emotion out of the decision making.

He pulled up late in the semi-final with a muscle strain and it was always going to be a quick turn around. I kept the faith and was positive throughout the week, working day and night with him, however, I just couldn't progress him fast enough.

The beauty of the step-by-step system is you can see how much work there is left to do before you can safely send someone back to training or out into the real world. Unfortunately, on this occasion there was too much work to do.

Still, off we went in a private mini van and I could feel the tension in the air. We did our warm up and I spent a good 20 minutes taking the athlete through a graded exposure program that would have been very similar to all the exercises covered in previous chapters from the floor, to the slouches, to the bottom-up lunges to the hopping progressions. We then started the running progressions...

By the third set, the athlete made the call. He knew he couldn't push any further and admitted he was "no good". Decision made.

The beauty of the running progressions that I am about to share with you is that you can continue to push very safely along the graded exposure ladder without having massive setbacks like I had at my time with Leeds Rhinos. These running progressions will allow you to continue to "show" the patient's nervous system it is safe to tolerate load in a very controlled and logical manner.

By now you have taken the emotion out of the decision making and the patient has proven to you and themselves that they can tolerate similar loads and speeds of movements. They have had no negative reactions to the KPIs that you were using and they are moving with "thoughtless, fearless movement", with every muscle doing its own job, no more, no less.

Tempo runs versus continuous running

I first came across tempo runs through Charlie Francis, the controversial track and field coach, when I was working with Leeds Rhinos. What attracted me to the tempo runs was the ability to run an athlete on back-to-back days if we kept the intensity under control.

It also fits my bias of quality over quantity and I've kept them in my return-to-play progressions ever since. Most injuries happen at top-end speeds, pushing off, decelerating or changing directions. The muscles and joints are therefore more likely to be stressed in these movements in real life than slow continuous running where essentially you are using different muscles and coordination patterns for the most part.

I usually start my patient at the end line of a football or rugby field and start with straight line runs of 50–60 metres. I instruct my patients to walk back and take plenty of recovery. The first few running sessions are "diagnostic" in nature and ensure the nervous system can tolerate the load on the tissues; they are not aimed at increasing cardiovascular fitness. You want quality over quantity in the first few sessions in particular.

The outline of the running sessions would look like this:

1. Graded exposure warm-up focusing on exposing the tissues to the loads that will be tolerated in the highest-level activities in a step-by-step manner (15–20 minutes).

2. First tempo running set of 4 x 60-metre runs with a walk back between each run, starting at around the 40 per cent perceived exertion level. If you have GPS units to gauge – great! If you don't, don't worry, just use common sense.

3. We then do some deceleration drills in the sagittal plane, again around the 40–50 per cent intensity. It is essentially a "walk through" of the movements that the patient will be doing in later sessions at higher speeds of movement.

4. The next tempo running set would be another 4 x 60-metre runs, increasing the intensity to 50–60 per cent with a walk back between runs. The patient should feel comfortable and have no symptoms whatsoever.

5. We then do our second set of deceleration drills, increasing the intensity and adding in the frontal plane as well as the sagittal plane.

6. The final tempo running set for the first session would be another 4 x 60-metre run, increasing the intensity to hit 70 per cent on the last two runs. The patient walks back between runs and must be symptom free throughout.

7. The final deceleration set will include transitioning from the sagittal to the frontal plane before pushing off and adding in a transverse plane.

The deceleration drills are not only focusing on deceleration, but also restoring intent to push off with "thoughtless, fearless movement" during the transitions. If the patient is all good, you leave it there for the first session.

As you only go to 70 per cent intensity on the first session, you can run the patient the following day again, if you so wish. The first session is a great opportunity to get quality running, stress the tissues at increased rates of force production and force absorption, and reassess the following morning for any negative reactions without overdoing it and experiencing big setbacks.

If there are no reactions the following day then the next session may look like the following:

1. Graded exposure warm-up.

2. Running tempo set one: 4 x 60 metres (walk back between runs) starting at 50–60 per cent intensity.

3. Deceleration set: 1 x 60 per cent intensity.

4. Running tempo set two: 4 x 60 metres (walk back between runs) starting at 60–70 per cent intensity.

5. Deceleration set: 2 x 70 per cent intensity.

6. Running tempo set three: 4 x 60 metres (walk back between runs) starting at 70–80 per cent intensity.

7. Deceleration set: 3 x 80 per cent intensity (can add up and down off the floor and other open chain reactive drills as required).

8. Running tempo set four: 4 x 60 metres (walk back between runs) starting at 80–90 intensity.

9. Deceleration set: 4 x 90 per cent intensity (can add up and down off the floor and other open chain reactive drills as required).

At no point should the patient experience any symptoms. After this running session you again reassess your KPIs for any reactions the following day. Usually on this day you would keep the patient off their feet and allow them to recover.

The next and final graded exposure running session would look like this:

1. Running tempo set one: 4 x 60 metres (walk back between runs) starting at 60–70 per cent intensity.

2. Deceleration set: 1 x 70 per cent intensity.

3. Running tempo set two: 4 x 60 metres (walk back between runs) starting at 70–80 per cent intensity.

4. Deceleration set: 2 x 80 per cent intensity.

5. Running tempo set three: 4 x 60 metres (walk back between runs) starting at 80–90 per cent intensity.

6. Deceleration set: 3 x 90 per cent intensity (can add up and down off the floor and other open chain reactive drills as required).

7. Running tempo set four: 4 x 60 metres (walk back between runs) starting at 90–100 per cent intensity.

8. Deceleration set: 4 x 100 per cent intensity (can add up and down off the floor and other open chain reactive drills as required).

9. Running tempo set five: 4 x 30 metres (walk back between runs) starting at 110 per cent intensity (often a race or full 100 per cent intensity).

10. Deceleration set: 5 x 110 per cent intensity (full intent, no hesitation).

At no point should the patient experience any symptoms. If the person is preparing for a contact sport, then the contact integration will also be done over the three sessions in a graded exposure with a predictable to unpredictable progressive manner. This means, from a logical point of view, you know the patient can tolerate the loads and rate of force production and absorption and can now focus on getting match or sport-specific fit.

After this running session you again reassess your KPIs for any reactions the following day. This example is the "ideal scenario" for a low-grade muscle strain. For a higher-strain injury, you may choose to spend two sessions nudging into 90 per cent intensity before then doing your final session at 100 per cent.

For an ACL-type injury where the patient has been off their feet for a long time, you may choose to do two to three running sessions peaking at 70 per cent intensity in the first week, followed by 90 per cent in the second week and then nudging into higher intensity again in the third week.

Once the patient has hit 90 per cent intensity and has had no reactions, you may choose to do some additional tempo runs at no higher than 70 per cent intensity, with little rest between runs to target the cardiovascular system.

A big mistake I've seen over the years when I consult with professional clubs is that once the athlete hits 70 per cent intensity, for example, the team then "condition" the athlete at their 70 per cent pace. However, you must remember the "perceived load" from the nervous system's point of view. If you haven't done a 60kg bench press for a long time, and go back benching again, 60kg is going to feel "very heavy" on the nervous system. You'd adjust your ribcage, and probably lock up your neck and back in an attempt to gain some stability to get the job done.

To then say, "OK, I can bench 60kg, let's now do this for lots and lots of reps" is risky. You'll find a way to get it done but at what cost?

Contrast this with benching 60kg on the first day, then 70kg the next day, and then 90kg on the third day. Thereafter, you decide to go back down to 60kg for reps. At this point, the 60kg will "feel" very light to the nervous system. The same thing happens with running progressions. You need the nervous system to tolerate the load and for it to "feel light" before you worry about conditioning, otherwise, from my experience, the patient's nervous system will cheat and you'll often end up with tight muscles, niggles or little joint effusions that slow down the overall progress. Always focus on quality over quantity. The principles are the principles. Use common sense and progress your patient through a graded exposure ladder as you have been doing to date.

A further note is that the directions of loading can be biased further, just as you have done the whole way through the graded exposure plan, by using the hands, for example, to further challenge the body's base of support if needed.

Performing your tempo runs with the hands overhead will stress the ankle joint and hamstring muscles more. Leaning the ribcage and hands to one side will shorten the hip muscles on that side and make the ankle joint and adductor muscles work harder. Once you understand the principles, you can progress or regress any tissue to tolerate load.

The following is an example of a template we give our private practice patients. As you can see, it is not as aggressive as the pro-sport protocol I've outlined already, but still follows the same principles of progression.

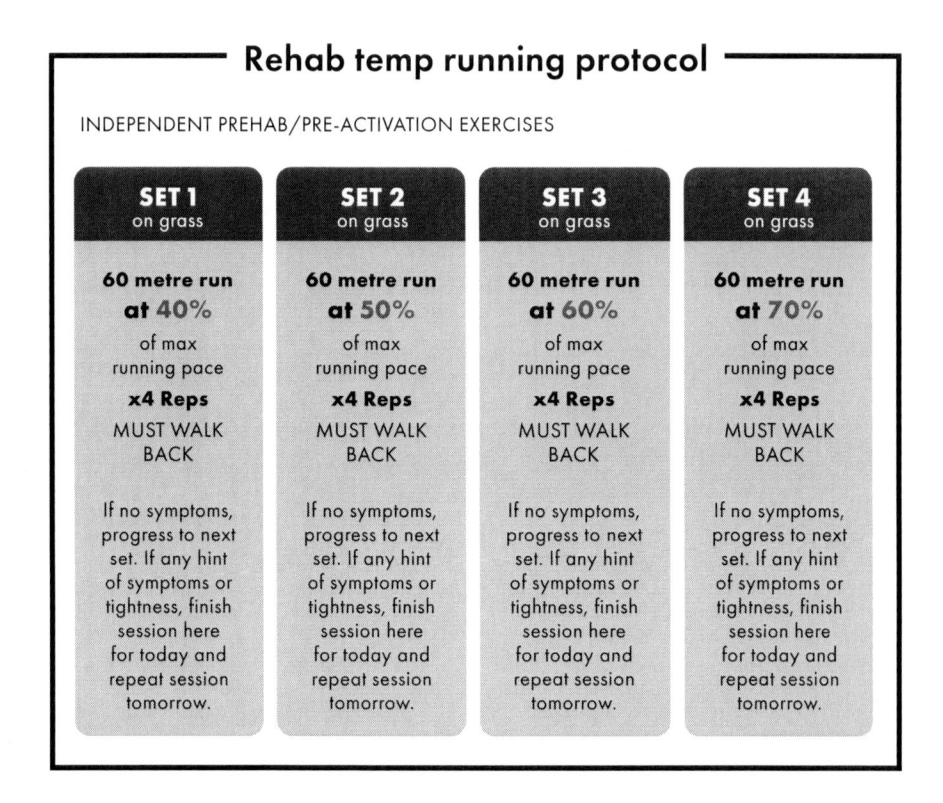

Rehab temp running protocol

INDEPENDENT PREHAB/PRE-ACTIVATION EXERCISES

SET 1 on grass	SET 2 on grass	SET 3 on grass	SET 4 on grass
60 metre run at 40% of max running pace	**60 metre run at 50%** of max running pace	**60 metre run at 60%** of max running pace	**60 metre run at 70%** of max running pace
x4 Reps MUST WALK BACK	**x4 Reps** MUST WALK BACK	**x4 Reps** MUST WALK BACK	**x4 Reps** MUST WALK BACK
If no symptoms, progress to next set. If any hint of symptoms or tightness, finish session here for today and repeat session tomorrow.	If no symptoms, progress to next set. If any hint of symptoms or tightness, finish session here for today and repeat session tomorrow.	If no symptoms, progress to next set. If any hint of symptoms or tightness, finish session here for today and repeat session tomorrow.	If no symptoms, progress to next set. If any hint of symptoms or tightness, finish session here for today and repeat session tomorrow.

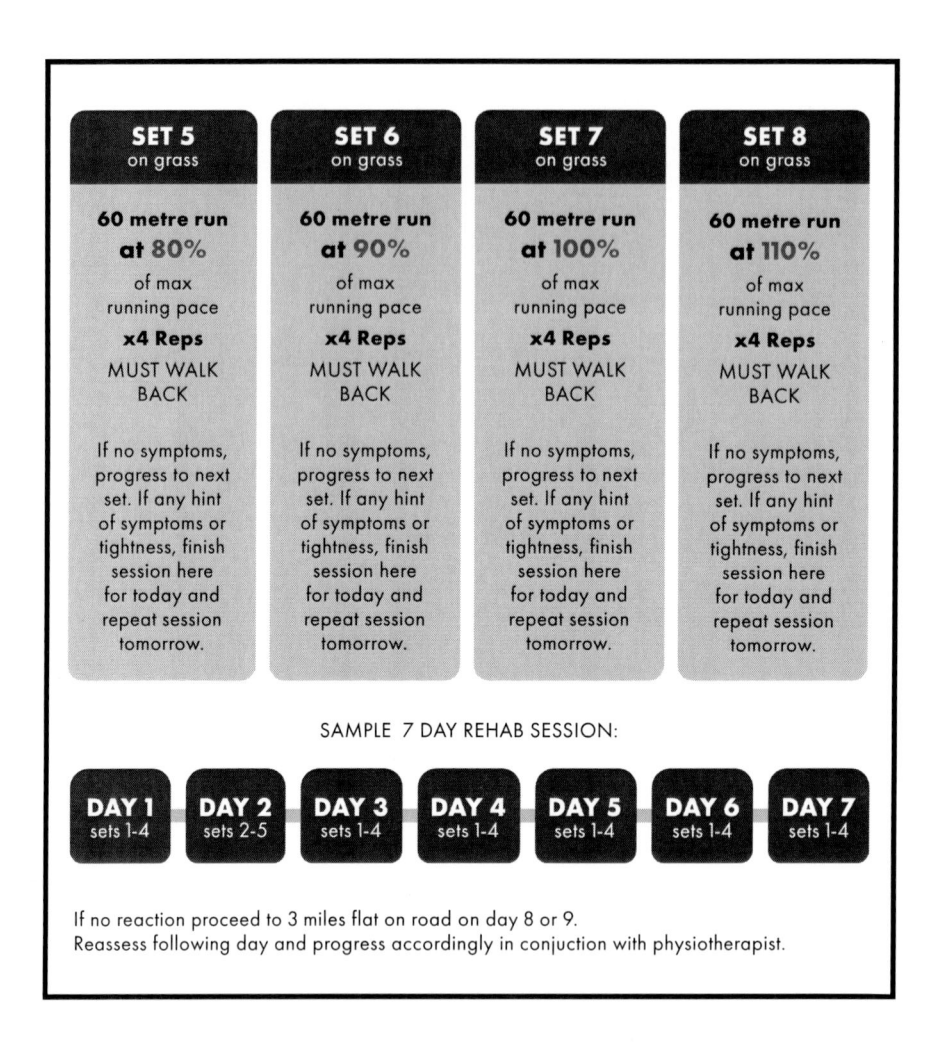

SET 5 on grass	**SET 6** on grass	**SET 7** on grass	**SET 8** on grass
60 metre run at 80% of max running pace **x4 Reps** MUST WALK BACK	**60 metre run at 90%** of max running pace **x4 Reps** MUST WALK BACK	**60 metre run at 100%** of max running pace **x4 Reps** MUST WALK BACK	**60 metre run at 110%** of max running pace **x4 Reps** MUST WALK BACK
If no symptoms, progress to next set. If any hint of symptoms or tightness, finish session here for today and repeat session tomorrow.	If no symptoms, progress to next set. If any hint of symptoms or tightness, finish session here for today and repeat session tomorrow.	If no symptoms, progress to next set. If any hint of symptoms or tightness, finish session here for today and repeat session tomorrow.	If no symptoms, progress to next set. If any hint of symptoms or tightness, finish session here for today and repeat session tomorrow.

SAMPLE 7 DAY REHAB SESSION:

| **DAY 1** sets 1-4 | **DAY 2** sets 2-5 | **DAY 3** sets 1-4 | **DAY 4** sets 1-4 | **DAY 5** sets 1-4 | **DAY 6** sets 1-4 | **DAY 7** sets 1-4 |

If no reaction proceed to 3 miles flat on road on day 8 or 9.
Reassess following day and progress accordingly in conjuction with physiotherapist.

If you are in private practice, then you may not be able to work on the tempo runs in the clinic for obvious reasons. However, an effective deceleration programme in three planes of motion can be executed in a ten-square-foot treatment room easily for the first couple of sessions and the patient can perform their tempo runs on a field independently provided you give them clear instructions to follow. You do not need to have a lot of space for effective deceleration work to really challenge the speed and load placed on the patient's nervous system.

Another nice benefit of this progressive step-by-step manner is that your patient's warm up for these running sessions is simply the exercises they have been performing over the past few sessions to get that graded exposure to load before the running takes place. The sets can essentially be reduced to one to two sets and the reps reduced to suit the athlete's needs as well.

You may also choose to integrate additional general mobility drills into the warm up if required. The patient is so familiar with the cueing of the exercises plus the ability to now decelerate efficiently, that the running sessions, from my experience, tend to go very smoothly, especially if we have not missed any "big elephants in the room" in the preceding sessions.

Other therapists are not necessarily wrong in their approach to running athletes as soon as possible, but I am personally in no rush to run the athlete as I prefer to build a solid foundation and decrease the risk of developing further motor adaptations while pain or nervous system adaptations are still present. Although this may look like it will take my athletes longer to get back, I actually find the opposite, as from day one post injury, I am working on his/her graded exposure to change of direction and force production for acceleration and top-end speed, specific to his/her needs.

As I am in no rush to run my athlete, I will spend a lot more time on earning the right to progress and the hopping progressions, so when the patient returns to running, they are more than capable of managing the ground reaction forces and perturbatory forces at said rate of force development.

It is imperative, in my opinion, that the patient is exposed to the loads and speeds of movement that they will be exposed to in training or games, before returning to these. I see so many athletes returning to training when they've hit 80 per cent max speed, for example, without actually hitting the top speeds and then they have protective responses when they do open up or move at a speed that they had not been exposed to previously in the rehab process. It is a risky way of working, and not one the 'Go-To' Physio would utilise to ensure consistently long-lasting results.

Once the patient or athlete returns to the training environment, it is also very important that they continue with the bespoke graded exposure warm up prior to taking part in the team warm up, especially for the first three to six sessions.

To keep it simple, you want to give them a graded exposure to the load and speeds they will need to tolerate in the training session. This will mean that, ideally, the first time they are exposed to these loads won't be in the training session. While it is impossible to ensure this every session, it can give you good direction for pre-training movement prep and injury prevention programmes.

The 'Go-To' Physio's patient's KPIs will also be monitored pre-training, if possible in the professional setting, depending on equipment requirements. For a groin pain patient, for example, the adductor squeeze and posterolateral hip force production may be monitored in the professional environment closely pre-training. For the weekend warrior, a simple "perception" of how their adductor squeeze feels while pushing their knees into their hand may suffice for getting a gauge of how much pre-training graded exposure may be needed. For something like an ankle injury you can teach the non-sporting patient to use a ruler to measure their knee to wall lunge test for gross ankle range of motion as a more straightforward method.

With regards to setting the ideal pre-training warm up, I believe this is down to an athlete's perception and personal feel, but certainly it makes sense to me to include a graded exposure to load and speed of movement to logically eliminate the chances of "perceived threats" kicking in. Once the patient is back successfully achieving the tasks that add value to their lives, then it is time to turn your attention to building some resilience in these tasks, especially under times of high stress.

Chapter 16:
Build Resilience Under External Loads and Increased Stress

Don't just focus on the results you can achieve for a patient in your nice, safe, comfy treatment room. Instead focus on the results you can get for your patients when they go back into the real world and into their most stressful situations. This is really what the top of the graded exposure ladder should be optimising for, or or, at the very least, an increased tolerance to the most stressful environments and/or situations identified for your patient during your subjective assessment questions.

Stress precedes pain and so you must go straight to the source and ensure your patients have a buffer or resilience to the everyday stresses they will experience. Stress can come in many forms and contain both physical and emotional stressors. An example of these two stressors combined is a case study patient that we have inside our 'Go-To' Physio mentorship program.

This patient, let's call her 'K', had failed with traditional approaches when I started working with her. There was a clear mechanism of injury that triggered her back pain many years before, as well as numerous motor adaptations, that I had to address and she was making good progress.

She was now able to sit for long periods without pain and walk for long periods without pain, amongst many other of her goals. However, about four sessions in, her progress stagnated and she had a setback after a hard day of work in the care home she was working in. Her work involved a lot of transferring patients where she had to tolerate a lot of the patient's weight (or external load) and it was a quite stressful environment in general as the care home was usually understaffed.

On this particular occasion, K went to work only to find out the other care worker had called in sick and she would have to do the full shift on her own that evening.

Truth be told, my treatment plan was not good enough at optimising for these stressful situations early enough in the program and had not considered the emotional stressors enough to prepare her for that situation. K had a small flare up which we were able to get under control, but more importantly, I was able to now optimise the treatment plan specific to her needs. This was a combination of controlling the emotional stressors through specific actions at specific times and also preparing her for the physical stressors to ensure she could tolerate the external load well throughout her body.

Emotional stressors

Ōita, Japan, 2019

England had just beaten Australia in the 2019 Rugby Union World Cup quarter final and were about to head back to Tokyo to play the All Blacks the following week in the semi-final. Everything was packed and all the staff and players were gathered in the dining room about to board the buses back to Tokyo. Eddie Jones addressed the group and said a phrase that really resonated with me: "How you think this week is how you will feel, is how you will behave."

At the start of the tournament we were all given a red notebook with our initials on it, and throughout the tournament I had been logging all my lessons learned and mistakes made as per usual. I immediately reached for my red book and made a note of that phrase.

Now, for the cognitive behavioural therapists, this won't be anything new, but it was a really powerful reminder for me.

Thoughts → Emotions → Behaviours.

Therefore, to improve your patients' behaviours, you need to influence their emotions. Going one step further, if you can break this cycle of thoughts to emotions to behaviours then you can help your patients be successful in the real world.

So how do you break the cycle? To quote Thich Nhat Hanh: "Breath is the bridge which connects life to consciousness, which unites your body to your thoughts. Whenever your mind becomes scattered, use your breath as the means to take hold of your mind again." This allows you to use the breath to break the cycle.

Karl Morris, the sports psychologist, taught me that your attention is either on something "useful" or "useless". If your attention or thoughts are on something "useless", then bring your attention back to the breath. The power of this is that when you focus on your breath you are in the present moment.

Ideally, you would anchor the breathing exercises whenever a patient has a "useless" thought, such as catastrophising about their pain experience or, as in K's case, when she starts to feel "emotional" about her work situation.

Identifying the triggers to the emotional response is key and it can be a person, place, thing or thought. Having awareness is the first step which allows you to get tactical and implement some strategies.

I am not a massive fan of trying to isolate the diaphragm with three sets of ten rounds of diaphragmatic breathing. The breath is governed by the autonomic nervous system and so I am sceptical that three sets of ten reps will be enough to lead to long-lasting changes.

Remember, intention first, then the muscles react. You can focus your patient's intention on making the breath "silent" and "slowing the air" as it comes through the nostrils when they are feeling stressed or have "useless" thoughts. I like to get patients to focus only on the air as it comes through their nose and find this external focus tends to take care of the diaphragm and pelvic floor nicely without accessory muscles taking over.

Another "tactic" I also like to use is humming! Getting patients to hum will usually treble, if not quadruple, their exhalation time, stretch the diaphragm and help the patient get into "rest and digest" quickly. It also makes them smile — which is not a bad thing! You can also hum silently to get the same benefits.

In K's case, to address the emotional component, I put a pre-work breathing routine into her day when she arrived at work and also a five-minute, post-work routine to allow her to completely switch off from work before she started the engine in her car. This allowed her to get back into "rest and digest" before she drove home. This small change to her routine allowed her to sleep better and we were able to break the cycle of work increasing her emotions, which increased the pain experience and which therefore made it more difficult for K to fall asleep; all of which then continued the cycle of increased pain.

The second component that I needed to address with K were the physical stressors of the external loads her nervous system needed to tolerate on a daily basis.

Physical stressors

When you think of physical stressors, you can consider internal loads, such as increased volume of load. For example, a marathon runner will need to increase their capacity to tolerate the load while maintaining the ability of all their muscles and joints to do their jobs, no more, no less. In this scenario, the same rules apply. It needs to be a gradual exposure to load, while you keep an eye on KPIs, and the patient needs to earn the right to progress.

You can also think of physical stressors with external loads, such as a weight lifted in the gym or a patient lifting their kids, taking the shopping bags out of the boot of the car or, as in K's case, helping patients transfer from bed to chairs etc. External load tolerance will usually fit into some form a squat, deadlift, lunge, push, pull, twist in specific planes of motions. Before I dive into the "tactics", let's continue to work smarter not harder by appreciating the principles.

External load principles

When your patient moves and has to manage an external load there are certain reactions that need to happen in the body to ensure that everything does its job, no more, no less. Before you focus on what should happen, let's look at the common motor adaptations that the nervous system may use that I see on a daily basis with both professional athletes and non-sporting patients.

A common reaction with athletes and non-sporting patients under higher loads is to maintain all the weight through a specific portion of the foot (usually either the heels or the opposite end of the foot, the toes). I personally believe the cue of "push through your heels" (or similar cues) is causing a lot of issues for people. The majority of personal trainers and strength and conditioning coaches these days are cueing patients to "push through the heel".

However, you only have to appreciate the gait cycle and the self-organising strategy that the body adopts to utilise elastic energy to appreciate the importance of each part of the body and, in particular, the importance of the full foot doing its job. When the weight is on the heel during the gait cycle this couples with the hip in flexion, but when the hip is extending, this usually couples with the weight going through the midfoot. At the end of the push-off, the weight is on the toes at the end of the hip extension.

Therefore, if the body self-organises this way, there must be some merit in these parts of the foot coupling with the hip movement for optimal management of ground reaction forces. Managing these forces throughout the body to utilise elastic energy to recoil back into the ground is a magnificent achievement that I think we need to also encourage in the gym.

Another method worth studying is the foot pressure during the Olympic lifting movements; the ability to organise the body and external loads to lift with such speed and power is glorious to observe. Again, you will notice the hip is in flexion when the weight is in the heels during these specific lifts and as the hip extends, the weight distribution transfers towards the mid – and front foot.

In fact, just prior to the most explosive part of the Olympic lifting movement, the second pull, the weight is on the midfoot, which makes sense when you think about the midfoot giving the athlete the ability to utilise all the muscles in the lower limb. If they use the heel instead they may lose the ability to plantarflex efficiently through the ankle joint, which will affect the lower leg muscles, distal hamstrings and possibly the glutes.

I believe that when athletes are lifting in the gym, the same weight distributions should follow gait or Olympic lifting to encourage movement variability, and help the self-organising ability of the nervous system deliver optimal movement efficiency, as can be seen during Olympic lifting.

However, from my own experience this coupling of efficient foot pressures and hip movements can often get mismanaged under higher loads and be cued ineffectively by the strength and conditioning or medical professional.

The two strategies that usually happen are:

1. Weight on the toes as the hip goes into flexion

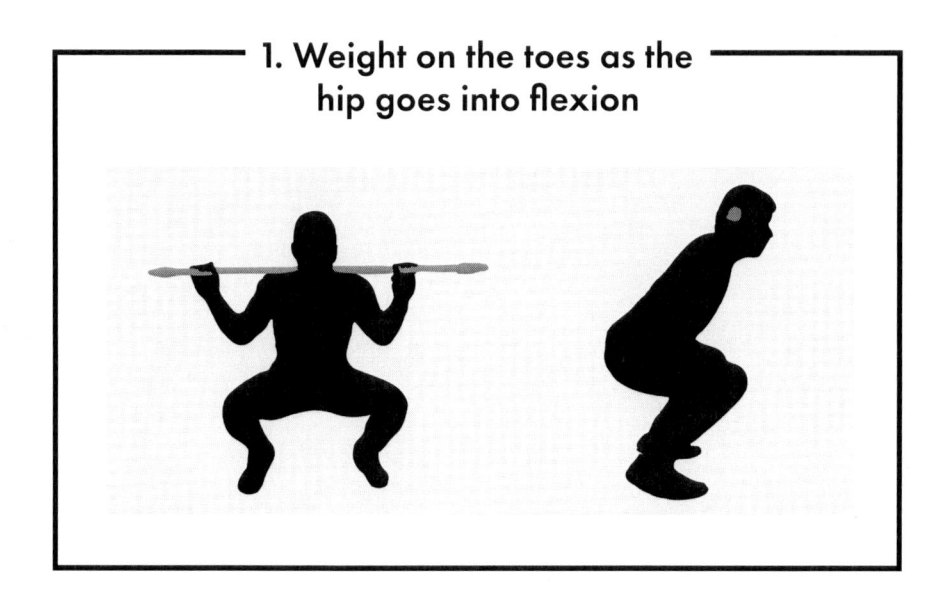

Notice the weight is excessively on the toes. The weight shift forward will cause the low back and knees to do work at the beginning of the ascent instead of the knees delaying knee extension and allowing the hips to do more work.

From my experience, this will usually result in excessive forward-travelling knees, limit true hip flexion (femur under pelvis rather than pelvis over femur) and increase the forward lean of the torso with the lumbar extensors having to react to maintain balance. This makes it difficult for the hamstrings to co-contract at the knee, with the quadriceps and soleus doing most of the work with the lumbar extensors. The lower back will also have to counteract the forward foot pressure to actually prevent the athlete from moving forwards.

If this type of patient presents with knee or back pain, is it the patella tendon's fault or the SI joint's fault that they become irritated? Will performing isometrics for the tendon or even eccentrics help if the patient returns to the gym and continues to lift like this?

2. Weight on the heels as the hips go into extension

Notice the athlete starts with the weight on the heels. This causes a reaction of excessive protraction of the ribcage forward to balance, which will increase lumbar extensor activity while also decreasing the ability to plantarflex the feet and utilise the distal hamstrings and proximal gastrocnemius, which are important to utilise through the ascent.

In an attempt to solve the knees going too far forwards, in the early 2000s the cue of keeping the weight through the heels became popular and this is the more common problem I see nowadays. The majority of athletes and patients are starting the lift with all the weight on their heels and this results in a lack of weight distribution through the full foot. This affects the ability of the distal hamstrings and proximal gastrocnemius to co-contract at the knee efficiently and to allow the hip joint to do genuine work due to a lack of plantarflexion forces and an inability to delay knee extension via a co-contraction at the knee joint. The quadriceps now tend to do excessive work and the knees "snap back", with the low back then having to hyper extend at the top of the lift and the athlete consciously squeezes the glutes.

Check this out for yourself, even in a seated position: push through the heels while placing one hand under the distal hamstring on one side and the other on the proximal fibres of the glute max with the other. You more than likely will feel little activity. Now push through the midfoot to forefoot as if squashing an orange through the floor while keeping the hands in the same positions. You should hopefully feel more of your distal hamstrings and gastrocnemius contributing to the movement and then a slightly delayed reaction through the glute max.

Would you rather a patient distribute the load evenly through the whole limb or use excessive muscles and joints to compensate for other tissues not doing their jobs? If the patient is coached to mainly push through the heels during the ascent, it is then common to see the lower back arching at the top of the lift and the athlete having to consciously squeeze the glutes. It is difficult to engage the proximal fibres of gluteus maximus consciously while the weight is on the heels. Give it a go. Now repeat while the weight is on the midfoot going towards the forefoot.

If the weight distribution travels forward towards the midfoot as the hip extends, you will naturally feel the proximal glutes engage during mid-stance and, more importantly, the distal hamstrings will continue to engage throughout the movement, similar to the sequencing we require when sprinting. If the weight stays on the heel, however, I usually see athletes snap the knee back with the quads and overarch the back in order to return to the start position.

The weight needs to start through the midfoot and then travel towards the heels as the hip goes into flexion so that the weight distribution goes towards the midfoot as the hip extends. This allows an opportunity for the athlete to manage perturbatory loads subconsciously and manage their base of support. It will also utilise the distal hamstrings and proximal gastrocnemius, as well as promote a more efficient co-contraction at the knee joint, delaying knee extension so the hip joint can do more work.

If you have athletes who present with proximal hamstring issues or patellofemoral pain, or the lower back continues to become irritated, will performing isometrics for the tendon and even eccentrics help if the athlete returns to the gym and continues to lift like this?

In both cases above, the 'Go-To' Physio appreciates that if the patient continues to lift like this under higher loads, certain tissues are becoming excessively loaded and ultimately over time may become sensitised, which may also result in subtle interactions and motor adaptation strategies.

You may then see further alterations in the athlete's movement strategies and the injury that eventually presents in the form of a tendon or muscle injury may be a further reaction. I appreciate there is a lot of theory here, but I'd just like to share my thought process.

Getting the patient to manage their base of support while handling external weight (both in the gym and the real world) is essential in order to reduce the likelihood of nociceptors becoming active, as this contributes to alterations in movement strategies that ultimately can lead to actual tissue injury or a pain experience, in my opinion.

While it is beyond the scope of this book to cover all the main movements patients will need to build resilience to, let's cover the deadlift as this was a big movement for K to be able to do well when managing transfers for her patients.

Deadlift

The start position of the deadlift needs to have intent through the midfoot to overcome all slack in the hamstrings prior to the ascent. As the bar comes up and the hips go into extension, there needs to be a genuine extension of the hips travelling horizontally over the midfoot towards the forefoot.

The deadlift start position is usually performed incorrectly among Rugby Union or Rugby League players. I rarely see players take up the slack in the hamstrings before initiating the lift. A lack of intent through the midfoot and too much weight on the heels is usually the result, in my experience.

Athletes or patients about to lift somebody or a "thing" usually tend to set themselves up with the weight too far back on their heels. This usually results in the athlete directing a lot of force through the proximal hamstrings and through the SI joint thoracic lumbar fascia, which I suspect may result in protective tension or tone through the lower back area due to not enough help from the gastrocnemius and distal hamstrings to allow forces to be directed through the knee joint and the hip from the ground.

An intent of "squashing an orange" through the midfoot while some weight is on the heels prior to lifting the bar will actually result in the hips going higher than the knees, slack being taken out of the hamstrings and a much more efficient strategy then being in place to distribute the load throughout the body. This will also help the midfoot contribute while the hip is extending, rather than extending the hips with the weight on the heels.

Give both versions a try and notice the differences in the reactions of the body and what muscles and joints have to do what. As the bar descends to the floor, the weight will naturally come towards the heels as the hip joints flex, adhering to our foot pressure principles and looking like a Romanian deadlift which we will cover next.

Romanian deadlift

The Romanian deadlift (RDL) start position (top of deadlift) should have the weight through the midfoot. As the bar descends, the weight should travel towards the heel while maintaining some pressure through the midfoot and forefoot for balance.

Most athletes or patients will again start with the weight on the heels, which makes it difficult to distribute more weight on the heels as the bar descends down the thigh. The ability to take up the slack in the hamstrings by having good intent with weight through the midfoot at the start of the top of the movement is also lost with this strategy.

Starting with the weight through the midfoot and then travelling back towards the heel while maintaining some pressure through the midfoot will create a movement that is genuinely challenging the athlete's base of support and will cause them to react subconsciously in order to maintain balance.

As the athlete descends with the barbell, the knees should straighten slightly to fully overcome hamstring slack while the humerus should externally rotate in order to take up the slack in the transverse plane of the latissimus dorsi by externally rotating the humerus.

Taking up all the slack allows the athlete or patient to transmit forces well through the hands, and the thoracolumbar fascia into the hamstrings and glutes.

As the athlete ascends and returns to the start position, I would ideally like to see the weight distribution travel forwards towards the midfoot and forefoot as the hips genuinely travel forward. A lack of intent through the midfoot and forefoot will usually result in excessive lumbar extension rather than true hip extension, and you lose the ability to stimulate the distal hamstrings and proximal glutes in the lift.

In addition, ensuring the weight travels forward will again force the athlete to manage their base of support as the weight shifts forwards with hip extension.

Other lower limb movement principles

Once you understand that the weight goes to the heel with hip flexion and the weight distribution goes to the midfoot and forefoot as the hip extends then the rest of the lifts are easy.

Movements such as squats and lunges follow the same principles in all three planes of movement. For example, a patient that needs to get out of a car on the left hand side is essentially performing a transverse plane squat, pushing through the midfoot as they ascend.

Once you start looking at movements as either a squat, deadlift or a lunge in three planes of motion, it becomes very easy to prepare patients to tolerate loads that will move them towards their dream outcome through the rehabilitation process.

Now that you have exposed your patient to both emotional and physical stressors, as well as helped the patient restore their movement variability and given them variance of movement, you've done everything in your power to genuinely build resilience.

We've covered a lot up to now and one of my biggest frustrations is spending hours and hours reading theory that I struggle to implement in the real world. With that said let's look at a case study of a real-life patient to demonstrate how to put this together from start to finish.

Chapter 17:
Putting It All Together with a Complex Patient Who Has Failed with Traditional Approaches

I recently read in a book about leadership from Larry Yatch[16] that the difference between entertainment and education is the ability to take action.

If you read this book and don't take action, you've been entertained for a few hours. My goal for this book is to share my mistakes as well as my successes, and educate you in a way that helps you help your patients who have failed with traditional approaches.

To best illustrate this, let's look at a simple case study I have used at one of my 'Go-To' Physio Mentorship Refresher courses so you can see how all of the different parts of the system fit together to help you become the 'Go-To' Physio who can help people who have failed traditional approaches.

---

[16] Yatch L., (2022), *How Leadership (Actually) Works: A Navy SEAL's Complete System for Coordinating Teams*, Lioncrest Publishing

Case study:
Lower back pain patient

Subjective Assessment:

68-year-old female presenting with persistent back pain for over eight years and progressively getting worse.

- No upper limb injuries previously.

- Old right-ankle injury (a bad sprain; she can't remember exactly when, but approx. ten years ago.)

- She has previously tried physiotherapy (massage, pain education, glute/core exercises) chiropractor (manipulation), massage therapist and pilates.

- No red flags.

Dream outcome/internal motivator:
Being able to do two hours of gardening per day.

Needs to be able to:
Lift/help husband off his chair daily.

Lift shopping bags up a flight of stairs.

Wants to be able to:
Sit pain free and watch TV.

Go up and down stairs pain free.

Sleep a full night's sleep.

Objective Assessment:

- No force transmission/load tolerance issues identified on assessment to the upper limb.

- Poor ribcage mobility into flexion with back pain present from the very start of the movement.

- Poor right side lower limb force steadiness when testing on the bed.

- Poor right leg intent with sit-to-stand and other position-specific assessments – uses lower back excessively to get up.

- Poor right side frontal plane force steadiness/load tolerance on testing (think glute medius muscle testing etc).

- Poor force steadiness/load tolerance through the abdominals on testing in supine.

Impression:

When you separate the symptoms (back pain) from the root problem, you clinically reason that the patient is not using her right leg enough throughout the day, thus increasing the load on the low back which may be contributing towards the sensitisation and hence the pain experience.

Breaking this down using the 80/20 rule, you would be looking to spend:

- 20 per cent of our time on the lower limb symptoms

- 80 per cent of our time – aiming to increase the load tolerance peripherally to the right leg.

You may choose simple diagrams like the following to help the patient understand the root problem and solution you believe will help them.

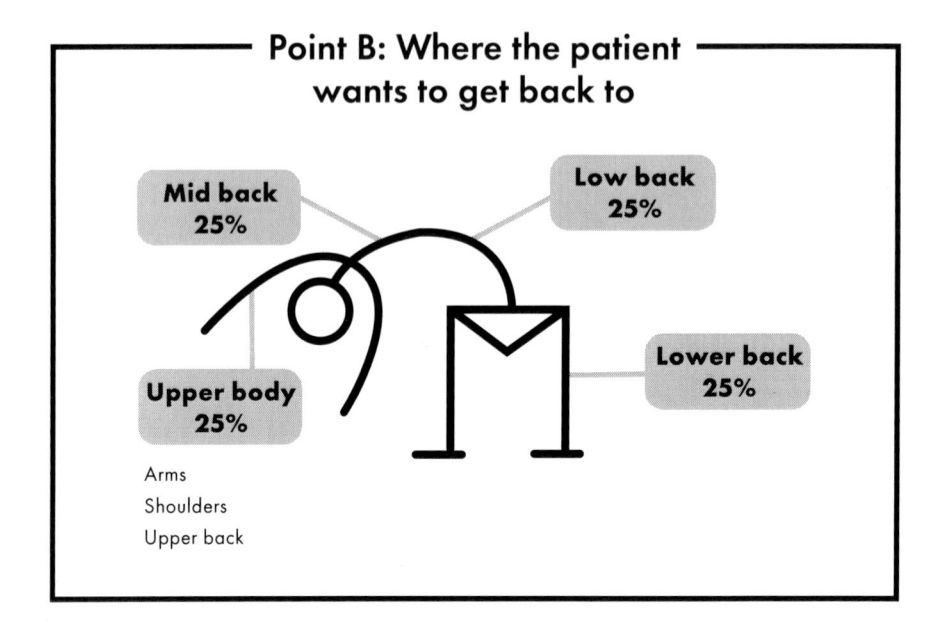

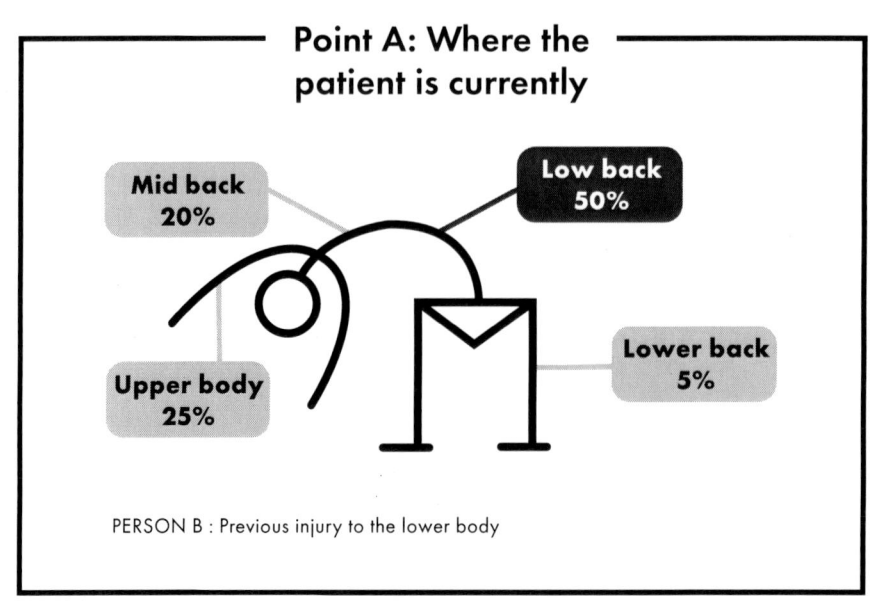

Point B: Where the patient wants to get back to

- Mid back 25%
- Low back 25%
- Upper body 25%
- Lower back 25%

Arms
Shoulders
Upper back

Point A: Where the patient is currently

- Mid back 20%
- Low back 50%
- Upper body 25%
- Lower back 5%

PERSON B : Previous injury to the lower body

So, where do you start to get results and allow the patient to "feel the difference" quickly?

The patient wants to be able to perform gardening for two hours a day. She wants to be able to sit and watch TV pain free, and also wants a good night's sleep. She also wants to be able to navigate the stairs pain free throughout the day.

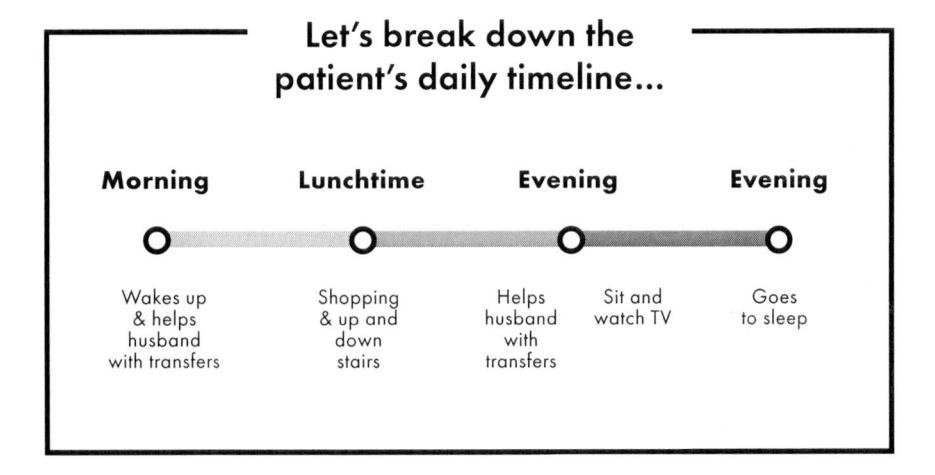

Let's break down the patient's daily timeline...

Morning	Lunchtime	Evening	Evening
Wakes up & helps husband with transfers	Shopping & up and down stairs	Helps husband with transfers / Sit and watch TV	Goes to sleep

Another great question to ask yourself is: **"Where could things go wrong?"** in getting the patient the results they want.

Wants to be able to...

Morning	Lunchtime	Evening	Evening
Wakes up & helps husband with transfers	Shopping & up and down stairs	Helps husband with transfers	Sit and watch TV	Goes to sleep

Needs to be able to...

Morning	Lunchtime	Evening	Evening
Wakes up & helps husband with transfers	Shopping & up and down stairs	Helps husband with transfers	Sit and watch TV	Goes to sleep

The ideal world

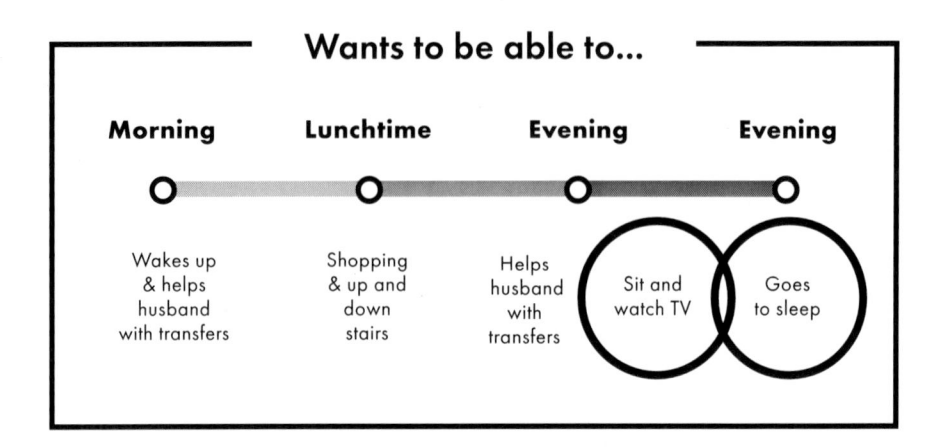

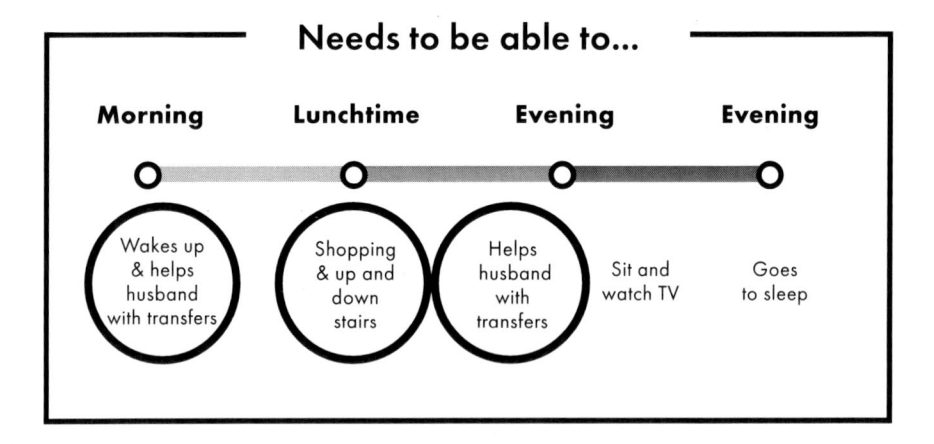

In the ideal world, you would start with patient education, some breathing exercises and helping the patient get back towards "rest and digest" in the evenings to help them get a good night's sleep using Module 4 of the 'Go-To' Physio Mentorship programme. There are a lot of great benefits to helping the patient get a good night's sleep, including more energy and potentially better tolerance of the pain experience.

You may also use a Peter O'Sullivan-inspired approach to help the low back relax, mobilise the ribcage and diaphragm and help the patient sit pain free watching TV.

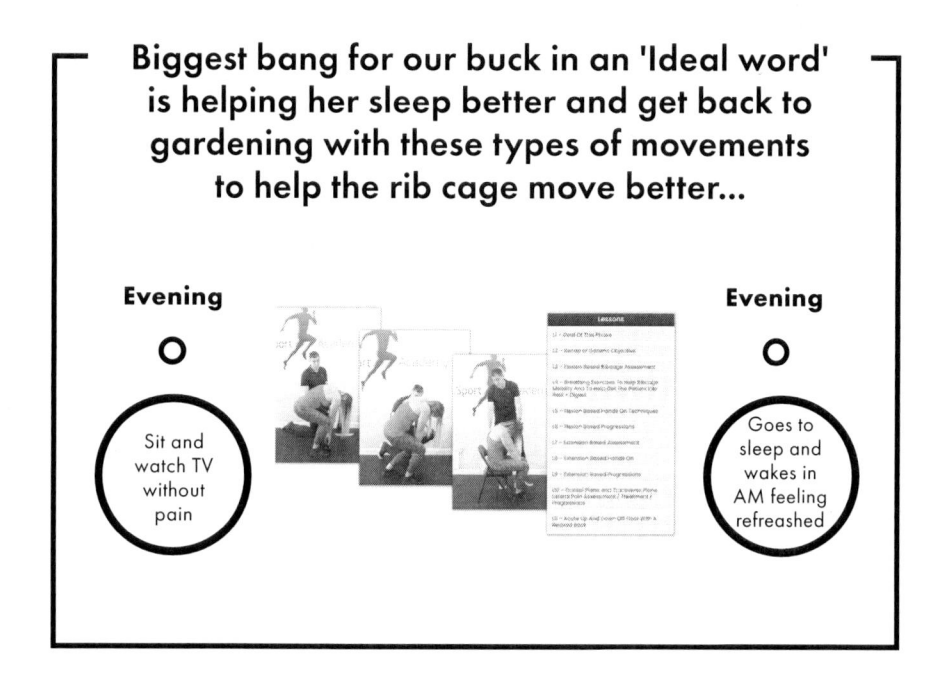

> **Biggest bang for our buck in an 'Ideal word' is helping her sleep better and get back to gardening with these types of movements to help the rib cage move better...**
>
> **Evening**
> ○
> Sit and watch TV without pain
>
> **Evening**
> ○
> Goes to sleep and wakes in AM feeling refreashed

All of these strategies are based on sound clinical reasoning in my opinion and I couldn't fault you for that approach.

In the real world

In the real world, if you map the timeline of the patient, focusing on sleeping, sitting and watching TV at night, without giving the patient strategies to be successful with the transfers of her husband and using the stairs, the chances are that the pain experience will be very much present throughout the day.

There may also be a chance that the pain is further sensitised/more irritable by the evening when you use your approaches to help the patient sit and watch TV or get a good night's sleep.

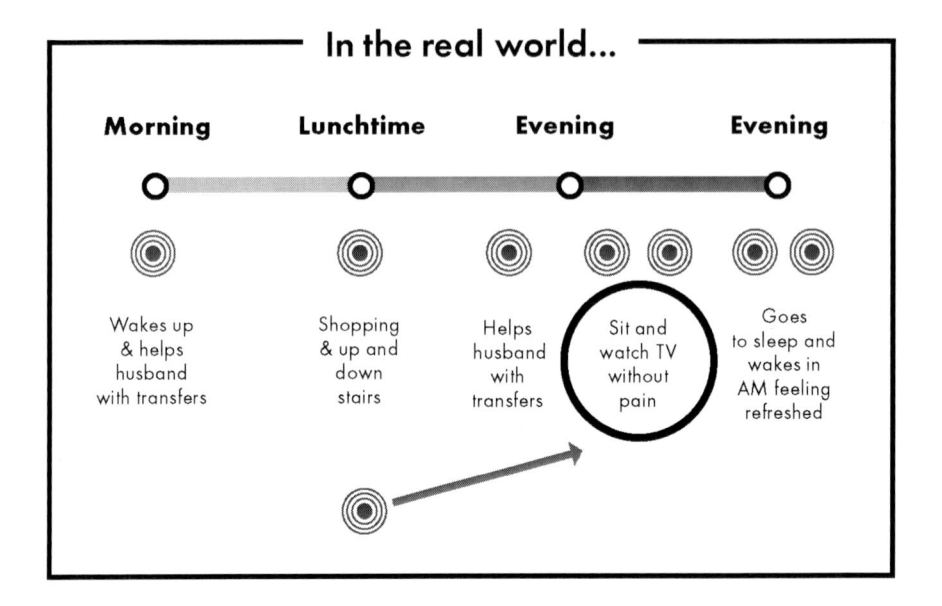

In the real world...

Morning	Lunchtime	Evening	Evening
Wakes up & helps husband with transfers	Shopping & up and down stairs	Helps husband with transfers	Sit and watch TV without pain	Goes to sleep and wakes in AM feeling refreshed

An alternative approach

Alternatively, you could look at the patient's daily timeline and focus on getting quick wins where the patient can "feel the difference" and start fast. To do so, you can focus your approach on what the patient has to do for prolonged periods of the day (six to ten hours) rather than just giving the patient an exercise they do for six to ten reps.

This is where we focus on our rental strategies to help her be successful throughout the day FIRST (6 hours a day vs just 6 reps)

Morning — Wakes up & helps husband with transfers

Lunchtime — Shopping & up and down stairs

Evening — Helps husband with transfers

Sit and watch TV

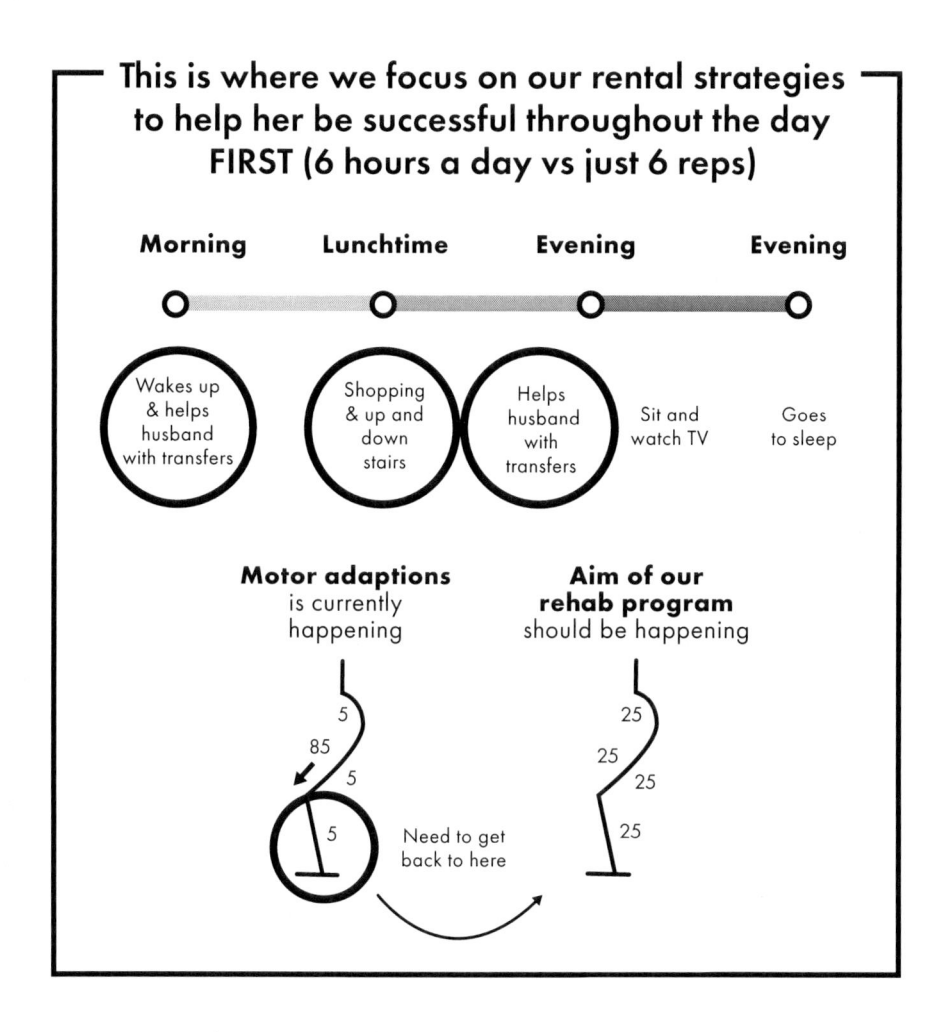

Goes to sleep

Motor adaptions is currently happening

5, 85, 5, 5 — Need to get back to here

Aim of our rehab program should be happening

25, 25, 25, 25

In the first session or two, you could instead go down a different treatment route and focus on helping the patient tolerate more load through her right leg to decrease the load tolerated on the low back throughout the day.

Focusing on getting results FAST!

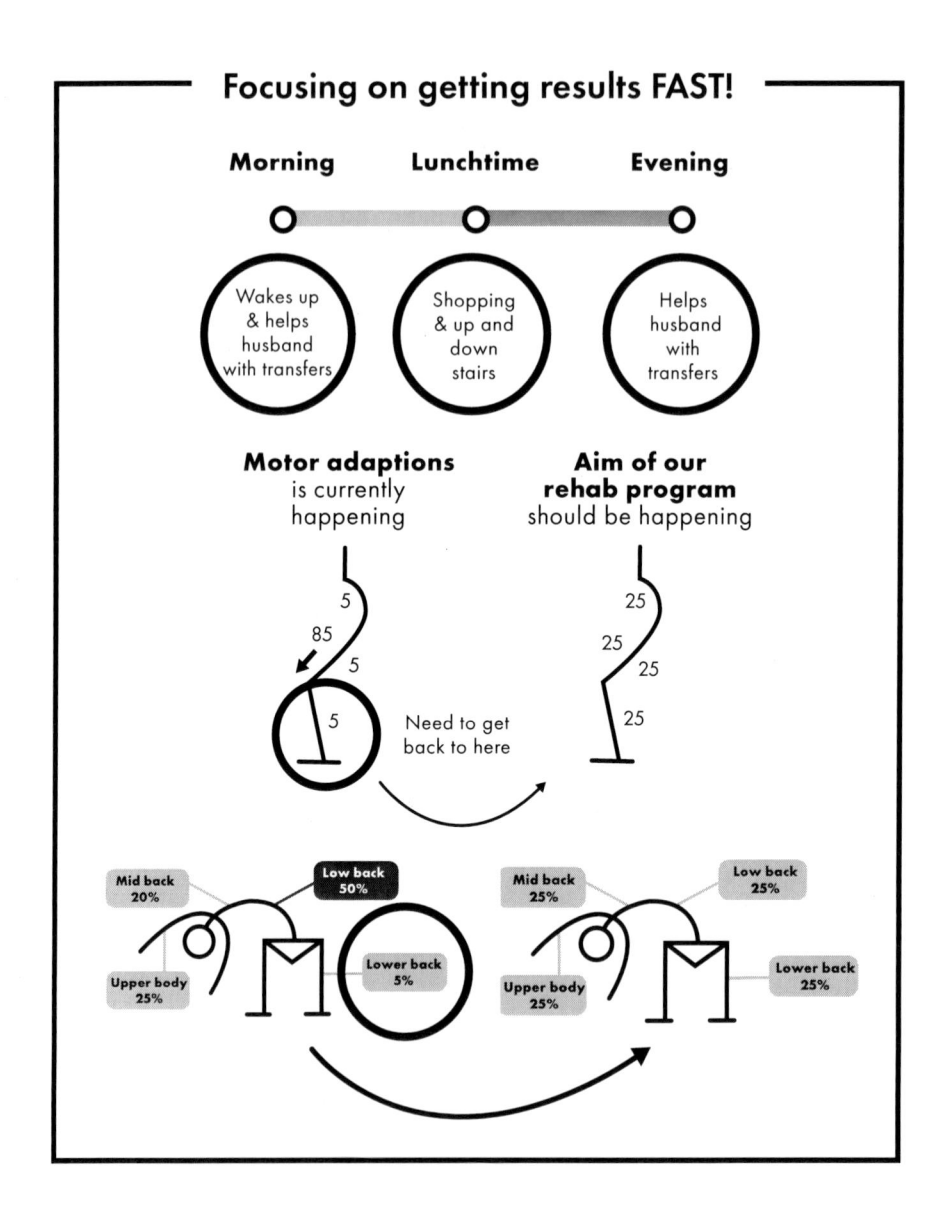

Morning — Wakes up & helps husband with transfers

Lunchtime — Shopping & up and down stairs

Evening — Helps husband with transfers

Motor adaptions is currently happening

5, 85, 5, 5 — Need to get back here

Aim of our rehab program should be happening

25, 25, 25, 25

- Mid back 20%
- Low back 50%
- Upper body 25%
- Lower back 5%

- Mid back 25%
- Low back 25%
- Upper body 25%
- Lower back 25%

This would then decrease the load tolerance on the low back throughout the day, where the patient can feel the difference, and the system may be less sensitised in the evening, also helping her when sitting and sleeping.

This means you would instead focus on Module 2 of the 'Go-To' Physio Mentorship programme, which involves helping the patient in positions specific to where they need to be successful throughout the day. You help her tolerate load through the right leg using a combination of hands-on treatment (if appropriate) and simple cues using a top-down, conscious cues approach initially to help the right leg do more work.

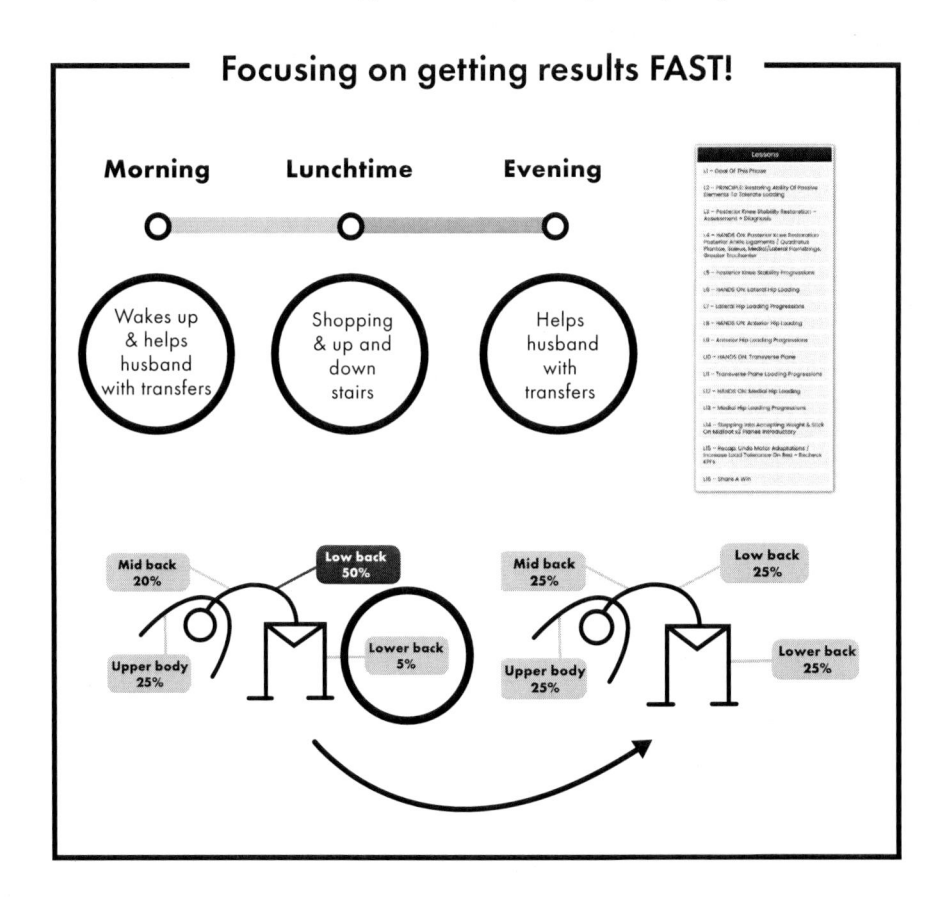

Focusing on getting results FAST!

Morning — Wakes up & helps husband with transfers

Lunchtime — Shopping & up and down stairs

Evening — Helps husband with transfers

Mid back 20% | Low back 50% | Upper body 25% | Lower back 5%

→

Mid back 25% | Low back 25% | Upper body 25% | Lower back 25%

This allows the patient to "feel the difference" quickly and you "start fast" by helping the patient get and see the results. As the sessions progress, you transition from top-down cues to a bottom-up approach where the patient does these movements without the need for conscious cues and moves towards "thoughtless, fearless movement" (Louis Gifford, 2014).

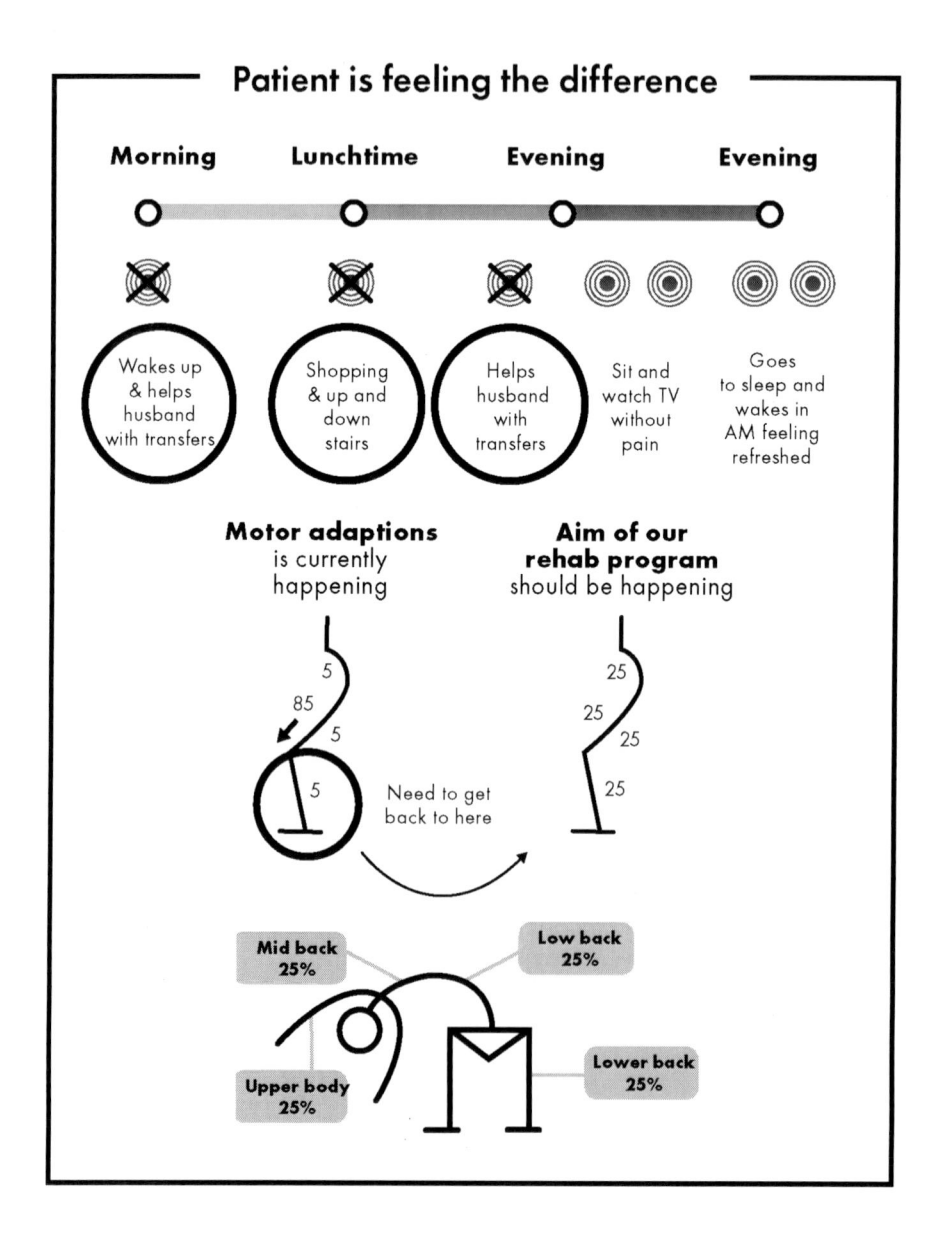

Patient is feeling the difference

Morning	Lunchtime	Evening	Evening
Wakes up & helps husband with transfers	Shopping & up and down stairs	Helps husband with transfers	Sit and watch TV without pain / Goes to sleep and wakes in AM feeling refreshed

Motor adaptions is currently happening

85
5
5
5

Need to get back to here

Aim of our rehab program should be happening

25
25
25
25

- Mid back 25%
- Low back 25%
- Upper body 25%
- Lower back 25%

As you progress through your treatment plan, you adhere to the five steps where the patient is clear on the plan and can see the small milestones being achieved on her way to her dream outcome/internal motivator.

5 steps to retain patients

1. Know your result/benefit
2. Map out milestones/progress
3. Pre-framing
4. Have a clear next step
5. Get them great results

Now that you have helped the patient "feel the difference" and be successful throughout the day, you can focus on helping the ribcage and low back with the potential "tripwires" (the right leg is now doing enough so the low back is not doing too much work) kicking in and affecting progress.

In the next few sessions...

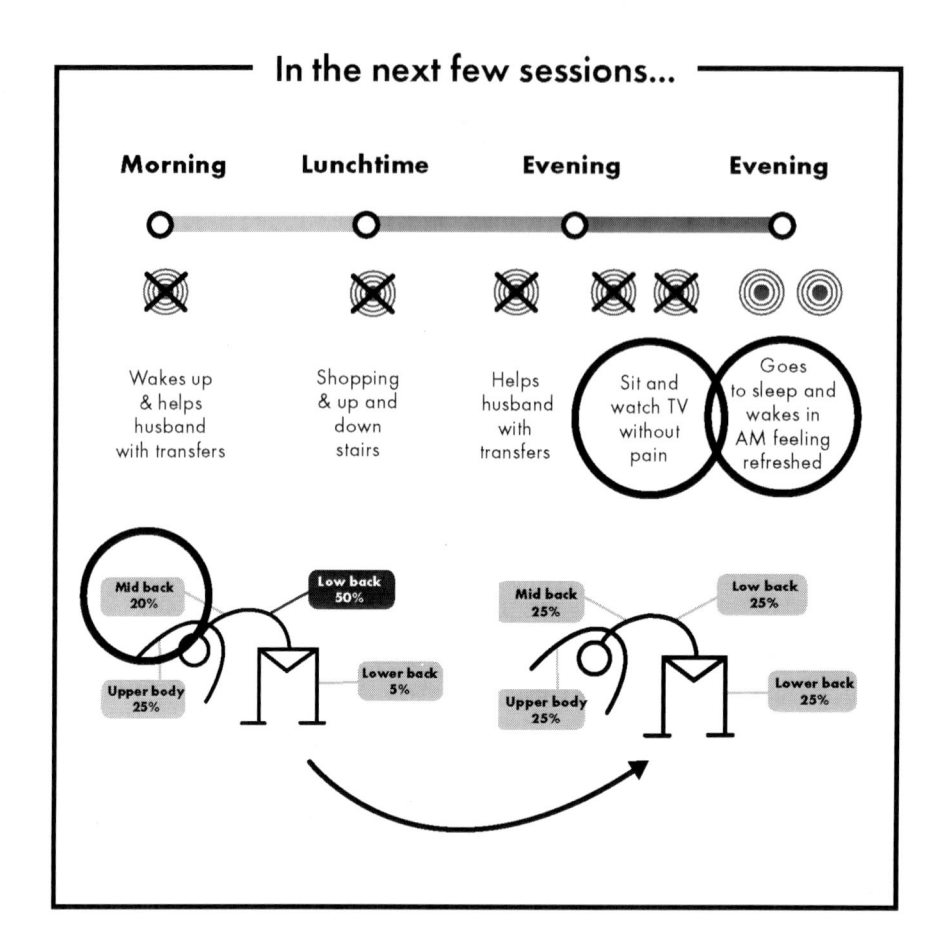

Morning — Wakes up & helps husband with transfers

Lunchtime — Shopping & up and down stairs

Evening — Helps husband with transfers

Evening — Sit and watch TV without pain / Goes to sleep and wakes in AM feeling refreshed

| Mid back 20% | Low back 50% |
| Upper body 25% | Lower back 5% |

| Mid back 25% | Low back 25% |
| Upper body 25% | Lower back 25% |

You would now focus more attention on helping the ribcage to mobilise better and helping the patient get into "rest and digest" prior to going to sleep using simple breathing exercises and other simple approaches.

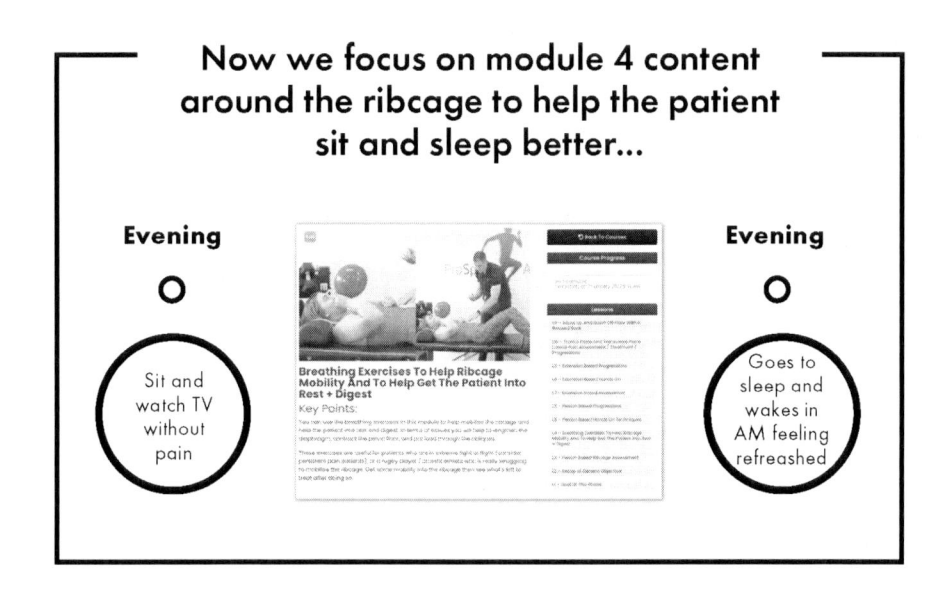

Now we focus on module 4 content around the ribcage to help the patient sit and sleep better...

Evening

Sit and watch TV without pain

Evening

Goes to sleep and wakes in AM feeling refreshed

You keep ticking off these milestones with the patient and they can clearly see the progress, as well as know there is more progress to be made.

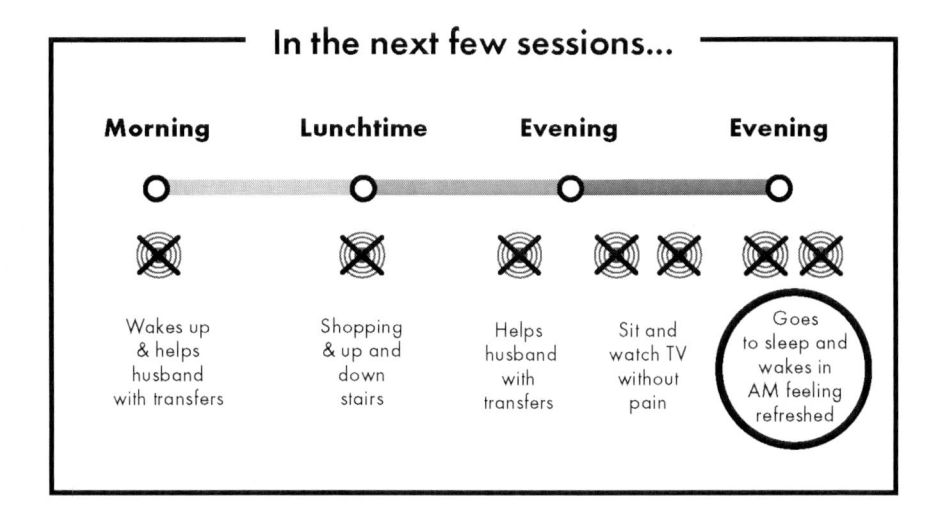

In the next few sessions...

Morning	Lunchtime	Evening	Evening
Wakes up & helps husband with transfers	Shopping & up and down stairs	Helps husband with transfers	Sit and watch TV without pain / Goes to sleep and wakes in AM feeling refreshed

The patient can FEEL the difference/progress!

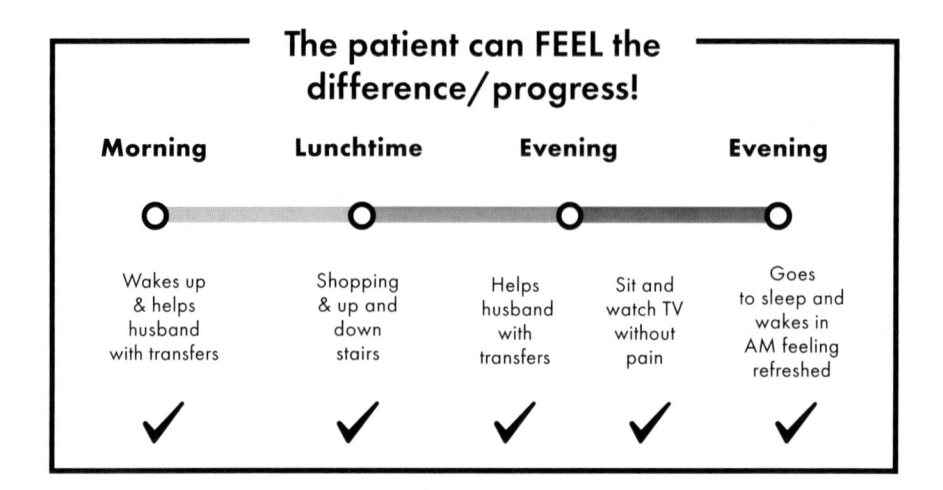

Morning	Lunchtime	Evening	Evening	
Wakes up & helps husband with transfers	Shopping & up and down stairs	Helps husband with transfers	Sit and watch TV without pain	Goes to sleep and wakes in AM feeling refreshed
✓	✓	✓	✓	✓

The patient is now able to move without fear or without kicking in any motor adaptation strategies throughout the day.

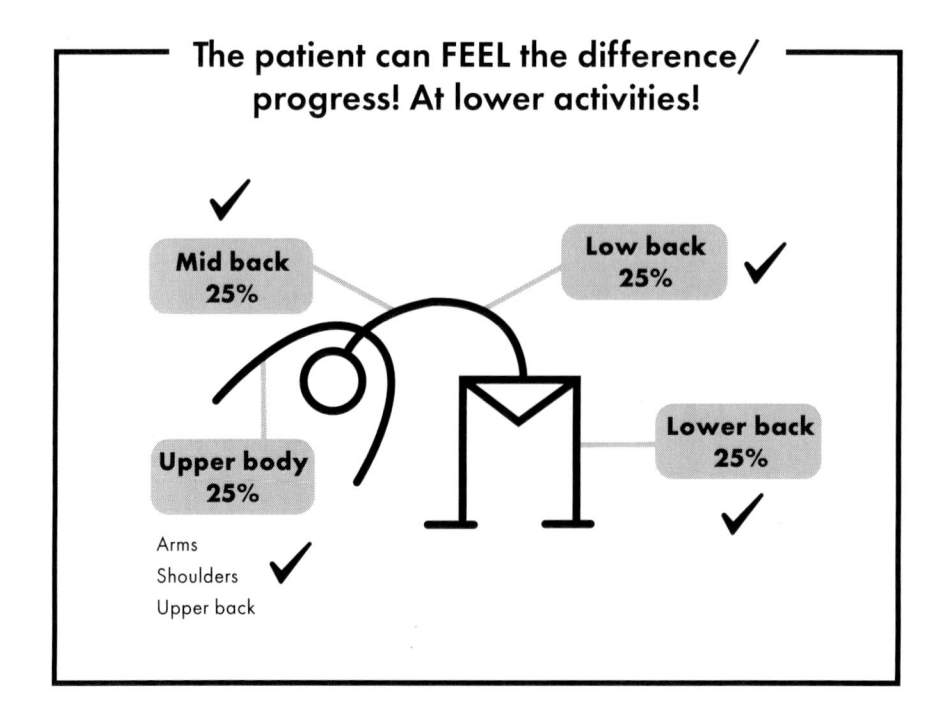

The patient can FEEL the difference/progress! At lower activities!

Mid back 25% ✓

Low back 25% ✓

Upper body 25%
Arms
Shoulders
Upper back ✓

Lower back 25% ✓

You keep the patient's dream outcome top of mind and you know the ultimate result the patient wants...

> **The dream outcome is gardening for 2 hours a day...**

You now need to ensure the patient has the "resilience" to tolerate two-plus hours of gardening and be able to maintain these positions while also tolerating load throughout the body. You will now use a combination of Modules 7 and 8 in the 'Go-To' Therapist Mentorship to bridge the gap from low to high-level rehab. This will also include increasing the load tolerance on the lower limb to help build that "buffer capacity" and "resilience" for the patient with the transfers of her husband.

We now need to bridge the gap from low to high-level rehab...

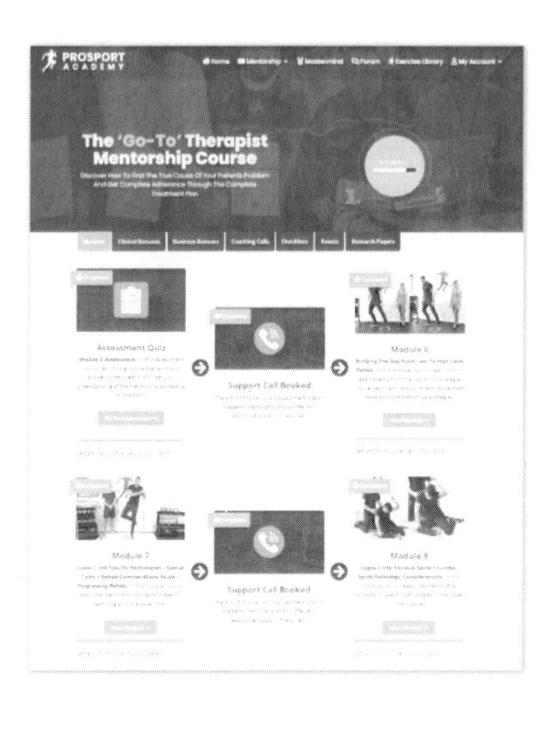

You now focus the final few sessions on increasing the load tolerance through the peripheral limbs so the low back muscles can "relax" for prolonged periods without feeling the need to kick in and help out. You would use simple strategies from Module 7 to bridge the gap and actually build resilience with the patient.

The dream outcome is gardening for 2 hours a day...

Lower limb eccentrics with relaxed back

You take the emotion out of the decision making and progress the patient logically. You introduce a graded exposure to gardening again and the patient has earned the right to get to two-plus hours a day of gardening.

She has earned the right to return to long lasting results and can tolerate gardening without daily life activites 'flaring her up'

✓

Mid back 25%

Low back 25% ✓

Upper body 25%

Arms
Shoulders ✓
Upper back

Lower back 25%

✓

✓

You then achieve Step 5 of retaining patients: Get them results!!

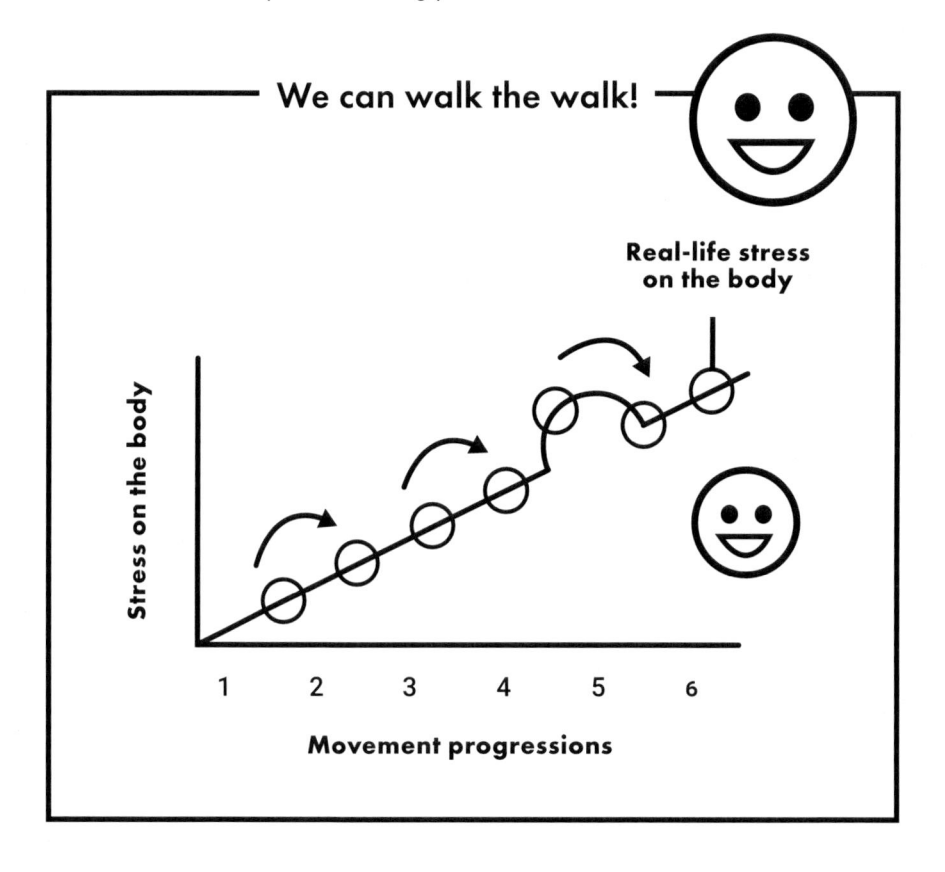

We can walk the walk!

Real-life stress on the body

Stress on the body

1　2　3　4　5　6

Movement progressions

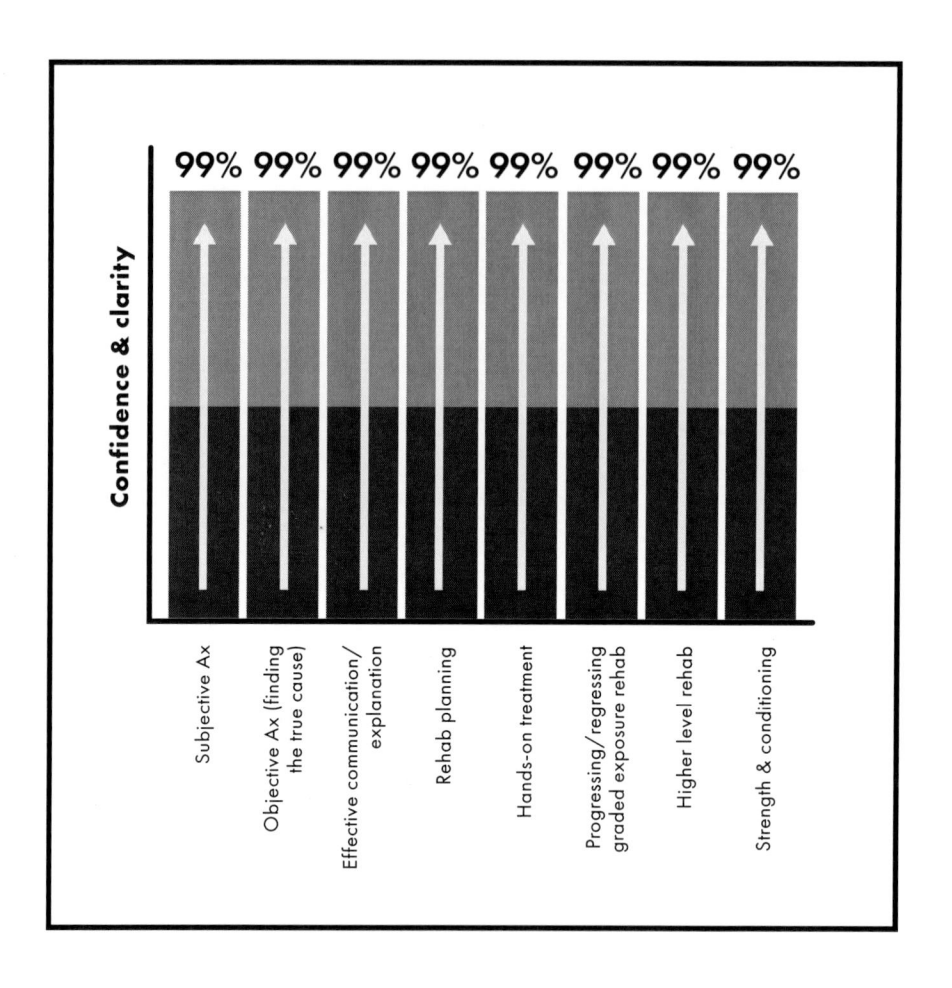

[Bar chart: "Confidence & clarity" on y-axis, with bars at 99% for each category: Subjective Ax; Objective Ax (finding the true cause); Effective communication/explanation; Rehab planning; Hands-on treatment; Progressing/regressing graded exposure rehab; Higher level rehab; Strength & conditioning]

Applying this approach in the real world…

Can it really be this simple?

I'm sure you may still have some hesitation about adopting this approach in the real world. Can this approach really work for you?

Nowadays I don't judge my step-by-step system by my results but more so by its ability to get my Mentorship therapists results. Here is an example below of one of our Mentorship therapists, Ollie, applying the principles in this book:

> **Ollie Attoe**
> 22 February at 15:46
>
> First big win through the mentorship outlining and explaining a full treatment plan in patients first assessment session, patient signed up to buy 6 treatment sessions up front! Was so thankful for a thorough explanation and clear map back to running (something she gave up on 3 years ago due to knee pain)
> Thank you Pro-sport team!
>
> You, Michael Szyczak, Laura Franklin Rehab and 6 others — 1 comment
>
> ♡ Love   💬 Comment
>
> All comments ▼
>
> **Dave OSullivan** Admin
> Awesome work implementing Ollie!!

And here is the end result after 'walking the talk'.

> **Ollie Attoe**
> 25m
>
> Small win this week already!
> Discharged 3 patients so far this week who had followed a full plan of treatment and progressions.
> I think this might be the first time I've ever formally discharged someone vs just saying 'do that and see how it goes'. So felt very good to see someone go fully through the plan, stick with it and get the results they wanted from session 1. Amazing what some structure can do!! I also asked each for a review too and they were more than happy to do so!
>
> View insights   45 post reach >
>
> Michael Szyczak, Charlie Cook and 5 others   2 comments

With the greatest respect to these therapists, if they can get these kinds of results, why can't you? All that is needed is for you to embrace the discomfort and take that first step on your journey to becoming the 'Go-To' Physio in your town.

Are you ready to become the 'Go-To' Physio in your town?

Part Five:
Growing and Scaling a Private Practice Sustainably

"With great power comes great responsibility!" – Uncle Ben, *Spiderman*

Now that you have the eight fundamental skills to confidently help any private practice patient who walks through your doors, you have some decisions to make. You will naturally begin to attract more and more people who have failed with traditional approaches and your clinic and reputation will naturally begin to grow also.

As your clinic grows, you will need to hire some additional therapists to cope with the demand and this is where you have some decisions to make.

This final section of the book will highlight some of my biggest business mistakes and how you can avoid them. It will also show you the most simple and direct path to having a successful private practice that can naturally grow without consuming your life and having everything rely on you. It will also share with you a simple model to ensure you continue to grow naturally, while remaining profitable and not having to worry about finding new patients every single week to fill your therapist's diaries.

The final chapter of the book will talk about the biggest obstacle that you will encounter on your journey and how to avoid it.

Chapter 18:
Choosing the "Right Way" to Grow Your Reputation, Clinic and Impact

---

I felt sick.

I had just handed over £12,000 to a business coach for 90 days of coaching to help me grow the clinic and academy. He got me on a call, promised me the world and took my money while, 90 days later, delivering absolutely nothing. Truth be told, I didn't even tell my wife how much the coaching was.

I was embarrassed. I had used all the business' and ProSport bonus money I had saved on this coach to help me grow my clinic. It was one call a week for 90 days and access to some of the latest "marketing secrets" designed to grow my business faster than I ever could have imagined. This experience is a big part of why I have such a distaste for these high-pressure sales calls people are doing these days.

I was one of the first to experience them in 2015, before they came so common, and I was left with empty pockets and nothing to show for it. To make sure this doesn't happen to another therapist, at the ProSport Academy we ensure we first have a coaching call with the therapist or clinic owner for our 'Go-To' Physio Mentorship and 'Go-To' Clinic Mastermind programmes.

This is to ensure they are genuinely a good fit for the programme, that we can actually help them and therefore that we give them a massive amount of value regardless of whether they want to be considered to be put forward for either of our programmes that help 'Go-To' Therapists build 'Go-To' Clinics.

I believe the best way to reduce scepticism is to actually help people get results and I live and die by this belief in how I run both my clinic and my academy. This was also my first exposure to the false belief that you must have loads and loads of new patients, highly complicated sales funnels and spend loads and loads of time on these special marketing techniques to grow your business.

While the majority of this book reveals my biggest clinical mistakes, I want to finish this book also revealing my biggest business mistakes so you don't have to go through the same stress and pain that I had to endure.

The truth is you can grow your private practice in a number of ways. The biggest lesson I have had to learn the hard way is that, regardless of the model you choose, a successful, scalable and sustainable private practice **is not built** on how many new patients you can get each week, but on how many you can keep.

Let's recall Jay Abraham's model of three ways to grow a business (as I explained in the Introduction). You can grow your clinic in only three ways:

1. By increasing the number of new patients you attract.

2. By increasing the number of sessions (ethically) a patient has.

3. By increasing the number of times patients buy more products/services (return with new problems or for upsells like pilates, massage, gym programs etc).

If we revisit this:

> ## Double your revenue and save hundreds of hours by not having to always find new patients!
>
> **100** of your patients having an average of 3 sessions each
> **£50/Session = £15,000**
>
> **100** of your patients ethically having an average of 6 sessions each
> **£50/Session = £30,000**
>
> Double you revenue **WITHOUT** having to waste time & worry about **finding 100 new patients to earn the same revenue!**

You'll see that by choosing option one of increasing the number of new patients as the primary strategy to grow your clinic, you will need to put in a lot of work, time, effort and money to focus on finding 100 new patients for your practice.

It makes more sense to me to choose option two and increase the number of sessions (ethically) your patients, who are already in your clinic and diary right now, need. This is the *easiest* and *simplest* way to grow .

I'll repeat, these patients *ARE ALREADY* in your schedule right now. Applying the principles of this book and making sense of each patient's symptoms, explaining the problem, solution and place to your patient, making a fast start and hitting milestones along the way to the dream outcome is the quickest, easiest and most effective way to grow a practice.

Option three is then closely linked to option two. If you do not get results for your patients when they come and see you, then it is highly unlikely they will return to your clinic for more of what they already got or for other products and services.

Therefore, by now you should be seeing that helping patients get great results is the foundation upon which a scalable and sustainable clinic is built. The simple fact is, getting patients life-changing results while giving them so much more value than you take in payment will solve most problems in your business.

Results equals reviews, referrals, retention and revenue.

This makes your marketing easier, your new patient numbers higher, your total appointments per week higher and easier to deliver and your ability to be profitable easier.

Said another way, the root cause of most problems in your business will be the inability to keep patients on track and progressing without cancelling or dropping off.

Look at it this way... how much bigger would your clinic be right now if you had delivered a great result and seen every single patient who had come through your door return due to future problems, while actively feeling compelled to tell everyone they know about you?

Keith Cunningham asked a great question in his book, *The Road Less Stupid*, to focus your mind on this:

"How would I run my business if 100 per cent of my future growth was by referral and repeat customers only?"

Delivering a world-class experience to every patient

The next thing you need to focus on is how to DELIVER a great experience to your patients to ensure that you ethically keep them progressing to their dream outcome so they will come back in the future.

As I like to remind my 'Go-To' Clinic Mastermind members (our business coaching program that helps our 'Go-To' Physios gain the confidence to grow a profitable clinic the right way and gives them the personal and financial freedom to then treat patients on their terms), you can have anything you want, you just can't have it all!

Quality, time and price now become three interchangeable aspects to consider when choosing your private practice model. Let's start with the price.

You can choose to be the cheapest clinic in your town. The problem with the cheapest is that someone can always undercut you, so it is a race to the bottom. With this model it is hard to deliver genuine quality while growing a profitable clinic. As you grow you will need bigger premises, more therapists to help with the demand, an admin team and other costs. This makes it hard to be the cheapest and give your patients the best quality in the shortest possible time.

Think of the McDonald's model – they optimise for time (speed) and price but the quality has to suffer. They therefore have to go for volume and with that a lot of work, systems and moving parts. The equivalent of a McDonald's model for a 'Go-To' Clinic is one that is the cheapest clinic, with the shortest appointment times and a low patient visit average, which is constantly worrying about finding new patients. If this clinic tries to be the cheapest, give patients the longest appointments and the best quality, it will, quite frankly, be pretty much impossible to grow and remain profitable (without considerable outside investment).

The patient that you would like to target and treat will also be important to consider when choosing the model for you. If your target market is six to 16-year-old kids (think students), then a McDonald's strategy may be right for you. If your target market is females in the 50–70 year old bracket, then a McDonald's strategy may not be the most attractive for this clientele.

While money is very often not a big motivation for therapists, a business needs to make money to keep the lights on, and the more money a business receives, the more it can choose to grow. This means you can help more and more people who have failed with the traditional approach.

Before discussing the other option, it is important to address a common misconception that people naturally buy the cheapest option. That is true for a small percentage of people but not the majority. Think about your current situation. If this was true, we would all be wearing the cheapest clothes, buying the cheapest foods and using the cheapest laptops and phones. People choose quality over price and simply want value for money combined with how the purchase makes them FEEL!

The other option is charging more money, which results in being able to give patients a better customer experience and more value. This therefore makes growing easier and you have fewer moving parts. That means less stress and a great work-life balance while delivering an amazing experience for your patients and always giving more in value than you take in payment.

To execute this model, you will adhere to the principles outlined in this book and become the 'Go-To' Physio that builds a 'Go-To' Clinic. This means you focus on delivering high-value treatment plans that get results. This will ensure your patients naturally tell their friends they have to come to see you and that they also come back and buy more of your services. So, where do you start?

The Perfect Private Practice Growth Model

The reality is that you can grow your practice, your patients, your revenue and your profit any number of ways.

I personally adhere to Keith Cunningham's growth funnel and his model of the eight ways to grow your revenue (as explored in *The Road Less Stupid*). Here is an adapted version of the growth funnel, with the order modified specific to a private practice to give you an idea of where to start.

1. Keep more patients.

2. Increase conversion percentage of initial assessments to rebook.

3. Increase transaction size of each patient visit by ethically increasing the patient visit average.

4. Enhance and train the sales process.

5. Increase referrals and repeat purchases.

6. Increase the frequency of purchase by ascending patients to the next product or service on their journey to their dream outcome.

7. Define and enhance certainty of success.

8. Increase leads and drive more traffic to your website.

1.Keep more patients

According to Cunningham, the common reason businesses fail to grow is not that they are not getting enough customers, it is that they are not keeping enough customers. He recommends that, rather than focusing on exclusively trying to get new patients, instead you focus your efforts on meeting and exceeding your current customers' needs and expectations. The previous chapters in this book as a whole outline how to do this from a clinical point of view, with the addition of some business systems that will be covered in the next book in this 'Go-To' Physio Perfect Private Practice series.

2. Increase conversion percentage of initial assessments to rebook

Now that you have addressed the low-hanging fruit and the patients already in your world, the next thing to focus on is the new patients who have booked in and are coming into your world for the first time.

Improving your initial assessments to ensure that a greater percentage of these patients rebook for another session is the next order of attack to hit the lowest-hanging fruit. Chapters 5 through 10 will help you with this process. To get patients to actually turn up will require some business systems in place that will be covered in the next book in this 'Go-To' Physio Perfect Private Practice series.

3. Increase transaction size of each patient visit by ethically increasing the patient visit average

While keeping more patients is focusing on the big picture overall and combining both the clinical and business systems, it follows that increasing the transaction size (ethically) of each patient visit by ensuring a high-value treatment plan is designed and a clear next step is in place is vital. Chapters 8, 9 and 10 in particular will help with this section clinically.

The biggest barrier to this section will usually be bridging the gap between low – and high-level rehab and prescribing the right exercise at the right time to keep your patient progressing. There will also need to be some business systems in place for the clinic to ensure you give yourself the best chance of doing this.

4. Enhance and train the sales process

Now you focus on what happens when potential patients ring your clinic. If you have admin staff, how do they speak to the patient? What happens before the patient arrives at the clinic? What happens when the patient arrives prior to going into the treatment room? All of these things require time, energy and effort, and will be addressed in the next book in this 'Go-To' Physio Perfect Private Practice series.

5. Increase referrals and repeat purchases

If you do a good job with number one, then this strategy is a whole lot easier. Remember Cunningham's question to help you focus: "How would you run your practice if 100 per cent of your future growth was by referrals and repeat business only?" It is a genius question to help focus your mind and, again, a big part of the answer to this question should lie in this book with the rest revealed in my next book in this series.

6. Increase the frequency of purchase by ascending patients to the next product or service on their journey to their dream outcome

After you have solved the patient's current problem, what other problems do they have that you can solve? This is now looking at other services you offer, such as: sports massage, pilates, yoga and gym services to name but a few.

7. Define and enhance certainty of success

While the concept of "keep more patients" is higher level and focused mainly on the patients already in your world, I like to think defining and enhancing the certainty of success focuses more on communicating to your potential new perfect patients that you understand what they want and increase that certainty of success. Doing this step before you spend money, time and energy on marketing will mean you will get more value from your efforts. It combines creating a unique space in the marketplace, sometimes termed a "blue ocean", for your business along with other principles such as lessening the risk of doing business with you for the customer.

Cunningham asks another powerful question to help you focus on this section by asking yourself, "What has to happen so the potential patient will say I'd have to be crazy to go somewhere else for treatment?" Once you figure this out, your marketing will become a whole lot easier and more effective in returning an investment for your time, energy and resources.

8. Increase leads and drive more traffic to your website

By now you have increased your ability to get results for patients and increased referrals and repeat business. You've also cleaned up your sales process and differentiated your clinic from others, while communicating clearly to potential patients that you understand what they really want and are certain you can give it to them while lessening the risk on their part. Now you are ready to focus more time and effort on getting more new "cold" patients who have not previously known about your clinic.

This will ensure that you work smarter not harder and get the most return on your investment of time, energy and money into your marketing efforts.

How to ensure you protect your clinic's reputation as it grows

Now that your clinic is growing and your practice is fully booked, the next question is how do you continue to grow while maintaining the quality of service without burning out? In the next chapter I will share how to grow your clinic and still be able to switch off at night while having energy to play with your kids or look after your own health.

Chapter 19:
Systemising Your Business for Ultimate Freedom

When I started out in private practice, I would be exhausted by the time my final patient left the treatment room. I'd scribble down their notes and try to get out of the clinic as fast as I could. I knew my energy, and hence the quality of my treatments, dropped significantly as the day went on. My final few patients were not getting my best and it played at the back of my mind.

I'd get home and just sink into the sofa, my hands and the rest of my body exhausted while my mind would still be racing, worrying about how the patient would be when they came back the following week. I'd struggle to get to sleep that night and it'd start all over again. It wasn't until years later and I started to become obsessed with developing a full step-by-step system that this would unknowingly solve this problem for me.

Systems

> "Your patients do not rise to the level of their goals, they fall to the level of your systems!" – Adapted from James Clear.

As you'll probably know by now, I am big into systems. A system is a collection of processes or components that are organised for a common purpose. A system can be simple, such as a few steps involved in sending an email, or more complicated, such as taking a new patient and progressing them all the way through to the final session. Said another way, a system is a method of solving a challenge in a consistent and repeatable way. This is good news for you and me if we want to get a consistent and repeatable result for even our most complex patients.

At the end of the day, think of systems as building blocks. When you put multiple systems together, it allows everything in your treatment approach (and business) to come together to achieve the goals. The following are just a few of the benefits of implementing a step-by-step system into your practice:

- **Saves time by giving you clarity and focus:** When a system is defined, it is then easier to implement and follow it. Instead of trying to do everything in the one session, you are focused on getting to the next level of the graded exposure plan. This squashes the overwhelm of not knowing where to go next, gives you clarity and focus, and therefore allows you to work smarter not harder. As you work to optimise the system and look for ways that you can improve, it takes less time overall to get the patient to the next level in the graded exposure plan so you need less time overall in sessions. Many therapists have been able to cut their appointment times as they now have a clear plan and system to work towards in each session without trying to treat everything.

- **Improves consistency:** Without a system, each time a task is performed, it may be done in a different way. A system, especially an optimised one, provides the simplest and most direct path to achieve a result. So, by following the same system each time for your subjective and objective assessments, treatment plan design and patient explanation, the outcome is going to be a lot more consistent. This ensures it does not matter if it is your first or last patient of the day, they will still get the same consistent care.

- **Enables delegation:** As your patient results improve, your reputation and clinic will naturally grow. You will then need to hire more therapists to help with the demand. There can often be this chicken vs. egg scenario where you are so busy that you need to delegate, but you don't have time to delegate. By capturing the systems that you are already using, it can ensure you can hire and onboard therapists much more quickly and easily, while ensuring it doesn't matter which therapist your patients see, as they will receive the same expert quality of care. This will protect your hard-earned reputation and give you the confidence to let other therapists treat your patients, knowing they are happy and progressing.

- **Less energy drain/decision making:** Without systems, you have to make a lot of decisions, many of which are small. This can lead to decision fatigue, which basically means that the quality of decisions and your energy goes down as you have to make more and more decisions. By having systems, you avoid this and save your energy for important decisions. Think again of your final patient of the day, this will ensure you have high-quality energy for these patients. Many of our 'Go-To' Physios report one of the biggest benefits they notice after implementing the step-by-step system is having more energy leaving work to go home and be present with family or to look after their own health.

The 'Go-To' Physio step-by-step system allows you to make sense of any patient's symptoms who walks through the door, explain the problem and solution to the patient for maximum buy-in and adherence, and then walk the talk by delivering the dream outcome. This is what really differentiates this system from any other CPD/CEU course or resource out there in that it teaches you how to put it all together in the real world and get results for even your most complex patients.

This 'Go-To' Physio step-by-step system does not just teach you "tactics" or "techniques", but rather a complete set of high-income skills.

Confidence & clarity

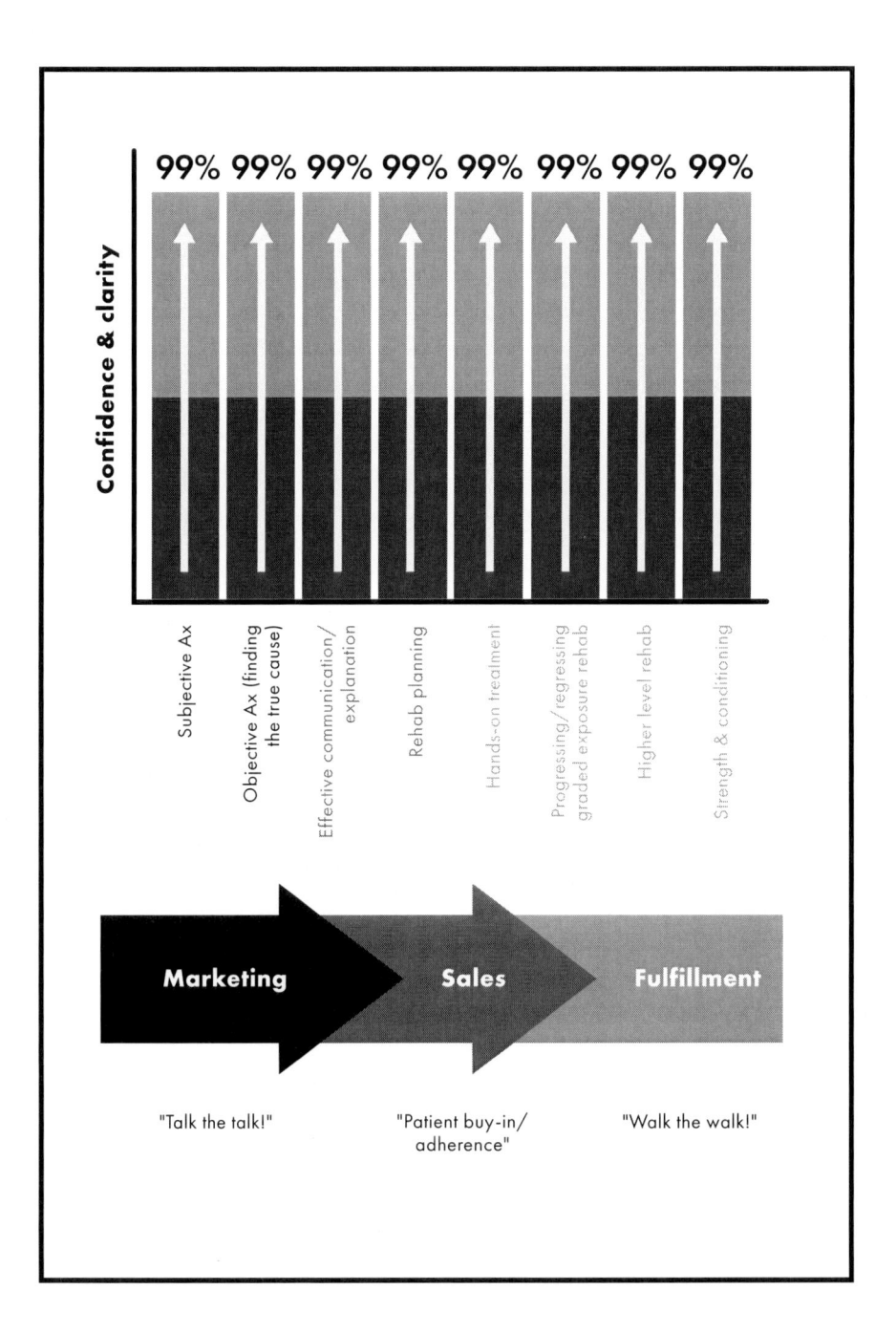

99% 99% 99% 99% 99% 99% 99% 99%

- Subjective Ax
- Objective Ax (finding the true cause)
- Effective communication/explanation
- Rehab planning
- Hands-on treatment
- Progressing/regressing graded exposure rehab
- Higher level rehab
- Strength & conditioning

Marketing → **Sales** → **Fulfillment**

"Talk the talk!" "Patient buy-in/adherence" "Walk the walk!"

Business systems versus a 'Go-To' Physio step-by-step system

As you grow and potentially hire a business coach, most business coaching programs will teach you to implement some business systems and collect some metrics on how your practice is doing. The problem is that the business systems will only tell you the "symptoms" in the business.

From 14 years of growing a private practice, I have found the true cause of the problem is usually people. To illustrate this point, let's look at arguably the most important number you would want to know to see if your business is growing – even if you were stuck on a desert island and could only receive one metric each week, I reckon this is the one you'd choose – total patient appointments per week.

This metric is an indicator of how close you are to a fully booked diary. If the number is going up every week, things are good. If the number is dropping every week, you know there is a problem in the business.

NOW		TARGETS	
#NPs		#NPs	
#Total apts		**#Total apts**	
PVA		PVA	
IA Rebook		IA Rebook	
Cancelled DNR		Cancelled DNR	
NPS Score		NPS Score	

If we break it down, the critical drivers or activities that will lead to the outcome of total patient numbers growing are the initial assessment to rebook percentage, the patient visit average, the cancelled did not rebook, and ultimately the net promoter score.

If all these things are going in the right direction, then the total number of appointments per week will take care of itself.

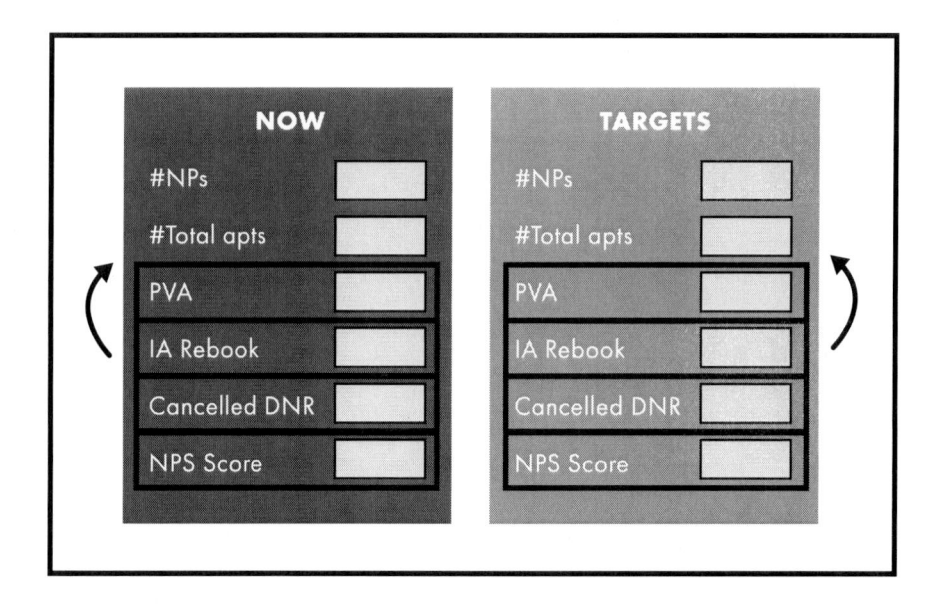

NOW		TARGETS	
#NPs		#NPs	
#Total apts		#Total apts	
PVA		PVA	
IA Rebook		IA Rebook	
Cancelled DNR		Cancelled DNR	
NPS Score		NPS Score	

The business systems will tell you "where" the problem is, but you will require the 'Go-To' Physio step-by-step system (or equivalent) to identify what the true cause of the problem is. Nine times out of ten, it is due to a lack of clarity and confidence from the therapist or a poor explanation of the problem and solution and therefore poor buy-in and adherence from the patient.

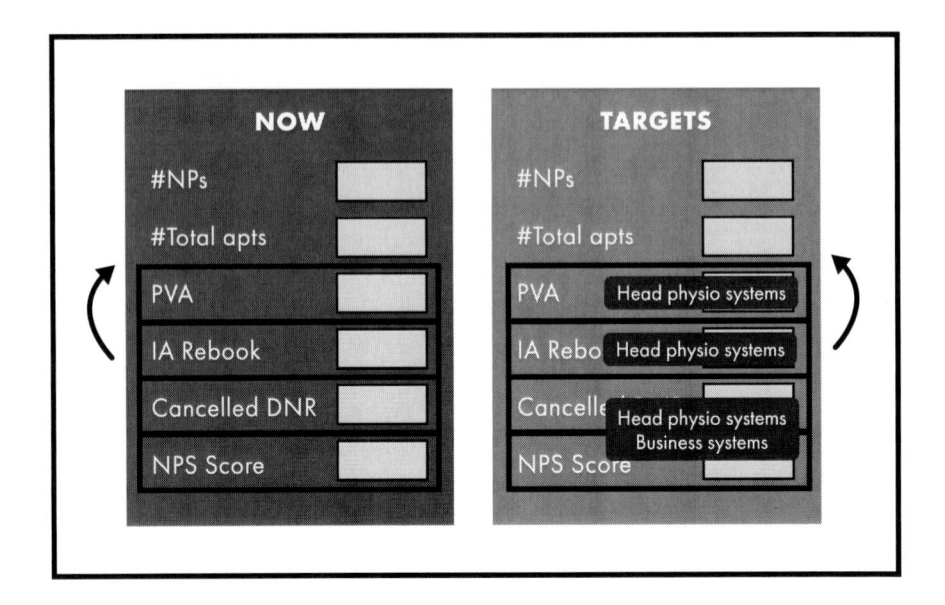

NOW		TARGETS	
#NPs		#NPs	
#Total apts		#Total apts	
PVA		PVA	Head physio systems
IA Rebook		IA Rebook	Head physio systems
Cancelled DNR		Cancelled DNR	Head physio systems / Business systems
NPS Score		NPS Score	

The true cause will usually be something that has not been done under the 8 Pillars of the 'Go-To' Physio.

You need different skills to thrive as a therapist in session one versus session six

The ability to differentiate your weak spots is critical if you want to grow a successful private practice. When you have a problem in your practice with initial assessments not rebooking, you'll require a completely different solution from what you would if you had a problem with patients cancelling three to four sessions in. You have the same symptoms, but a different root problem. Therefore, business systems are useful yet ultimately you want to work smarter not harder by solving the problems at source.

Once you address your weak spots or your therapists' weak spots, you can then minimise drop offs and cancellations by keeping the patient focused on the next steps while they can see the value and "feel the difference" throughout their day.

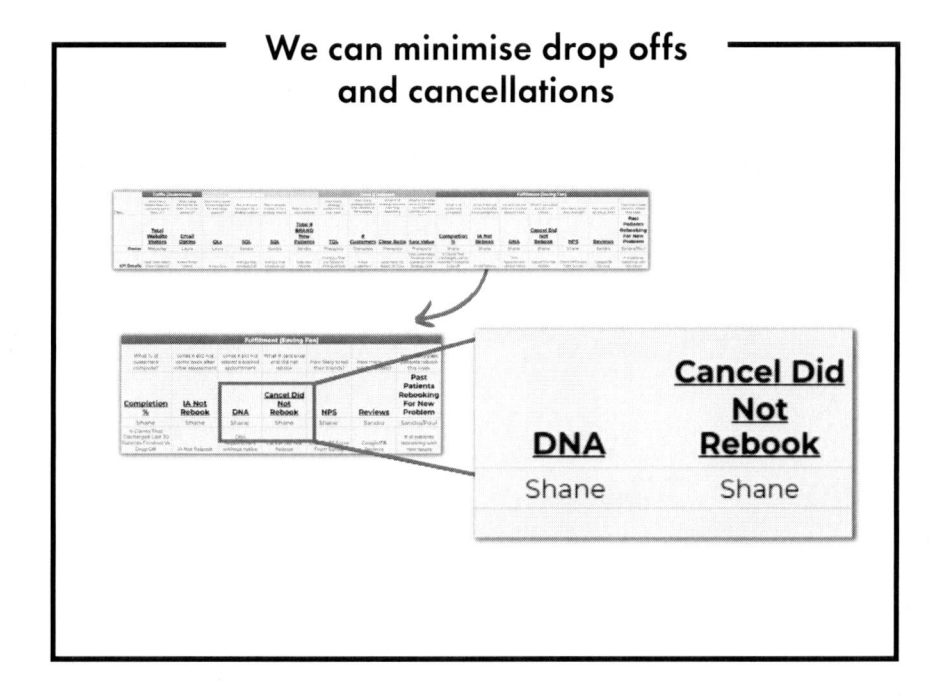

You can "walk the talk", and in doing so have a massive impact on people's lives and create raving fans (with the appropriate business systems in place to measure raving fan status and solve problems/unhappy patients early if required).

We can create raving fans...

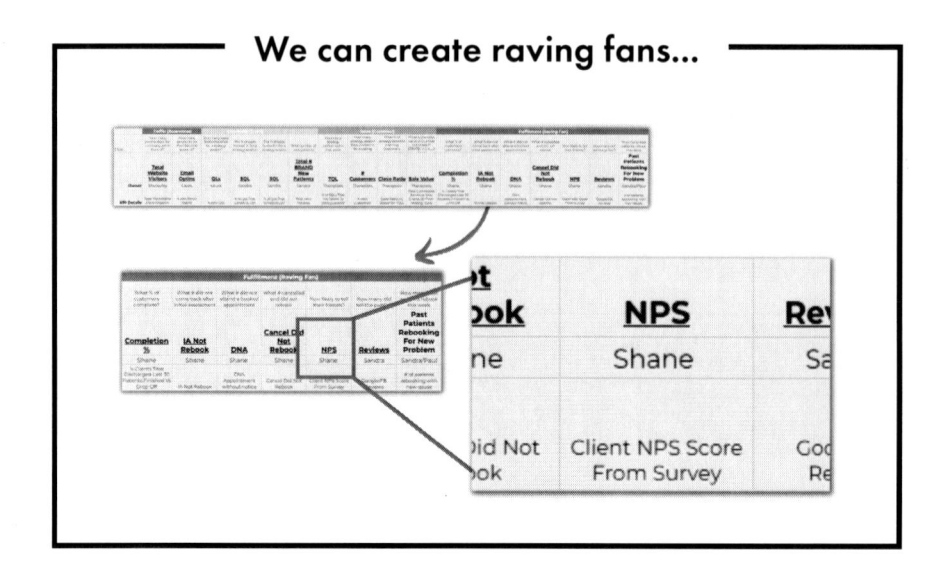

You can then get reviews which help your marketing. It is far more powerful for someone else to tell people how great you are than you having to tell them!

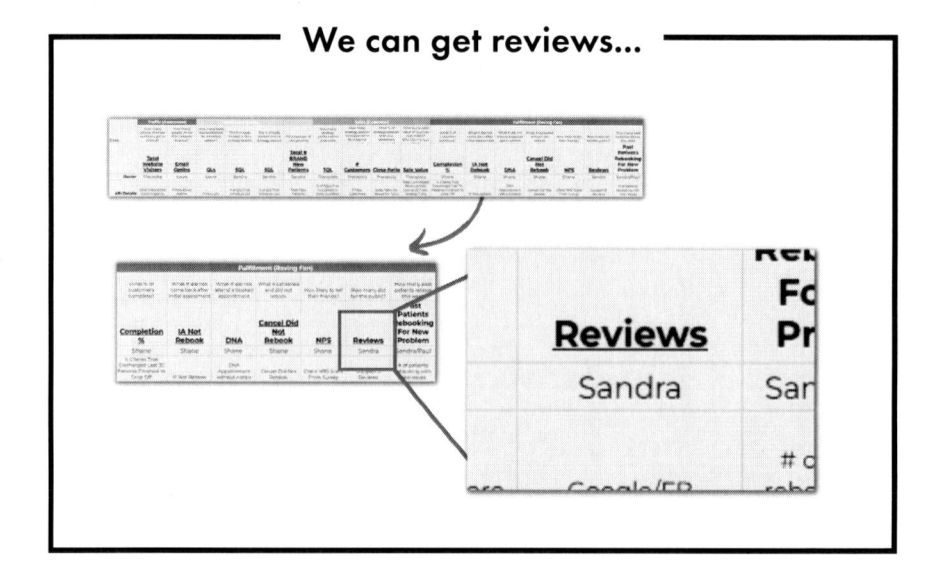

We can get reviews...

You will have patients who know, like and trust you. You solve their problems and you deliver more in value than you take in payment, thereby creating customers for life.

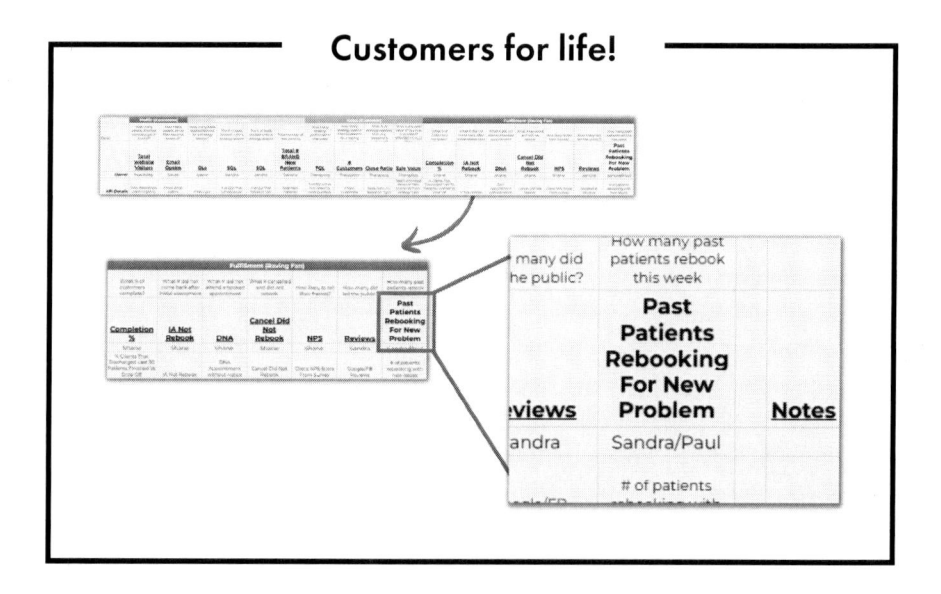

Customers for life!

The patient has 'CONFIDENCE IN YOU' to get results. Remember, it is a RISK for a patient to tell a family member or friend about you. They need to have confidence that you can actually help their friend or family member. No one wants to refer people to you and see them waste money, time and energy by not getting the result. This can cause embarrassment for the referee. The patient having confidence in you as a therapist and the ability to get results is a non-negotiable first step getting referrals.

We get referrals!

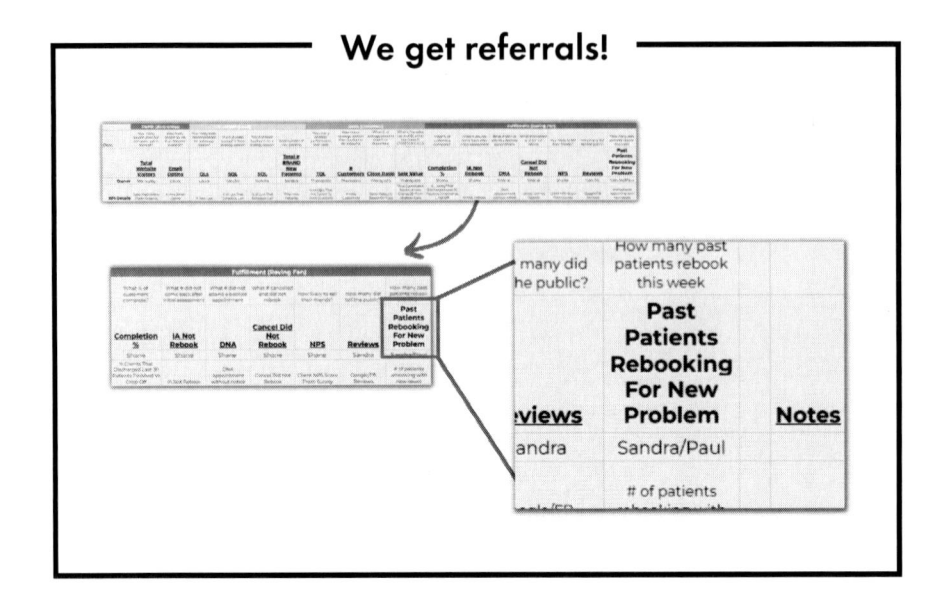

This is where you will build a 'Go-To' Clinic that has a reputation for helping people who have failed with traditional approaches by addressing these key areas...

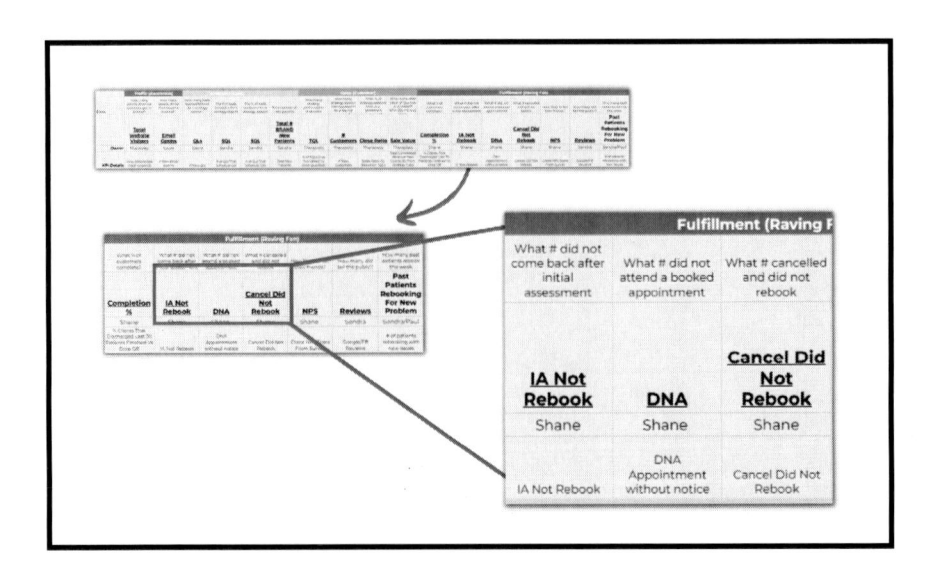

But it all starts with having a step-by-step system in place where you can take a patient on a journey from the minute they walk in the door, make sense of their story, get patient adherence and buy-in and keep that patient progressing each session to their dream outcome.

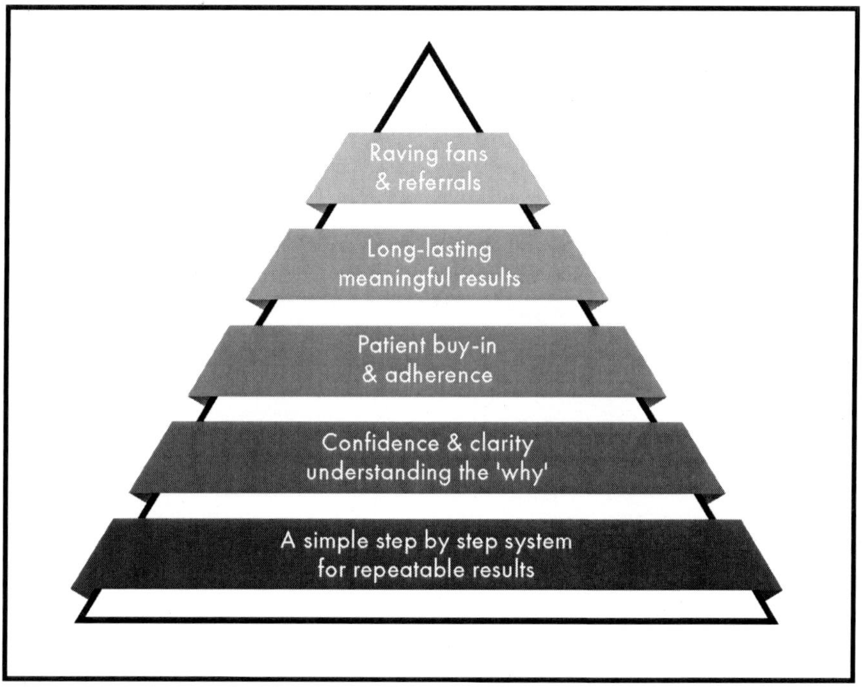

Raving fans
& referrals
Long-lasting
meaningful results
Patient buy-in
& adherence
Confidence & clarity
understanding the 'why'
A simple step by step system
for repeatable results

Confidence & clarity

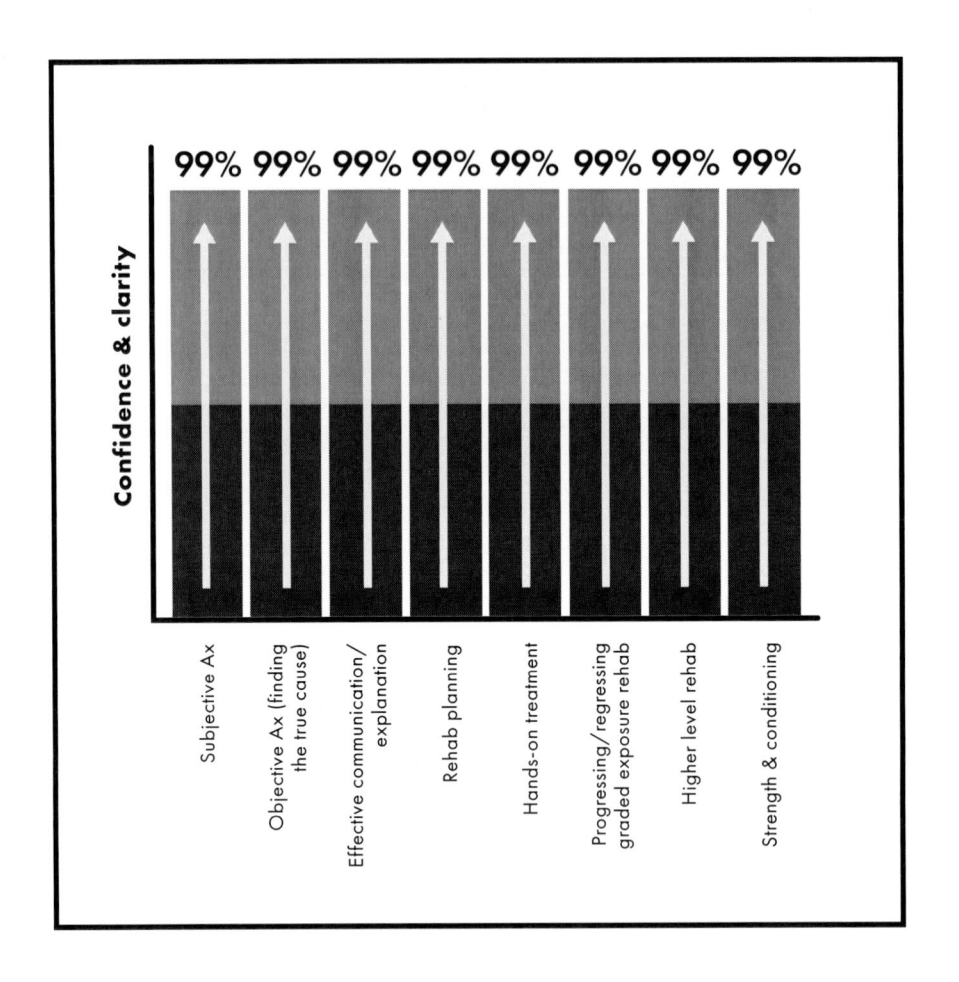

99% 99% 99% 99% 99% 99% 99% 99%

- Subjective Ax
- Objective Ax (finding the true cause)
- Effective communication/explanation
- Rehab planning
- Hands-on treatment
- Progressing/regressing graded exposure rehab
- Higher level rehab
- Strength & conditioning

'Go-To' Therapists build 'Go-To' Clinics when there is a consistent standard of care, a common treatment language and consistent results.

The 'Go-To' clinic

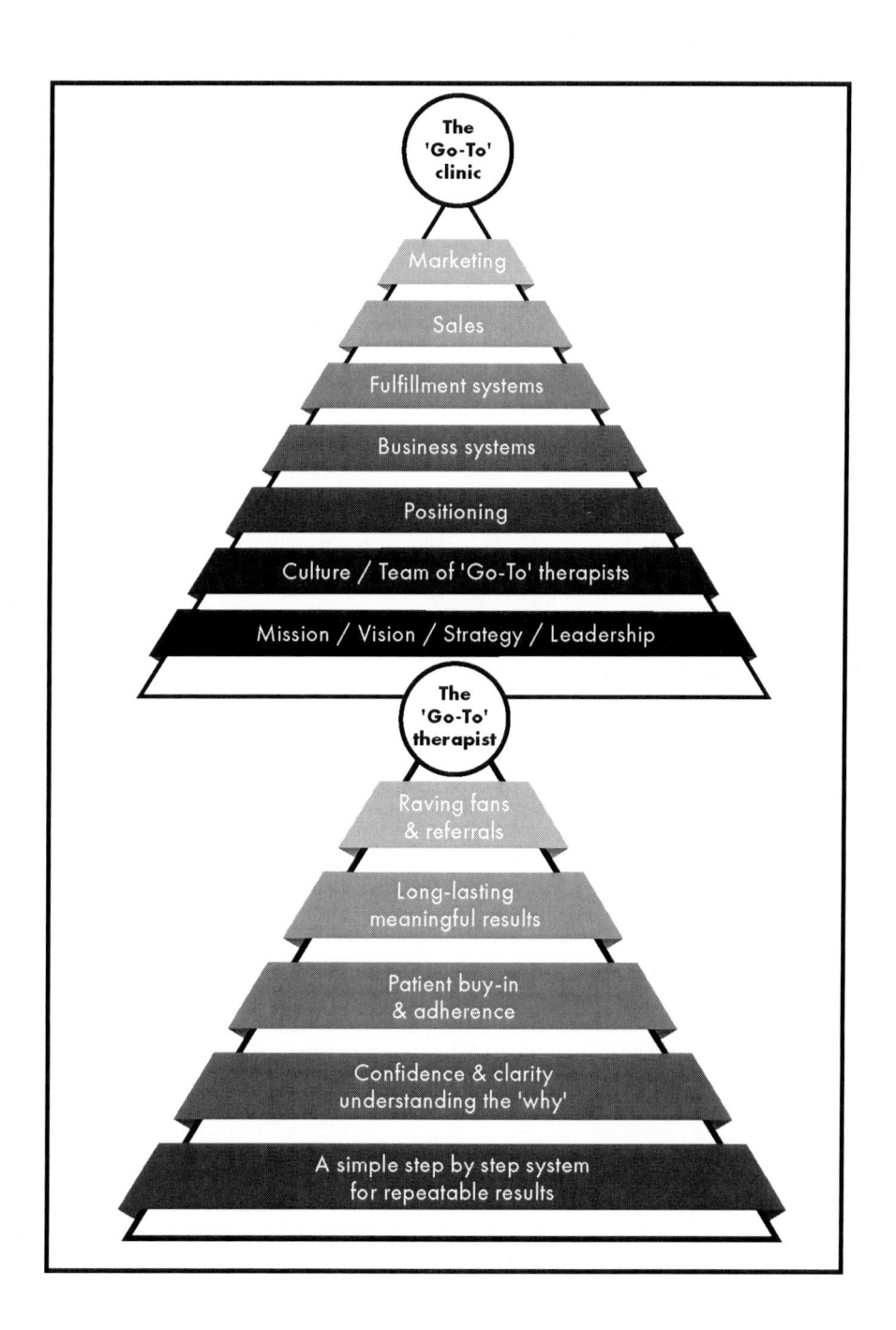

- Marketing
- Sales
- Fulfillment systems
- Business systems
- Positioning
- Culture / Team of 'Go-To' therapists
- Mission / Vision / Strategy / Leadership

The 'Go-To' therapist

- Raving fans & referrals
- Long-lasting meaningful results
- Patient buy-in & adherence
- Confidence & clarity understanding the 'why'
- A simple step by step system for repeatable results

A step-by-step clinical system is the quickest and easiest way to grow your practice as you naturally have to give up some control while it grows. A step-by-step system ensures you have a consistent and repeatable way to get even more complex patients great results so you don't have to "fire fight" or get involved with your therapists' caseloads as your clinic naturally grows.

Now that you have everything you need to become the 'Go-To' Physio in private practice that builds a 'Go-To' Clinic, the next question is what is really possible for you when you implement this step-by-step system? We will cover this in the final chapter.

Chapter 20:
What Is Possible for You and Your Practice with a Step-By-Step System?

I'm going to let you in on a little secret... In 2005, in my first year at the University of Huddersfield, I failed my neurology module. I had to carry the module into my second year and even then, I only just passed the exam.

I wasn't the smartest student in university. In fact, in the majority of my placements I scored mid-50s to early 60s; the only exception being my last placement at Bradford Bulls Rugby League Club where I scored 90 per cent. I was an average student who came away with a 2:1 degree. I wasn't particularly good at writing essays and assignments, yet I was obsessed with becoming the best physio in the real world.

Every research paper I read and everything I continue to learn to this day, I always ask myself the question: "How can I apply this in the real world with real patients?" Focusing first and foremost on developing a step-by-step system that gets results in the real world has allowed this kid from Cork, Ireland, who wasn't smart enough to study physiotherapy in his own country and who then nearly failed in his first year in the UK, to experience two World Cup finals – one in Australia with England Rugby League at the Suncorp Stadium, Brisbane in 2017, and the other in Japan with England Rugby Union in Tokyo in 2019.

If I can travel all over the world working with teams like England Rugby Union and Rugby League, professional golfers and other professional athletes and organisations then so can you if you wish to do so.

The ability to help patients, who have failed with traditional approaches, get long-lasting results quickly is a special gift that allows you to have a massive impact in this world. If you are good at what you do and can help patients who have failed with traditional approaches then you will never be out of work.

If I can build a 'Go-To' Clinic from a "shabby treatment room" above a running shop and then go on to build a successful private practice with six therapists (at the time of writing) working in the clinic, then so can you. I've shared my biggest clinical mistakes and also my biggest business mistakes up to now.

It is now time for me to share the personal mistakes that I have made so you can hopefully avoid them in the future as you look to grow a 'Go-To' Clinic. There is one big thing that I must warn you about, because it is something you need to be aware of as it will sabotage your success on this journey to becoming a 'Go-To' Physio who builds a 'Go-To' Clinic that has people travelling from all over to see you.

The one thing that will sabotage your success...

The one thing that will sabotage your success is you! Fix your mindset and everything else will follow.

In January 2021 I set goals for myself and the business for the year ahead... I failed miserably! In fact, halfway through the year, coming back from England camp in July, I knew I was going to fail miserably (personally, and with the clinic and academy) and that the second half of the year would be tough. No one likes being part of a losing team and I had set my staff up for failure due to my lack of leadership.

I let my therapists in the clinic down. I neglected them due to being away with teams, instead of focusing on my own academy team...

We were in new territory as we grew and my leadership was lacking. I knew I wasn't good enough first and foremost. I was doing everything half-heartedly. I was drinking more and more alcohol, eating more and more crap food and neglecting my sleep. I wasn't present with my wife and kids when I was at home because I was then stressed about the business. It was a vicious cycle.

To get my clinic and academy to the next level, I knew I personally needed to grow and get to the next level. I had heard the phrase numerous times before, and it finally resonated with me that, "We can't expect the same skills that got you and me to this level to get us to the next level." I tried that and it didn't work.

Upon searching for answers and the solution to my problems I came across *75 HARD*[17], a book by Andy Frisella, and in January 2022 I took the controversial 75 Hard challenge to strengthen my mindset and regain my discipline. When I came through the other side, I had a stronger mindset and better focus and clarity.

I found my purpose and mission again; and this book is a direct result of this focus and clarity. I want to help as many people who have failed with traditional approaches as possible and the simplest way I can do that is by helping therapists all over the world gain the clarity and confidence to help as many people who pass through their doors as possible.

Then I want to help as many therapists as I possibly can around the world go on to build 'Go-To' Clinics that have teams of 'Go-To' Therapists helping people who have failed with traditional approaches. By doing this, I can positively impact even more people who are suffering in pain needlessly. What's more, I also want to help you, as a therapist, charge what you are worth, have a comfortable life and get well paid for solving people's biggest problems while always giving more in value than you take in payment, but in order to achieve this you and I need to do the work!

---

[17] Frisella A., (2020), *75 HARD: A Tactical Guide To Winning The War With Yourself*, 44Seven Media

The work comes before the belief

I would love to tell you that you just need to watch the movie *The Secret*, visualise your dream clinic and bang, it will appear. I wish it was that easy. Joel Barker, the American futurist, said it best: "Vision without action is merely a dream. Action without vision just passes the time. Vision with action can change the world."[18]

Remember that the difference between entertainment and education is the ability to take action. You must take action and implement the content in this book. I came across an email from Andy Frisella, which I also thought summed this up perfectly, so I shared it immediately with my 'Go-To' Physio community:

> **"The Work Always Comes Before the Belief**
>
> *When you actually get a glimpse of how great you can be...*
>
> *Doing the work required is no longer a problem.*
>
> *It's the work required to get to the point where you get that glimpse that people have a hard time with.*
>
> *Buckle down, and understand this...*
>
> *The work always comes before the belief."*

I thought that was a pretty powerful message for the final chapter of this book. I was scared s*%tless the first time I applied the 80/20 rule with my patients. I was

---

[18] Barker J., *The Power of Vision* (1991 video)

scared s*%tless the first time I used an effective explanation. I was scared s*%tless the first time I told a patient that I NEEDED to see them next week even though their pain was gone. I was scared s*%tless the first time I hired another therapist…

Yet, as Andy says, when you do the work first, step outside your comfort zone, and things work – that's where the belief comes from!

Becoming a 'Go-To' Physio

To help you become a 'Go-To' Physio, here are some simple personal principles that I try my best to live by. I hope they will serve you well while avoiding the biggest mistakes I've seen therapists make on a daily basis.

Focus on taking imperfect action. As the saying goes, progress over perfection. There will never be a "perfect time" or "perfect environment". Life is full of ebbs and flows and so you must keep moving forwards taking imperfect action.

Life happens for you, not to you. Having two Munster players retire on my watch happened to ensure that I keep my candle burning deep inside of me to continue to further refine my skills and develop my own step-by-step system. It is critical that you move from a fixed mindset to a growth mindset in order to become a 'Go-To' Physio.

Learn from doing and not by watching. In our weekly in-service training, we have one rule: "Show me, don't tell me!". You must learn by taking action and doing. There will always be another research paper to read, another book to read, another webinar to watch. At some point you need to take action. Even if you don't have all the pieces of the puzzle yet, take the first step and figure out the rest as you go along.

Use numbers and logic wherever possible to take the emotion out of the decision-making process. When emotions go up, intellect goes down. Use data to make better decisions than just relying on your "gut". Your brain can trick you. We track a lot of metrics in our clinic to take the emotion out of the decision making so we can improve as therapists and as a business. The numbers usually don't lie.

Small daily actions done well consistently compound. Do the basics extraordinarily well. This ties into the idea that work comes before the belief. It is not one big thing that will change your confidence, your profits, your revenue, your life; it is small things done really well each and every day that consistently compound.

Focus on yourself and don't ever compare yourself to anyone else. In a world of "Instagram highlights" it is so easy to feel inadequate and not good enough. Protect your mindset at all costs and stay in your own lane. Once you are taking action on a daily basis and improving even one per cent every day then you are winning. Remember, the work comes before the belief!

The most dangerous words in the English language are, "I already know this". If I catch myself thinking this, I quickly redirect myself. The second you find yourself thinking this, you are losing any opportunity there is to improve and learn. You might already know this but you only know what you have to show for it! Another one of my former coaches, "K", once told me, "You hear it, you know it and then you finally understand it!".

Avoid shiny object syndrome at all costs. There is always going to be a "new" technique or spin coming out claiming to solve all your problems. Remember no amount of hands-on treatment can overpower a nervous system that doesn't want to tolerate load through certain tissues in the real world. As Sun Tzu once said: "Strategy without tactics is the slowest route to victory. Tactics without strategy is the noise before defeat." A step-by-step system allows you to use any tactic successfully, as long as it is used at the right time in the right order.

Embrace overwhelm. Overwhelm is good. Overwhelm and a little bit of stress is good. Think of anything in life that is worth having. There is always going to be some overwhelm and stress involved. When I work out in the gym, if I go through the motions and lift a light weight, chances are my muscles won't grow and I won't get the outcome I want. I need a little stress. I need my nervous system to feel overwhelmed, it can then adapt and grow. There is a big difference, however, between a little bit of "good" stress and "good" overwhelm and being stuck, which brings us to the final principle that I try to live my life by...

Ask for help from someone who is two to three steps ahead of you. I'm a huge advocate of mentorships because my mentors changed my life. Work smarter not harder. Find someone a few steps ahead of you who has already got to where you want to go and learn from their biggest mistakes and what they would do differently now in your shoes. With the right mentor and framework to look at the body as a whole and bridge the gap from low to high-level rehab effortlessly, you'll be amazed at how quickly your confidence and clarity will dramatically improve whilst having a fully booked diary ethically. All the while you'll be making a massive impact on this world by getting life-changing results for your patients.

Here are some final questions I ask myself before choosing a mentor:

1. Is this person a few steps ahead of where I'd like to be?

2. Has this person made mistakes that I am probably making now or could potentially make in the future and can help me avoid them?

3. Has this person learned from their mistakes, overcome them and gone on to progress in their career or business?

4. Does this person walk the talk and implement what they teach or JUST TEACH THEORY that sounds good on paper?

5. Who has this person helped get the results that I desire?

6. Does this person have a plan in place and know how to get me from where I am now to where I want to be?

I have held nothing back in this book. I have given you the clinical, business and personal principles that I do my best to live my life by every single day. I am not a guru. I still make mistakes and fu&k up and I am sure I will continue to do so. That means I'm pushing myself, I'm continuing to grow and continuing to learn.

I achieved every single professional goal I set for my career within ten years of starting out as a newly graduated physiotherapist. I've flown all over the world in business class and stayed in some of the nicest hotels around the world because of my skills as a physiotherapist. Yet when all that is said and done, I'm just a lad from Cork who wasn't smart enough to study physiotherapy in Ireland. I failed exams in my first year studying physiotherapy. I was a middle of the road student. If I can do this, then so can you!

Get your mindset right and the rest will follow. The question now is are you willing to do the work before the belief kicks in?

But if not now... then when?

If not you... then who?

Epilogue

In 2017 I boarded a plane for Perth, Australia for the Rugby League World Cup and again in 2019 for Tokyo, Japan for the Rugby Union World Cup, leaving my private practice, academy and staff behind for months at a time to run without me.

Most clinic owners believe they couldn't leave their clinic for a week without everything falling apart. Yet the saddest thing of all is that most clinic owners get into the profession because they want to help people improve their health, but, ironically, in the process put their own health at risk.

All too often I see clinic owners have some success, build up a busy caseload and then hire staff to help them with the demand. In theory what should happen is the new hires should help take the majority of the caseload away from the clinic owner so they can spend some time working "on the business" and have the freedom to treat patients on their terms.

In reality what happens is this: the clinic ends up consuming their lives while they work 50-plus hours per week. Their week is mostly filled with treating patients, hence them having to spend additional time outside of the clinic working on the business side of things. They experience substantial stress, fear of failure, overwhelming anxiety, burnout, disillusionment. This then turns into feeling unsupported and believing they can no longer rely on someone to take leadership and responsibility and help drive the clinic forward. They believe they can't take a holiday for two weeks because the clinic would not be able to run without them.

They soon become the bottleneck in the business as too many patients only want to be treated by them. They believe the physios they hired aren't providing care to a high enough standard and hence aren't able to generate referrals and don't have an adequate repeat booking ratio due to limitations with the quality of care, all of which inhibits the growth of the clinic.

Shortly after this scenario emerges, the clinic is not generating enough revenue, primarily because the physios that were hired aren't generating enough referrals either because of the quality of their care or because they are not being proactive enough about asking for referrals. The clinic is not generating enough rebookings from initial assessment and/or is unable to generate more than three to four sessions per patient ethically. The wages to gross revenue percentage is way too high and the clinic can't generate enough profit. The outgoings are now too high and it doesn't leave much money left over for the clinic owner to take home a fair wage.

All of a sudden, the once successful therapist now starts to not feel good enough. They struggle with leadership and keeping staff motivated as their diaries are quiet. They are spinning too many plates and also struggle with the business, marketing, administrative and sales side.

All of a sudden they are seeing all the patients, doing the vast majority of the work and getting paid the least amount of money each month, while their therapists and admin are getting paid more money for having empty diaries.

So, how can I leave my clinic and go away for months at a time to work with professional organisations and athletes while other clinic owners are afraid to take a week off? It goes back to that key word: systems!

While I have covered the step-by-step clinical system in-depth in this book, starting from the minute the patient comes into the initial assessment to the moment they will be discharged, there are also some other higher systems that will need to be plugged into your practice to ensure you build a great customer experience. This, in turn, allows you to build a 'Go-To' Clinic and that gives you the personal and financial freedom you deserve.

When we break it down, all private practices simply need to do five things, really:

1. Find new potential patients.

2. Talk to potential patients.

3. Sell to patients.

4. 4.Deliver the result for patients.

5. 5.Retain these patients for future purchases.

Each of these steps will contain various systems, and when combined will ensure a 'Go To' Clinic that gives the clinic owner the freedom to treat patients on their terms with a great work-life balance.

1. Finding potential new patients

Every business needs to find new patients to grow. You will need a simple system for finding new patients and communicating your clinic's differentiating factors while increasing the certainty of success in a simple marketing message to compel them to take action and reach out to your clinic.

2. Talking to potential new patients

Every business will need a system for how to talk to patients. That will ensure that you can communicate to them that you understand their needs and wants, and increase the certainty of success. This will also ensure you can clearly communicate how your clinic is different and therefore overcome objections such as price so you can charge what you are worth. In this day and age you will need to communicate to patients in multiple forms – phone, email, direct messaging and in person, to name but a few.

3. Sell to patients

Nothing changes until a sale is made. Whether we like it or not, we need to sell ourselves and our treatment plan to the patient in order to get buy-in, adherence and ultimately the results. We have covered this in-depth in pillars 1–4 of the 'Go-To' Physio in previous chapters. In addition, you may need some other systems if you sell treatment plan packages or systems to reactive past patients that cancelled and did not rebook.

4. Deliver the results for the patient

The 8 Pillars of the 'Go-To' Physio will take care of this for you and we have already covered this in depth in the previous sections. In addition, you may need some additional systems in place for what happens to a patient between sessions. For example, in my own clinic, after each session the patient will receive video links to their exercises. This is a key part of the customer experience. Therefore, a simple and repeatable way of ensuring this happens for every patient needs to be in place, in order to give us the best chance of delivering the result for the patient.

5. Retain these patients for future purchases

Now that you have delivered great results, you need some simple systems in place to ascend these raving fans to the next step on your customer journey. That could be a pilates class, a sports massage or a six-week gym program, depending on your clinic size. For a lot of therapists starting out, this step may not be in place yet so just keeping in touch with these past patients will be important in order to stay top of mind so that, if they do have any future problems, they will contact your clinic.

Growth and control are inversely proportional

Whether you like it or not, as your clinic grows you must give up control. If you want freedom from your business then, unfortunately, you will also need people to help give you this. Truth be told, as I hired staff, I struggled with this for the first few years. This is where most clinic owners go wrong and they struggle to turn these assets (staff) into revenue, into profit, into cash.

Peter Drucker is reported to have famously said: "What gets measured, gets managed." This is where it is important to have people, numbers and systems in place for each of the five elements of a growing 'Go-To' Clinic.

In the 'Go-To' Clinic Mastermind, we install a simple dashboard with metrics to track the journey from finding new potential patients all the way through to the final step of rebooking or ascending to your next product or service. This allows clinic owners to take the emotion out of the decision-making process and keep control of the business while it grows.

Some numbers to track at each phase may include:

1. Find new potential patients

Website visitors

Number of new leads/email optins

2. Talk to potential patients

Number of website enquiries

Number of inbound phone calls

Number of direct message conversations

3. Sell to patients

Initial assessment to rebook

Percentage of initial assessments to packages

Cancelled, did not rebook percentage

Did not attend percentage

4. Deliver the result for patients

Net promoter score/patient satisfaction score

Number of reviews

Number of referrals

5. Retain these patients for future purchases

Number of past patients rebooking

Number of patients ascending to pilates

Number of sports massage appointments

These are by no means exhaustive lists, but should give you a starting point to look at to manage your practice.

People and accountability

With the numbers defined, you now need people in charge of each of these key elements. No more than one person can be in charge of each number or else no one will be in charge! Once you have the people and the numbers defined along with the targets, you can now build out the systems that you need in order to ensure that we can have a repeatable and consistent outcome for each element.

This ensures that you empower your staff to be successful in hitting their targets and have a clear "definition of done" for each process or system. This sets the team up for success and allows you to give recognition and praise at every opportunity.

Business systems versus head physio systems

While clinical reasoning is king for a therapist who helps patients who have failed with traditional approaches, critical thinking skills are king for a 'Go-To' Clinic owner who has a successful, profitable and growing 'Go-To' Clinic that can function for months at a time without them.

There will always be problems in a business. It is the ability to use the numbers to find the biggest bottleneck and then define the root problem and solve it at source that will be the difference between you being a stressed, overworked, and overwhelmed clinic owner and a calm, confident leader who has the freedom to treat patients on your terms while your team are rowing in the same direction to move the business to your vision.

While the business systems will tell you the symptoms, the majority of time the problem will be people – this is where you will need Head Physio Systems to define the root problems and then fix those problems at source.

My next book in this *Perfect Private Practice* series will cover the 'Go-To' Clinic Step-By-Step Business and Head Physio Systems in detail so you can enjoy owning a successful and highly profitable private practice that has a highly-motivated team of 'Go-To' Therapists helping patients who have failed with traditional approaches while you have the freedom to treat patients on your terms.

Until then, keep booking patients in, helping them progress and transforming people's lives.

About the Author

Dave O'Sullivan is a professional sports physiotherapist, private practice clinic owner and mentor to over 900 therapists in over 30 countries around the world. He holds a degree in physiotherapy from the University of Huddersfield and a masters degree in strength and conditioning from St Mary's University.

Dave quickly found out that traditional physio approaches taught in university were limited in their ability to help real patients get real-world results and, after struggling with some complex cases in pro sport, went on a journey to develop his own step-by-step system that looks at the person as a whole and not just the site of pain.

Headhunted to work in two World Cups, one with England Rugby Union at the 2019 Rugby Union World Cup in Japan and the other with England Rugby League for the 2017 Rugby League World Cup in Australia, Dave has therefore had the unique honour of being involved in a World Cup Final in both Rugby League and Rugby Union. He has also worked with other professional sporting organisations such as Leeds Rhinos, Munster Rugby, Huddersfield Giants, Warrington Wolves and Leicester Tigers.

Dave is also the clinical director of ProSport Physiotherapy in Huddersfield where he and his team of 'Go-To' Therapists help both sporting and non-sporting patients who have failed to see results with traditional approaches to get long-lasting relief and live happy, healthy lives.

The ProSport Academy 'Go-To' Physio Mentorship was set up by Dave in 2015 to give therapists an opportunity to learn how to confidently make sense of their patients' symptoms and design value-based treatment plans that keep patients progressing to long-lasting meaningful results. Dave has a passion for helping people who have failed to see improvement with traditional approaches and, through his work in his own clinic and through his mentoring of 'Go-To' Physios all over the world, aims to help millions of people around the world to live happy, healthy lives.

Dave is married to Georgina and has two daughters, Ava May and Ruby Rae. Dave is originally from Cork in Ireland and now lives in Huddersfield, in the North of England. When Dave is not teaching or treating, he enjoys playing Gaelic football, hurling, strength training and tennis.

THE GO-TO PHYSIO MENTORSHIP

Discover Dave O'Sullivan's step-by-step method to rapidly improve patient adherence and progress — while skyrocketing confidence in your clinical care!

" The Go-To Physio Mentorship is one of the most comprehensive, forward-thinking personal development programs available to physical therapists.

Dave and his team are phenomenal. I went from struggling to feeling confident in my abilities virtually overnight . This also took my client numbers from 10-15 a week to 15-20 to 20-30 in the first 3 months — I now struggle to fit them all in the diary!

I would recommend The Go-To Physio Mentorship to any therapist who is willing to go that extra mile to succeed. "

TONI STANTON

Scan the QR code now to find out more about how The Go-To Physio Mentorship can help you and your business grow!